The Reflexive Classroom Manager

Dr. Thomas Ryan

DETSELIG
ENTERPRISES LTD

Reflexive Classroom Manager

Library and Archives Canada Cataloguing in Publication

Ryan, Thomas

The reflexive classroom manager / Thomas Ryan.

Includes bibliographical references.

ISBN 1-55059-292-0

1. Classroom management. 2. Action research in education. 3. Teachers--Inservice training. I. Title.

LB3013.R94 2005 371.102'4 C2005-902351-1

Detselig Enterprises Ltd.
210, 1220 Kensington Road NW
Calgary, Alberta T2N 3P5

Phone: (403) 283-0900
Fax: (403) 283-6947
Email: temeron@telusplanet.net
www.temerondetselig.com

We acknowledge the support of the Government of Canada through the Book Publishing Industry Development Program (BPIDP) for our publishing program.

We also acknowledge the support of the Alberta Foundation for the Arts for our publishing program.

COMMITTED TO THE DEVELOPMENT OF CULTURE AND THE ARTS

SAN 113-0234
ISBN 1-55059-292-0
Printed in Canada

Cover Design by Alvin Choong

Acknowledgments

I would like to thank my family for being there and fellow educators, action researchers, and community members who have provided words and actions that have moved me both physically, spiritually and mentally.

Thank you, as well, to all the students and teachers who contributed their experiences and reflections, and demonstrated just what it means to be a reflexive classroom manager.

About the Author

Dr. Thomas G. Ryan, H.B.P.E., B.Ed. (Lakehead), Specialist (Special Education – Ontario A.Q.), M.Ed. (Sask), Ed.D, (OISE/UT) has been teaching since 1985. He began instructing at the college level on Reserves in Northern Ontario before moving to the Secondary level to teach Physical Education, Law, History, and Special Education. Next, he entered the Elementary level teaching mostly within Special Education (Resource K-8).

Thom is currently teaching Classroom Management, Physical Education, Special Education, and has been teaching graduate level courses. Previously, Dr. Ryan taught within the Faculty of Education at Lethbridge (Evaluation, Research Methods) and recently authored and taught on-line for the Campus Alberta Graduate Program (Research Methods).

Dr. Ryan has completed research in Alberta, Saskatchewan, and Ontario, and is a frequent speaker at conferences and workshops. He has published articles and hopes to help as many people along the way as possible.

He can be reached at thomasr@nipissingu.ca or by mail at

Nipissing University
Faculty of Education
100 College Drive
North Bay, Ontario P1B 8L7

or visit his web page:
http://www.nipissingu.ca/education/thomasr/genesis/index.htm

Table of Contents

Chapter 5 *Secondary Reflections*

Chapter 6 *Teaching and Classroom Management*

Chapter 7 *Nonverbal Communication*

Chapter 8 *Verbal Communication*

Preface

The *Reflexive Classroom Manager* has been written to support and facilitate professional development of both in-service and pre-service teachers as they plan, teach, and reflect recursively throughout the day, week, month, and year. Teaching is a mode that can create angst and at the same time teaching serves to motivate, stimulate, and provide many rewards. The first chapter illuminates "The Educator's Toolbox: Action Research" in a manner that is easy to comprehend yet challenges the reader to become an active, reflective teacher researcher. The many tools, theories, and modes used to construct an action research effort are revealed and examined in detail to ensure that each teacher can make use of each one as they refine and improve not only their classroom management but also their professional practice.

The following chapter puts forward a number of points concerning the collection of data and supplies several possibilities a teacher researcher can entertain while envisioning an action research project. The next chapter, "Analyzing Action Research Data," guides and supports while offering several choices in this critical area. In Chapters 4 (Elementary) and 5 (Secondary), reflections from pre-service teachers are included which highlight the reflexive 'voice' of new classroom managers within Elementary and Secondary classrooms. These chapters also expose teacher ethics, improving practice, professional development, and teacher action via the construction of classroom policy and practice centred on classroom management.

Chapter 6 takes the reader further into teaching, classroom management, and the world of the *Reflexive Teacher*, as teaching is defined and authentic pre-service classroom management philosophies are provided. These initial efforts to construct classroom management philosophies shed light upon understanding the perception of classroom teaching. From here, Chapter 7 develops the image of a teacher as a nonverbal communicator who is constantly sending and receiving messages whether he or she is aware of this or not. Nonverbal communication is presented as a powerful tool in education. Following this, naturally, Chapter 7 is devoted to verbal communication, the other channel that is vital in our classrooms, schools, and our communities.

Chapter 9 delves into "365 Days of Teaching." This chapter reminds us that teaching is not an event but a lifestyle that needs careful monitoring. In this chapter, a systematic and strategic examination of the school year is completed using a unique paradigm in order to provoke substantive thoughts. These thoughts cause readers to question both their current stance and the possibilities for the future. Finally, in Chapter 10, numerous scenarios, role plays, interventions, problem-solving, and mediation situations are offered. The activities encourage both pre-service and in-service teachers to move into the performance mode which can help them prepare for the drama unfolding in schools today. Acting and getting into character are opportunities to rehearse both mentally and physically what can or may happen within an educator's role. Being prepared is not only a good motto, it can serve to alert and remind teachers daily. Lastly, a resource section demonstrates just how deep and wide (Reflection/Teacher Research) Action Research is in Canada and elsewhere. It is hoped that these chapters will propel the new and veteran educator forward to increase not only their utility of practice but also enrich professional life hereafter.

The Reflective Educator

Reflection is the process or act of looking back at what you did (actions), what you thought at the time (cognition), and how you felt at the time (affective domain) in order to generate new understandings. "The practice of reflection has the potential to lead to significant growth as an educator. These thoughtful considerations of your teaching and student learning will lay the groundwork for a successful career in education" (Henniger, 2004, p. 369). As a professional educator you are required to make decisions that impact the lives of others and your ability to reflect upon your experience is essential as this can promote the active construction of new knowledge, skills, and attitudes to help you grow and move forward. As you research teaching via reflective tasks and generate new perceptions, awarenesses, and approaches, you are critically evaluating not only the practicum but also yourself within that context. In fact, one might conclude that the entire pre-service experience is about getting to know yourself better as there are many reflective tasks, peer feedback requirements, and mentor evaluations.

As an outcome "intern teachers are better prepared to teach and learn if they use critical reflection as a tool to enhance their performance as professionals" (Goethals, Howard & Sanders, 2004, p. 181). Within each Faculty of Education program there are a number of models that acknowledge and facilitate the achievement of these outcomes.

> In the developmental model, a successful pre-service program is not a teacher-building factory, but rather the first step in a

> long, collaborative, and reflective process that influences the professional development of a teacher's career. A pre-service program can either set this process in motion with the appropriate tools, attitudes, and expectations, or it can set the novice up for a dizzying fall from the heights of unchallenged naive idealism. (Russell & McPherson, 2001, p. 8)

Moreover, in a recent conversation with the Dean of Education from Nova Southeastern University in Florida, I learned that the state required all education students, including graduate students, to complete an action research (applied research) project before they can graduate. Similar requirements (reflection, action research, applied research) can be found in most schools of education, in North America, the United Kingdom, and Australia. This requirement – to reflect on practice – can be traced back to the work of John Dewey (felt need), Donald Schon (reflective practice), and others who put forward the notion that reflection is a critical function of successful teaching and learning.

Reflective Classroom Management

We begin our developmental journey by considering what we are attempting to do in this course, our classroom, and our profession. Some students may want to know from the onset: what are the most important key understandings, knowledge, skills, and values that we need to study as a pre-service educator examining classroom management?

In our course (classroom management) as in most education curricula, beliefs are deliberately exposed via tasks. I attempt to lead each pre-service student to conclude that classroom management is not limited to a classroom or a rigid stance; it is a flexible disposition that needs to be embraced and maintained in order to modify and evaluate each day's events. I believe all teachers aware of this must make efforts to reach beyond their grasp, to attend to the needs of not only the student but also the community. Indeed, a classroom reflects the larger community. A goal in our classroom management course is to illuminate the *purpose* of education, and that is to nurture and prepare students to become caring, responsible, contributing members of society. This citizenship emphasis means that all teachers must be able to address not only the curricula (content) but also the curriculum (whole person in the community).

The informed teaching of citizenship addresses social skills, morals, and values; however, this realization places an even larger burden on all educators. My own research (Joong & Ryan, 2004; Ryan, 2001) has shown that the greatest threat to teacher success is the lack of time to put into practice what each teacher plans, in theory, to undertake. I point out to each of my students that one approach or solution is to become more efficient, proactive, and aware of how to achieve these ends given the obstacles of time, facilities, and number of students per class. In our management class I *reflect* on the lessons I have learned, recalling ways in which I became efficient and proactive. I do this reflecting in order to question my current understanding, wisdom, insight, and philosophy. I am reminded that teachers do indeed teach who they are. My stories are practical lessons, my voice is confident (lived experiences), and the messages within are often universally applicable to all grades. For example, I relate how I handled a student who verbally abused me and suggest ways to frame this event in order to help both the student and teacher cope with emotional injuries sustained. It is critical that educators move through times of turbulence and tension with poise and understanding.

We examine classroom management as something undertaken in a systematic and strategic manner. Our communication strategies and human systems are of pivotal importance in education. Educators use human communication channels, the non-verbal and the verbal – usually in that order – constantly. Communication theorists such as Galloway (1976) and McCroskey (1992) have argued that our communication actions are largely non-verbal (80-90%). We practice using our communication abilities in class as pre-service teachers, 'give the eye' to one another, or motion for quiet during whole class dramatizations. I regularly ask students to learn more about management and themselves via role-play and case study discussions. Classroom practice involves the use of a specific intervention in order to be able to modify observed behavior. The outcome of this exercise causes students to use new language, terms, words, and phrases such as token economy, response/cost, contracting, pre-correction, the turtle technique, self-management, behavioral self-control, cognitive modelling, the timer game, and so forth. Armed with new knowledge, students are eager to apply certain techniques during a practicum. Students then *reflect* upon their overt and covert experiences and produce written evidence of their classroom management actions, reflections, and plans to revise these same actions. The opportunity to discuss and debate our *reflections* and philosophical positions brings about clarity and it is rewarding to hear a student speak about an experience they had during a practicum in which they discovered something useful. Conversely, I sometimes hear students who have quickly become fearful of classroom management due to a challenging practicum.

During discussion of a challenging practicum, I remind students that educators must deal with at least two realities at the classroom level and need to take time to reflect upon and revise their approaches. These omnipresent realities are *dilemmas* and *problems*.

Dilemmas require coping strategies in the form of individual pupil plans that are program specific and offer unique curriculum (community) supports. As well, dilemmas are often formally identified via an Individual Placement and Review Committee (IPRC). Dilemmas are school team concerns as an identified student (IPRC) can have a social worker, child development counsellor, psychologist, and a teaching assistant providing support and insight.

Alternatively, educators deal with problems. A *problem* could be a particular student's behavior; for example, one who refuses to work (contrary). Usually this student can be approached and convinced to complete the work, or at least be less contrary. Problems are readily solvable whereas dilemmas are situations requiring coping mechanisms. I illuminate the area of special education by describing my successes and my frustrations as IPRC labels sometimes cause more problems if we choose to look only at the label and not at the person as we guide and support them. Having a means to frame presenting issues provides functional mindsets for new and experienced educators.

My students gradually come to appreciate that discipline – or 'disciplino,' the latin root – actually means to instruct. It is from this orientation that I encourage pre-service teachers to use a variety of **instructional approaches** in order to bring out the best in students. To do this often requires a *multiple-intelligences approach* to instructional planning and teaching. The curricula can be infused with instructional novelty, authenticity, and energy to ensure that each student will have the opportunity to learn in a manner that engages their specific intelligence(s). For example, the science lesson becomes an opportunity for some students to use their artistic abilities to illustrate what they see on site, and other students may see science as a way to use their oral abilities in a small group presentation or make use of technology to make their point. The engaged student who is able to succeed causes positive energy to amass, and this becomes a motivational force pervading not only your class but also the larger community. Success displaces anger and resentment.

Management classes are filled with constructivist philosophy as I attempt to 'activate' previous learning in my students and guide them to use new scaffolding to construct new understandings which are supported by their own previous learning. This approach is compatible with many cultural groups and meets the needs observed in management classes; after all, what I am on a daily basis is more important than what I teach.

Students hear me talk about getting to know yourself as a teacher and knowing your limitations, standards, and vulnerabilities. I encourage them to listen to their inner voice and be reflexive in a positive manner. I put forward the notion that it is important to have a personal life that is private, a professional life that is open and healthy, and at all times, be aware of their political lives.

Being an educator is exciting with professional, political, and personal responsibilities, yet it carries tensions and turbulence from time-to-time. In order to add context, the class becomes involved in scenarios that provoke thought and cause new and active constructions. Our lively debates expose positions that are often adjusted by reflection and dialogue. Students realize that boundaries are required, as is self-discipline (appropriateness), and positive, rational self-talk. I challenge my students to become a student of their students.

Empowering students is a positive endeavor. It is not a matter of herding students into neat rows or looking for rule infractions. It is about establishing an environment that supports learning and in fact, most of your efforts are directed towards the maintenance of that healthy environment. Being a teacher who can take the pulse of the class will enable that teacher to precisely act and react as necessary. We teach and we coach. Coaching students is not entirely a science, however much some may want to argue that it is; coaching and teaching are in part artistic efforts that require informed practice, *critical reflection,* and constant revision throughout each educator's career.

When the last class ends, I look towards the empty seats and I reflect on the things that once were. I ask myself, "Did I miss anything?" My answer is yes, because I cannot take all of my knowledge, skill, and experience and simply pass this on. Instead, I hope that each pre-service (student) teacher now has an opportunity to further his or her education via experience as a full-time reflective educator. It is well known that theory informs practice and practice infuses the theory put forward in Faculty of Education classes. It is my hope that all of our education students will successfully establish and maintain healthy classroom environments where all students achieve and grow.

Chapter 1

The Educator's Toolbox: Reflection via Action Research

Introduction

In this first chapter, action research is illuminated via a series of definitions and a brief history. Praxes are defined and various action research modes are explained and illustrated. Specific action research roles are described, as are various conceptualizations of these which will support educators as they seek to improve their practice and grow professionally.

Action Research: A definition

By defining action research, ambiguity is reduced since "the dictionary is full of words [which] are almost all ambiguous in the sense that they have many meanings"(Adler & Van Doren, 1972, p. 97). The term, used here, indicates a specific, singular, contextual meaning. The phrase *action research* is the very foundation of this text and needs to be understood in a manner that brings forward a common understanding. Consequently, to ensure accuracy and increase comprehension of my intended usage, I have chosen to include the thoughts of seminal action researchers who suggest:

> The shortest and most straightforward definition of action research is given by John Elliott (1991:69), whose work has been influential in this 'movement': action research is 'the study of a social situation with a view to improving the quality of action within it.' This simple definition directs attention to one of the most essential motives for doing action research. It lies in the will to improve the quality of teaching and learning as well as the conditions under which teachers and students work in schools. Action research is intended to support teachers and problems of practice and carrying through innovations in a reflective way. (Altrichter, Posch & Somekh, 1993, p. 4)

To more completely ensure understanding we need to consider that most teachers undertake some action to improve their practice at many points in their career. For experienced educators, it is second nature to constantly attempt improving their practice, understanding, and ultimately the situations in which such practice occurs (Carr & Kemmis 1986). As teachers engage in teacher research (Hopkins, 1993), which can be described as a trial and error way of life in education, it is natural for teachers to wonder and reflect upon further refinements. Often the process of reflection can be a social enterprise, which leads to the Carr and Kemmis (1986) view that:

> Action research is simply a form of self-reflective enquiry undertaken by participants in social situations in order to improve the rationality and justice of their own practices, their understanding of these practices, and the situations in which the practices are carried out. (p.162)

Generally, as a teacher, if something doesn't work, you make changes until you are satisfied with the outcome. As you do this you take certain actions in order to ensure desired outcomes. This action, combined with reflection, becomes a praxis (habitual practice), which is necessary in action research. The action for improvement may stem from a new theory, program, initiative, curriculum, parent suggestion, staff goal, administrative guideline, government directive, or personal reflection. The teacher acting as action researcher "is interested in the improvement of the educational practices in which he [or she] is engaging. He [or she] undertakes research in order to find out how to do his [or her] job better" (Corey 1949, p. 509).

Sometimes a teacher's actions may be solely individualistic yet it may be that a group of teachers have undertaken substantive action in order to achieve better results. Action research may operate independent of the number of people involved; it is the action which is important, as it enables people to take control via critical theory (emancipation).

> Action research is, therefore, a deliberate way of creating new situations and telling the story of who we are. Action research consists of deliberate experimental moves into the future, which change us because of what we learn in the process (Connelly & Clandinin 1988).

Yet, there are those who contend that action research is currently in a state of flux, with several writers (McNiff, Lomax, Whitehead, 1996; Stringer, 1996; Zuber-Skerritt, 1996) attempting to further define its nature and role. As a cautionary prerequisite, we are told: "Action research is not a method or a procedure for research, but a series of commitments to observe and problematize through practice a series of principles for conducting social enquiry (the praxis of a social science?)" (McTaggart, 1996, p. 248). Consequently, a simple and universally accepted definition may seem unattainable today, in some social research circles. Action research is "best thought of as a large family, one in which beliefs and relationships vary greatly . . . it is a group of ideas emergent in various contexts" (Noffke, 1997, p. 306). Even the *Action Research International Journal* (1997) has felt the need to detail a definition for contributors which demonstrates several similarities to the previous definitions described in this section, the journal suggests:

> **Action research** *consists of a family of methodologies, which pursue outcomes of both action (change) and research (understanding).* It uses a process that alternates between action and systematic reflection, or achieves theory-practice integration by some other means. It is usually, though not universally, collaborative and qualitative. Its many forms include such varieties as participative action research, emancipatory action research, action science, and soft systems methodology, among others. [emphasis added] (p. 1)

While this definition would suffice in some cases, Carr and Kemmis (1986) augment the meaning of action research by pointing out three minimal requirements:

> Firstly, a project takes as its subject-matter a social practice, regarding it as a form of strategic action susceptible of improvement; secondly, the project proceeds through spirals of planning, acting, observing and reflecting, with each of these activities being systematically and self-critically implemented and interrelated; thirdly, the project involves those responsible for the practice in each of the moments of the activity . . . and maintaining collaborative control of the process (p. 137)

What seems fundamental to this definition and many other conceptualizations (models) of action research is that action research involves participants talking about everyday things in the life of education and unpacking these for their historical and ideological baggage (Connelly & Clandinin, 1988; Noffke, 1995).

Action Research: A Brief History

Action research has been conducted in many countries and in many fields of endeavor since the 1920s. "The story of action research is traced out almost as a family tree, with clearly identifiable descendants and some debate over who is the patriarch" (Noffke, 1997, p. 311). As a result of this growing family tree, it has achieved widespread popularity across cultural boundaries. As McLean (1995) points out, the history of action research shows several major influences.

> Action research is historically credited to Kurt Lewin in the . . . 1940's . . . Ron Lippitt in the early 1950's . . . [and] in the 1970's . . . Lawrence Stenhouse and John Elliott . . . expanded Corey's concept of action research by emphasizing its aim as adding to the understanding of the solution and the development of a theory of teaching as well as solving practical problems. (p. 4)

As a consequence of this long and varied history, in several sociocultural contexts, action research has become more theoretically sophisticated (McTaggart, 1991, p. 33). Some major influences on its development include farmers in rural areas of Scotland and New Zealand, community development programs in Africa and Asia, and its use in education in North America, Australia, and England (Deshler & Ewert, 25 May 1995 On-line, p. 1). As well, there are several variants of educational action research that are illuminated for discussion in this section.

Action Research: Praxes

The term praxis, used as a noun, has two meanings. **Praxis** in the first sense can be *the practical application or exercise of a branch of learning*. **Praxis** in the second sense could indicate *habitual or established practice, as in a custom or classroom*. The plural form of praxis is **praxes**, and this could be used to indicate *several branches of learning or established practices and customs*. Melrose (1996) has explained its use within the action research paradigm:

> Critical theory has regenerated the Aristotelian concept of praxis, the idea that personal theory and practice grow, develop and adapt in unison and are not artificially separated. . . . A critical practitioner is in effect a researcher into his or her own practice who develops and redevelops personal theories cyclically, as a consequence of putting these theories, as they arise, into active practice and then reflecting on that practice and the learning which has taken place. (p. 52)

Therefore, in most educational pursuits learning occurs in unison with theory and practical development. Take for example, the praxes of assessment (gathering data), which then can be examined, changed, and effectively transformed via the application of the action research mode. Teachers can learn by doing and by participating with others as they develop their individual practice(s). Thus, the science teacher, for instance, learns to assess better by *doing* assessment, participating and *reflecting* on the assessment, and *revising* assessment as experience accumulates. Most often, the improvement is aided by critical friends, which some would argue is the essence of action research (social enterprise aimed at improvement). This intertwining of action research and praxes is well illustrated by McNiff et al. (1996):

> To be action research, there must be praxis rather than practice. Praxis is informed, committed action that gives rise to knowledge rather than just successful action. It is informed because other people's views are taken into account. It is committed and intentional in terms of values that have been examined and can be argued. It leads to knowledge from and about educational practice. (p. 8)

The development of committed self-critical groups of teachers permits the examination of policies, practices, and schools as problematic elements within the community (Carr, 1986). This is important to teachers at all stages of their career as any "approach to teacher education which does not encourage teachers to critically reflect . . . will be either inherently conservative or dangerously doctrinaire" (Carr, 1986, p. 6). As the educational community action research experiences manifest themselves, each participant enjoys the whole, rather than just a part or pieces, of the experience. This educational-focused research will then "build excitement, confidence and insight – and these are important foundations . . . of personal and professional development" (Adelman & Carr, 1988, p. 6) for teachers.

Action Research Modes

As noted earlier, there are many ways to address the term *action research* and its definitions are beset by variant conceptions. Many researchers (Altrichter et al. 1993; Carr, 1995; Carr & Kemmis, 1986; Elliott, 1991; Hopkins, 1993) have proposed and implemented models of action research. Most are socially-driven modes, which incorporate action and reflection in recursive cycles in order to realize improvement. Each conception allows researchers to work as practitioners, or closely

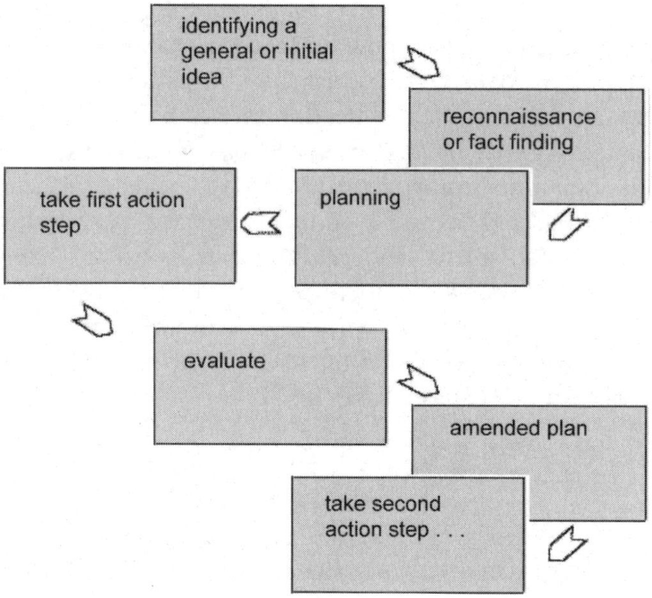

Figure 1. Kurt Lewin's model requires a recursive spiral of steps, 'each of which is composed of a circle of planning, action and fact-finding about the result of the action'. Smith (2001)

with practitioners to systemically monitor the issues and problems of changing practice (Elliott 1991). Lewin (1946) is often recognized as the person who first used the term action research and proposed a model (Figure 1).

As time passed various researchers modified action research and it was simplified. Stringer (1996) proposed only a three-phase model of action research (Figure 2).

Each model aims to help participants learn from experience. These models appear rigid on paper yet it has been suggested that although "action research is one way of restoring and enhancing professional confidence . . . we must, however, be aware of problems associated with too prescriptive a framework for action and the values that are embedded within it" (Hopkins, 1993, p. 56). Hence, we need to keep in mind that even scholars are at odds with the very elements of action within each conception of action research.

Action research is a means to combine researchers and practitioners in a process that permits a high degree of coalescence. Nichols (1997) adds:

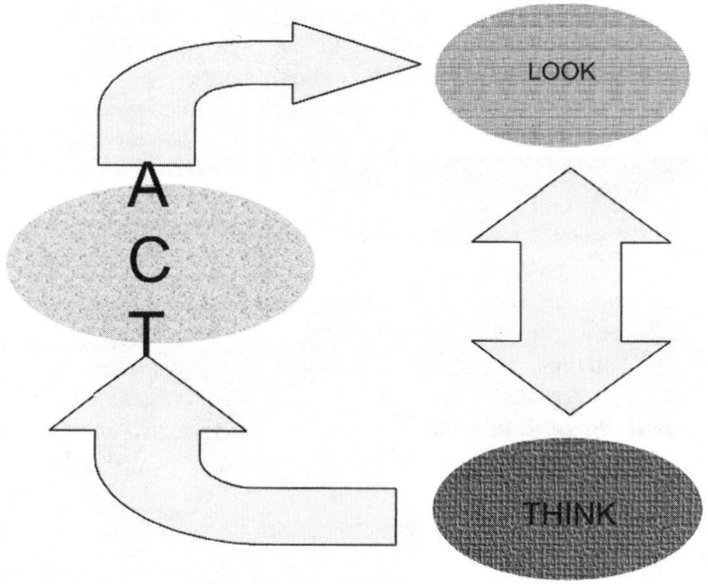

Figure 2. Stringer's (1996) model of the action research. *Look* at the problem, *think* about the problem, and then ***act*** on the problem. The researcher then repeats the cycle thus it is said to be recursive.

> Approaches to action research place emphasis on the full integration of action and reflection, and on collaboration between those involved in the enquiry process. Action research methodology bridges the divide between research and practice. It directly addresses the problem of the persistent failure of research in the social sciences to make a difference in terms of bringing about actual improvements in practice. It does so by rejecting the concept of a two-stage process in which research is carried out first by researchers and then applied by practitioners. Instead, the two processes of research and action are integrated because the findings of action research are fed back directly into practice with the aim of bringing about change. (p. 186)

While there is a great deal of practical usefulness in the notion of research-practitioner it leads to many questions of image. For instance, what actions are now possible and necessary given the new title of research-practitioner? Answers can be varied and distinct from one another. This can lead to uncertainty as research-practitioners pursuing guidance may encounter conflicting images of action research. Help can be found in some typology as detailed by Zuber-Skerritt (1996) who suggests three images of action research, as follows:

> *Technical* action research aims to improve the effectiveness of educational or managerial practice. The practitioners are co-opted and depend greatly on the researcher as a facilitator. *Practical* action research, in addition to effectiveness, aims at the practitioners' understanding and professional development. The researcher's role is Socratic and to encourage practical deliberation and self-reflection on the part of the practitioners. Action research is *Emancipatory* when it aims not only at technical and practical improvement and the participants' better understanding, along with transformation and change within the existing boundaries and conditions, but also at changing the system itself or those conditions which impede desired improvement in the system/organization. It also aims at the participants' empowerment and self-confidence about their ability to create 'grounded theory.' (p. 2-3)

The images are useful to the action researcher as they further detail possible outcomes and modes for each study or project. While it is generally accepted that this classification originates in the work of Carr and Kemmis (1986) it has been adopted and modified by others in their efforts to develop further conceptions of action research. However, the roles for these types of action research are quite different and each has its distinctive theoretical underpinning. An action research study focused at the technical seeks to control, while the practical interest aims at the practitioner's understanding and professional development.

> In practical action research, participants monitor their own educational practices with the immediate aim of developing their practical judgement as individuals thus the facilitator's role is Socratic: to provide a sounding-board against which practitioners may try out ideas and learn more about the reasons for their own action, as well as learning more about the process of self-reflection. (Carr and Kemmis, 1986, p. 201)

In some studies the aim is not emancipatory, with a goal to changing the educational system, its culture, and the way in which teachers perceive and function in the school culture. Yet most action research studies can be a "stepping stone to emancipatory action research in which participants themselves take responsibility for the Socratic role" (*Ibid.*). Action research needs to be self-directed and participants need to be free to speak their minds; guidance often comes from a list of topics provided by a facilitator (researcher); hence, there can be role tensions with others and with oneself.

Action Research: Roles

Context and Action Research

One can argue that just as the educational context should define the nature of curriculum, so too should the educational context define the nature and conduct of action research. Action research roles are tied to context by the very purpose of the action research. As the context or setting changes, so can the purpose of the inquiry. Therefore, the role and commitments of the participant and the facilitator are very much tied to context, setting, and purpose.

To reduce and decontextualize the social world is to misrepresent the situation that is the focus of the study, argument, or question (King, 1988). For example, concern with accountability in education has resulted in attempts to break down the art of teaching into steps that can be measured, assessed, and ultimately made 'teacher-proof.' Consider the pre-service teacher checklists which attempt this feat (*Royal Commission on Learning*, 1994, Volume, III, p. 22), in contrast to the 'real' performance required each day in the classroom. Real teaching situations are multidimensional, idiosyncratic, and constantly changing. Therefore, a research approach that uses static models and sees problems as readily susceptible to rigorous analysis, is inappropriate. The real strength of action research is its capacity to recognize the complexity and uncertainty of educational contexts.

In addition, action research is the most appropriate research and development method to employ in education because it is *holistic*. It is concerned with the whole professional situation in which the teacher is located, not with some sub-set of observable, measurable behaviors. This holism gives action research efforts their power and educational impact. Hodson (1993) adds: "We need to guard against undervaluing that which we cannot measure . . . we can still make judgements, provide criticism and proffer advice" (p.143).

Education is a complex, multidimensional activity requiring a personalized, idiosyncratic, and context-specific approach. It follows that action research is the ideal approach – maybe the only approach – capable of effecting significant change and improvement. An action research approach allows researchers to embrace the 'whole' culture in a manner that produces useful professional development. This is possible because "professionals are engaged in work which influences the lives of others in significant ways, [and] their professional development ought to be an essential component of their work lives" (Yonemura, 1982, p. 234). As such, action research demands a further series of commitments; it is a journey of self, through reflective inquiry that is social in nature. We do it to improve, to illuminate, and to fully understand education. We desire to improve praxes and understanding within the contexts in which these understandings are implemented (Kemmis & McTaggart, 1988). Ultimately, holism and context determine the role of the action researcher.

Participant and/or Facilitator

Whether a person is labelled a participant, facilitator, or both, in an action research effort, one notion is omnipresent: the idea that each person is involved in strategic actions to carry out collective social action which can lead to freedom, justice, and rationality (emancipation) (Carr, 1995). While in pursuit of these ideals, via critical social science, it is suggested each person enter into "a process of reflection which requires the participation of the researcher in the social action being studied, or rather, that participants become researchers" (Carr & Kemmis, 1986, p. 149). Yet there is another way to define the role of the participant and the facilitator in action research efforts.

In *technical action research*, the participant is an equal member. Carr and Kemmis (1986) add: "this kind of action research . . . can produce valuable changes in practice – but the value may be in the eyes of the observer rather than the practitioners themselves" (p. 202). This is because each participant is encouraged to "work on externally formulated questions or test externally generated research in their classrooms. In essence, the purpose of the Action Research Group is the addition of new findings to external research literature" (Pedretti, 1994a, p. 76). This technical action research effort, which does not concern itself with self-development of the participant as a result of working together or thinking about the experience, is only one approach. However, the experience may cause educators to begin more critical reflection of their practices (Carr & Kemmis, 1986). In this mode of action research the facilitator is interested in improving the educational practice in general (Zubber-Skerrit, 1996, p. 4) and is not necessarily concerned with the individual participant's practice (Carr & Kemmis, 1986).

In *practical action research*, the participant's role is limited to improving effectiveness, just as it is in technical action research. Yet, in addition, aims at the practitioners' understanding and professional development. "The researcher's role is Socratic and to encourage practical deliberation and self-reflection on the part of the practitioners" (Zubber-Skerrit, 1996, p. 2). In this mode of action research the practitioner, or participant, is a collaborative member. The collaborative member generates useful knowledge concerning some problem identified either by the individual or another participant, yet cooperatively with other participants. Practical action research is "intended to contribute directly to change efforts on the part of participants . . . the major thrust is not primarily to create generalizable knowledge or 'basic' research that is unattached to particular circumstances, but to focus the knowledge generation on specific desired changes in a specific, often unique, situation" (Deshler & Ewert, 25 May 1995 On-line, p. 2).

In *emancipatory action research*, the participant's role benefits from the catalytic nature of the involvement of the facilitator. The facilitator "helps form a reflective and critical group of practitioners. However once this group is established, the participants take full responsibility and ownership for their direction, [and] development" (Pedretti, 1994b, p. 77).

> Emancipatory research is collaborative, critical and self-critical inquiry by practitioners (e.g. teachers, managers) into a major problem or issue of concern in their own practice. They 'own the problem' and feel responsible and accountable for solving it through teamwork and through following a cyclical process of (1) strategic planning, (2) implementing the plan (action), (3) observation, evaluation and self-evaluation, (4) critical and self-critical reflection on the results of (1)-(3), and making decisions for the next cycle of action research. (Zubber-Skerrit, 1996, p. 84)

Researcher Role

The role of researcher in this study can better be understood using terms such as facilitator, associate, and consultant. (Stringer, 1996) The role is to act as a resource and not as an expert who does research (Stringer, 1996). Flores and Granger (1996) add:

> The role of the collaborator in an action research project has characteristics that seem to run against the traditional connotation of the word 'collaborator.' In the face of ambiguity, a collaborator's role is to seek clarity, not reassurance, although this may increase ambiguity. The collaborator needs to remain an individual, and not 'blend' in one cohesive unit called a 'team' or 'group.' Finally, whereas one would think that it is necessary to adopt an equalized role of collaborator for all

> members of our group, our discussion appears to indicate that the action research collaborator should in fact emphasize his or her own individual role as he or she illustrates power relationships that are an essential component of practice. (p. 178)

The role of facilitator, associate, and consultant is one of support and collaboration. Metaphorically, the role can be likened to that of a leg of a chair, where each one can be shaped differently yet the function is that of support, and together these legs of equal length fulfill a role. Indeed, each action research project is unique. So, the appropriate role for the facilitator is determined by the group's composition and by the tasks in which it engages.

"Each professional group develops a characteristic stance towards the world, a language with which to interpret it and respond to it" (Lebacqz, 1985, p. 52). It is from this characteristic stance of the group that reflexivity can be viewed. *Reflexivity* is a semantic quality attached to all words, terms, and phrases used as a language. The words of a language have meaning as long as the receiver understands the stance of the group. If such understanding exists, the receiver can interpret and ascribe meaning to the words that the sender uses. Yet, the sender needs to have sufficient knowledge and experience to assign meaning to the words selected and used. Winter (1996) adds:

> The thesis of reflexivity . . . argues that most statements rely on complex, interpersonally negotiated processes of interpretation. Individual words only have effective meaning because of the vast array of knowledge of other words and their meanings, brought to bear by speaker and listener. (p.18-19)

As a result, researcher reflexivity is always of concern even though all participants share a common background (i.e., teaching a subject). For instance, when group members are in the school system, subject to the same experiences, and develop a common framework of understanding (and a language in which to express it), concern for researcher reflexivity is still high. A researcher from another school may have different meanings to common terms (lab, quiz, test, and portfolio). Hence, it is likely that communication problems will surface. In particular, there may be significant chunks of implicit meaning to which there is no access.

Some educators are accustomed to a traditional hierarchy in the school and system, and the fact that a person, not on staff, is joining to facilitate or consult, may instill a sense of threat and unease not unlike that of an external evaluator. Openness is the key to lessening the impact of an unfamiliar person in the work environment. This can be done by proactive explanatory communications. This is important in the formation of ethical relationships within what Noffke (1997) has suggested are the "interconnected spheres of the professional, personal, and political dimensions" (p. 333). For instance, trust is established by being forthcoming, sincere, and leaving no questions in the minds of participants concerning motive or treatment of data in or outside of school. Consequently, it is important to make the agenda clear on the first day, by addressing the purpose of an action research effort. Most such efforts seek to support and facilitate growth and professional development in the areas of attention, and make it clear that no information would be communicated outside the group unless all participants approved of its release.

Action Research: Paradigms

This section embraces an attempt to further conceptualize action research beyond what was detailed earlier. Also included are two outcomes of action research. Each has something to offer and, as a result, most studies can best be described as a practical action research projects (improvement-focused agenda plus the promotion of understanding and professional development). However, it is necessary to reiterate, that fundamentally, there are many forms of action research.

Action Research: A Model

As noted in earlier sections, the notion of action research is something that often eludes simple definition. It is a mode that really transcends boundaries inherent in categories or terms found in various texts (Somekh 1989; Noffke, 1995). It is the *action* of doing something and the reflecting upon the action that produces a unity, which leads to a sense of freedom. The effort of action and reflection in order to act again is often labelled *praxis* (Carr & Kemmis, 1986). This repetitive cycle involves commitments that are linked to all facets of life. Each action research effort can change (or augment) the very understanding of action research in accordance with its application. As a result of this trait "action research needs to be conceptualised more broadly in terms of social theory, and . . . curriculum theory needs to be invoked to sustain and inform the work of action researchers" (McTaggart, 1991, p. 40).

Babbie (1983) explains:

> Social scientific theory has to do with what is, not with what should be. I point that out at the start, since social theory for many centuries has combined these two orientations. Social philosophers mixed liberally their observations of what happened around them, their speculations as to why, and their ideas about how things ought to be. Although modern social scientists may do the same from time to time, it is important to realize that social science has to do with how things are and why. (p. 17)

As action researchers focus and reflect upon the *how* and *why*, they use past experiences and current observations to move towards improvement and understanding (Grundy, 1996; Kemmis & McTaggart, 1988a). They acknowledge the multidimensional nature of action research and the connectedness of their educational practices (Noffke, 1995). As action researchers investigate social theory, they commonly call upon understanding of curriculum theory. This understanding can best be framed by suggesting they are aware of what *is* taught, what is *not* taught, and what is learned *just by being there* (Connelly & Clandinin, 1988). From this awareness, educational action researchers can theorize and reflect in a manner akin to social scientists, integrating theory and practice of action research. By moving along this continuum of understanding and awareness, we can reach a realization similar to what Noffke (1995) suggests:

> Action research then, is about taking everyday things in the life of education and unpacking them for their historical and ideological baggage. It is similar to, but not the same as, the everyday process of improvement, in that it is public and collaborative. It highlights process with content, rather than content alone. It allows for a focus on teaching, in addition to student outcomes, and on the interplay between the two. (p. 5)

Action research discussions revolve around what can be done to enhance curriculum theory, practice, and understanding of theory and practice as it unfolds in specific environments (Kemmis & McTaggart, 1988a). Often, this cycle is repeated in order to refine and improve outcomes. Hence the entwinement of curriculum and social theory which produces "a conception of teachers as professionals whose practice includes not only curriculum development but moral, yet not necessarily political, deliberation" (Elliott, 1987). Some suggest "action research is simply an extension of the notion of curriculum inquiry and is built on the idea of potential in curriculum materials. It names the process that innovative teachers do as a matter of course" (Connelly & Clandinin, 1988, p. 152). Action research is about producing desired change.

Participatory Action Research

Building on what has been detailed thus far, it is necessary to look at features of action research that seem to accommodate alternative models.

Action research, as noted earlier, is a means for teachers, in this case, to improve (Altrichter et al. 1993; Elliott, 1991). As action is undertaken, a better way of doing things is often realized. Reflection is necessary following these actions in order to move forward towards improvement. As progress is made via this praxis (action\reflection) a sense of freedom can be experienced (Carr & Kemmis, 1986). When one person is working in solitude some features of action research seem much more straightforward yet when a number of people participate confusion can often arise. To safeguard the process we must define both participation and involvement (McTaggert, 1997). "Authentic participation in research means sharing in the way research is . . . practiced. . . . It means ownership, that is, responsible agency in the production of knowledge and improvement of practice. Mere involvement implies none of this" (*Ibid.*, 28-29).

In most projects each participant has 'control.' This means that each member collaboratively develops the data collection schedule and to some extent the research agenda (mode). As well, each participant can opt out at any point and would be made clearly aware of this. Most action research efforts collaboratively collect data (journals, interviews, group discussions, artifacts/tests, and conversations), participate jointly in the analysis of data, and approve the final written reports cooperatively. This process is part of the professional development agenda which is often tied into personal (self-improvement), political (school role), and professional (educational praxes) dimensions. Each participant may have different reasons for being involved and each will fulfill the commitments as they see fit.

Many researchers such as Kemmis and McTaggart, 1988; Grundy, 1996; McCutcheon and Jung (1990) have argued:

> Action research is characterized as systematic inquiry that is collective, collaborative, self-reflective, critical, and undertaken by the participants of the inquiry. The goals of such research are the understanding of practice and the articulation of a rationale or philosophy of practice in order to improve practice. (p. 148)

As most studies refine praxes both theoretically and physically, the benefits become obvious. A veteran action researcher characterizes teacher research aims this way: "The refinement of professional skills is generally achieved by the gradual elimination of failings through systematic study" (Stenhouse, 1975, p. 39). To achieve these ends most action researchers work via a participatory work ethic where "conversation was not only a research method used by teachers for data collection and analysis, but was also their stance toward research and a way of generating knowledge and understanding" (Feldman, 1999, p. 141). Action research is about sharing, meeting, conversing, and generally being social in a strategic and systematic manner.

The Practical Action Research Paradigm

Practical action research has several virtues, for example, it is well-suited to bringing about professional development (McNiff et al. 1996, p. 10) in the area of education. It does not attempt to "change the very system itself or those conditions which impede desired improvement in the system " (Zuber-Skerritt, 1996, p. 3). It is 'practical' in the sense that it promotes change within constraints imposed by outside authorities (Board / Ministry).

Practical action research is a means to facilitate collaboration (Sagor, 1992) which is essential if participants are to improve self-confidence (Hargreaves & Fullan, 1998). It enhances understanding and may change participants' practices collectively (Rosaen & Schram, 1997) by allowing teachers to control the inquiry as the process is shared, guided, and collectively directed (Hodson, 1994, p. 93). "Some see it as an overall perspective, a series of commitments to problematizing social practices (including that of action research itself) in the interests of individual and social transformation" (Noffke, 1997, p. 307). It is participatory and akin to the aims of practical action research.

Another rationale for choosing practical action research can be found in *The Royal Commission on Learning* (1994), which realized, after much deliberation and consultation with Canadians:

> We know that teachers need to continue to learn and develop throughout their careers, and it turns out that one of the best vehicles for such growth is the school itself. One of the most effective ways of promoting both teacher growth and student learning is for teachers to work in a setting that emphasizes two things: continuous improvement of teaching, and regular monitoring and feedback about results. In other words, a

> 'collaborative culture' focused on instruction and student achievement is a powerful force for improving schools . . . in-school professional development. (Volume III, p.6)

It seems odd that the term, *action research,* was not used in the Royal Commission's Report. Perhaps this is because this mode of inquiry is still in its infancy in Ontario and its language would not be familiar to the general public. However, the action research process is developing slowly but steadily via university, school board, and teacher union support. One of the best ways to achieve a stronger collaborative culture is for all teachers to engage in practical action research. By becoming teacher/researchers, teachers learn first-hand what skills are essential and also learn to fine-tune their capacity to facilitate inquiries. Hargreaves and Fullan, (1998) add:

> Teachers today need to do much more learning on the job, or in parallel with it – where they can constantly test out, refine and get feedback on the improvements they make. They need access to other colleagues to get learning from them. Schools are poorly designed for integrating learning and teaching on the job. The teaching profession must become a better learning profession. (p. 83)

Similarly, Hodson (1994) states

> It is my contention that effective curriculum development and implementation requires that groups of teachers who know students, the locality and the school environment well, are brought together to work on theoretical and practical issues related to the design and implementation of a new science curriculum in a critical and supportive environment. (p. 93)

As well, McNiff, et al. (1996) explains: "An important principal of action research is for the research to be educational in the sense of self-developing. It is through enquiring into our own practice that we are able to create a living form of educational theory" (p.10-11).

Community-Based Action Research and Roles

The *community* in community-based action research can be best understood as an organization or group, who seek to better understand and solve a problem, or problems, that may confront them (Stringer).

Further, Stringer (1996) suggests:

> Community based action research . . . is ultimately a search for meaning. It provides a process or a context through which people can collectively clarify their problems and formulate

> new ways of envisioning their situations. In doing so, each participant's taken-for-granted cultural viewpoint is challenged and modified so that new systems of meaning emerge that can be incorporated in the texts—rules, regulations, practices, procedures, and policies—that govern our professional and community experience. We come closer to the reality of other people's experience and, in the process, increase the potential for creating truly effective services and programs that will enhance the lives of the other people we serve. (p. 158)

The social enterprise of community-based practical action research considers and embraces cultural differences. It does so via a systematic process of facilitation where participants may enjoy an enhanced life experience (Stringer, 1996) in teaching and in general. Community-based practical action research is then quite purposeful. It is from this recognizable purpose that it is often viewed as a professional development initiative (Hopkins, 1993). In community-based action research, each participant's role is of paramount importance. Stringer (1996) explains:

> Participation is most effective when it
>
> - Enables significant levels of active involvement
> - Enables people to perform significant tasks
> - Provides support for people as they learn to act for themselves
> - Encourages plans and activities that people are able to accomplish themselves
> - Deals personally with people rather than with their representatives or agents. (p. 32)

Each opportunity to examine another conception of action research causes further reflection. In Appendix A there are a few models that create differing roles and actions for those involved. The benefit of such consideration leads, eventually, to another rendering of action research. What follows is my rendering of an action research model.

An Action Research Paradigm

The concept of action research I have adopted "is one way of restoring and enhancing professional confidence. . . . Action research provides teachers with a more appropriate alternative to traditional research designs and one that is, in aspiration at least, emancipatory"

(Hopkins, 1993, p. 56). Action research efforts need to follow the principles that it does not interfere with the regular routines, was efficient, demonstrated commitment, was ethical, and was collaborative (shared vision) (Hopkins 1993). An action research study "combines substantive act with a research procedure; it is action disciplined by enquiry, a personal attempt at understanding while engaged in a process of improvement and reform" (Hopkins, 1993, p. 44). As an action researcher you need to be active in your "study of a social situation with a view to improving the quality of the action within it" (Elliott, 1991, p. 69). By acting in the above noted manner action research success can be assured, however, there is a need to further characterize action research.

The *action research paradigm* includes systematic inquiry, which is collective, collaborative, self-reflective, critical, and undertaken by the participants of the inquiry (Kemmis & McTaggart, 1988a; McCutcheon & Jung, 1990). Action research is, afterall, an exercise in participation, as noted previously, which often leads to elucidation, clarification, further communications, and commitments (Carr, 1995; Elliott, 1991). The implicit theoretical perspectives of teachers' assessment praxes emerge through discussions and observations which are often dialectic. These means of communication produce data which are then scrutinized, challenged, and refined through group activity (Hopkins, 1993). Feldman (1999) adds "that conversation can play a significant role in the establishment and sustention of collaborative action research groups, and that it can lead to the generation of new knowledge and understanding" (p. 141). However, it may be a lengthy and piecemeal process in which group members may fight tenaciously for the views they hold because they are embedded within a wider set of values that they hold dear. These value positions are challenged and through these exchanges, new positions may be assumed which sustain a sense of belonging in the group.

Summary

In summation, it is because action research can take on a variety of forms, either individual or collaborative, that it is necessary to label each enterprise carefully.

"Collaborative forms can be collaborations between teachers and outsiders, such as university researchers . . . or they can be collaborations among teachers" (Feldman, 1999, p. 125). Many action research efforts include only teachers and are directed towards improvement, as is the case with technical action research. Indeed, most inquiries are undertaken to improve the effectiveness of teacher praxes. Therefore, participants can be somewhat dependent upon the teacher-researcher as a facilitator as is often the case in collaborative undertakings. Still, if the aim is to enhance each practitioner's understanding and professional development in education, then one member's presence is not essential every time they meet. Roles are often Socratic and aimed to encourage practical deliberation and self-reflection on the part of participants, which constitutes practical action research and usually leads to improvement.

Chapter 2

Action Research: Collecting Data

Introduction

Action research has survived for many years via the support of enthusiasts, practitioners, and newcomers. Many new action researchers are in-service educators and some are education students. From pre-service to in-service and from undergraduate to graduate programs, there is a desire to become involved in action research projects related to education, teaching, and improvement. Enthusiasts seek out and request guidance and reassurance as they move forward towards educational goals and research outcomes. Even veteran researchers take note of new developments and observe both the quality and pace of evolution within action research efforts. The following was developed to address some of the needs of action researchers and to reexamine critical elements of action research such as the collection and analysis of data within action inquiries.

How to Collect Data

Data is a curious word which is actually the plural form of the noun, datum. This realization requires attention and careful consideration. When we read the word 'data'in a sentence, we sense a slight bit of grammatical uncertainty. For instance, I could say that the data are correct. To the person who is unaware of the plurality of the word, *data*, this sentence seems somewhat awkward or incorrect. We now know, however, that the sentence is fine. Therefore, when you read the word 'data' think of plurality and when you use the word data in a sentence reflect on its significance as a plural noun. Consider the question; do these data represent our students? It is useful to reread the sentence while checking your interpretation and comprehension, and then proceed.

Data are everywhere. Our observations (direct/indirect), experiences, and daily life provide a rich source of data. In my current role as an educator, I speak to many people and gather data on a daily basis.

In my research efforts, I may choose to speak directly to participants via informal conversation, or formal interviews which require me to ask questions that provide feedback and information. Each communication mode is a means and opportunity to gather useful data. I could communicate indirectly with participants via a survey, questionnaire, or instrument (psychological – projective test), as commonly used in Special Education areas. A third source of information emanates from colleagues. Colleagues, who interact with the research participants, can share their perceptions and observations of research participants. Lastly, the researcher (participatory or non-participatory) can provide observations and this information helps to build a picture, or record, that reflexively captures the context as perceived.

Within the community, I can pick up a newspaper, a magazine, or a journal and find data. If I locate the same data in different sources (corroboration) then we can suggest that information is somewhat credible (valid). I can elect to visit a business or school and from that experience gather data. In fact, we are constantly sensing data. It may be too cold or too warm, and if we take some time to record these 'facts' daily, or at least in some systematic and strategic manner, we can then say that we have collected data in a manner that is uniformly credible. Credible data is within many stories. For instance, if a study reported a 17-year-old female in the 11th grade ran a 100 meter race in 9.5 seconds we could then make use of this information. We need to corroborate these data in other sources in order to affirm the credibility. Yet, there are many pieces of data in this short excerpt. We now know that the participant was female. She is also 17 years old and she is, or was, in the 11th grade at the time of this study. This 17-year-old female also ran 100 meters in 9.5 seconds. The information recorded and/or provided by participants in a study, is a source of data for the researcher and those who read the research.

As educators, we live with evidence. It is in our conversations, emails, student products, video-tapes, audio-tapes, checklists, anecdotal observations, report cards, conference notes, staff meeting minutes, board documents, test results, and just about any artifact an educator can lay a hand on. What follows is a cursory look at some of these elements through the eyes of an action researcher.

Action Research Within the Classroom: Locating Evidence

Student Products

Student products include all of the products they develop via the curriculum tasks. These products prove they have learned and achieved. It is evidence, and these products symbolically represent their knowledge, skills, and attitudes at a point in time. This evidence surrounds a teacher in a classroom and much of it has been systematically collected. Students produce, among many things, evidence of their ability to process information, think critically and construct products. Teachers regularly make use of checklists and daily observations to document student progress. Weekly tests, monthly tasks, and yearly assessment and evaluation schemes aim to capture evidence of successful product completion.

Most teachers use a variety of means to gather data (assess) and eventually judge (evaluate) that data in order to decide the extent of teacher, student, and/or class progress and need. Data collection in the classroom is a multifaceted and continuous task that prepares teachers to become action researchers, as the teaching process is, in many ways, analogous to the action research process.

Some student products commonly take the form of a collection of writing (journals), videotapes (performances), audiotapes (oral tasks), computer demonstrations (technology usage), bulletin boards (captured via photography), and debates (recorded). By capturing these sources of evidence, students can demonstrate their understanding, skills, and attitudes. Teachers then judge the degree and level of growth in social and academic skills and attitudes.

Student (product development) tasks present an opportunity for authentic efforts. In other words, the products can be intended for real audiences. Some examples include:

- Creation and marketing of a food product;
- A letter to the editor and/or articles for a newspaper;
- Published work in periodicals/magazines;
- Displays in public places such as malls, businesses, and parks;
- Presentations to a city council, historical society, or naturalists society;

- Artistic performances for the community;
- Story telling at a library or bookstore;
- Creation of oral history tapes;
- Invention convention for the community or regional stage;
- Televised student discussion of a community problem;
- Business plans reviewed by business community; and
- Dramatization.

Teacher observations

Usually, traditional teacher observations fall into two categories: informal and formal. Within these two categories, it can be argued that teacher observations are largely driven by assessment and evaluation data collection goals. *Informal observations* may entail scanning a classroom for behavioral concerns, while *formal teacher observations* can involve anecdotal observations (checklists), specific work tasks, or controlled groupwork tasks such as tests, exhibitions, or performances. Classroom tasks, whether formal or informal, most often stimulate and instigate learning. These achievement opportunities can be recorded, documented, and used to inform the teaching process.

Within action research, there are multiple modes of observation. We can stand apart and be non-participatory while making observations, or we can be a participant and observe from within. Participatory teacher observation takes place when we engage fully in an activity; for instance, we join one side and play soccer during a physical education period. A third observational mode occurs when educators step outside of their direct responsibilities and attend another class to observe, or visit another school to make observations. This opportunity to observe passively while others teach means you are not responsible for the instruction. This is quite an opportunity and a privilege. Hence, the term *privileged observer* is often used to describe this mode.

We could argue that observation in our own research tends to bias our observations as we look for data related to our research problem(s) or hypotheses. This is something we need to write about, to make public, and explain our level of observational bias awareness. We also need to remind ourselves that just being alive renders us natural observers. As we move through our day, we make informal observations of others and our own behavior. Our data, perception, interpretation, and learning help us make sense of our world. They inform and guide our actions. Largely, our daily observation is habitual, principally unconscious, and unsystematic. Our lived experiences help us to maintain common sense interaction within our world. Our observations as educators are a research tool only when it is purposeful, planned, and recorded both systematically and strategically.

A lack of systematic and strategic control while observing in research brings about criticism as the data can be admittedly highly subjective, random, and scattered. The educational system actually helps action researchers in these areas, as systems in schools are highly routinized, strategic, organized, and systematic. Observer training in schools is part of their occupational role and is actually infused through curriculum initiatives. Timetables illuminate how each moment of the day will be used and lesson, unit, and year plans detail the content of these moments. Therefore, most educators are mentally prepared and have an understanding of observation which is important for all researchers. Yet, we simply do not move from participant to non-participant to privileged observer without embracing the elements, which keep each mode distinct.

Whatever the observational mode chosen, an observer is usually selective and attends to certain elements within the milieu. It is important not to try to attend to all elements within the research site, as it is overwhelming and even if a videotape was utilized, we would still be overwhelmed. We must attend selectively and focus. We work to become better and we search out means to improve in all occupations. A skilled teacher does not just happen; it takes a great deal of effort, practice, and refinement. In action research, you can learn to be a careful, strategic, and systematic observer. Preparing to be a skilled observer includes learning how to write in a descriptive manner. How to create a picture for the reader, which communicates context in a simple manner, is important in action research. Observing and writing what you perceive via the disciplined recording of field notes is not an easy task as you are attempting to recreate and reconstruct what you just observed. Knowing how to detach detail from trivia will permit your to construct a useful observational record.

To practice observing and recording is a necessary task. Strive to be a non-participatory observer in a public place and then challenge yourself to be a participatory observer in your work or social settings. Dare to be a privileged observer at city hall and record a council meeting. The apprenticeship process tests your abilities and each time you test yourself, you improve. You move from inexperienced to experienced just by applying yourself in a strategic and systematic manner. Compare your observations with others and read other people's accounts of experiences. Involve yourself in a class that requires observational tasks and build your competencies.

Observational Modes: 'D-E-L-I'

1. Define the behavior(s) to be observed.

2. Choose a recording mode, or recording strategy, and utilize it for that period of time. For instance you may choose:

> *Duration recording* – Observer records the length of time the behavior lasts.
>
> *Event recording* – Observer counts the number of behaviors that occurred during the observation period.
>
> *Latency recording* – Records the delay between instructions and start of task.
>
> *Interval recording* – Recorder divides the observation period into equal intervals and reports the frequency and duration of behavior during each interval.

Using the DELI provides a framework and a means to guide the teacher researcher.

Teacher Communications

A teacher is a communicator –whether he or she wants to be or not – who is obligated to reach out to parents, administration, peers, students, and the community. To do this requires knowledge, skills, and attitudes that are informed and refined. A teacher is compelled to utilize effective written, verbal, nonverbal, and visual communication techniques to foster active inquiry, collaboration, and supportive interaction both in the classroom and in the community. In doing so, vast amounts of data are created that can then be gathered, sifted, and examined. Our examinations can illuminate several realizations concerning teachers and communication.

We may realize that teachers understand communication theory, language development, and the role of language in learning as we read their report cards and Annual Education Plans (AEP). We realize that teachers understand how cultural and gender differences can affect communication in the classroom as we read Special Education forms (IEP's, IPP's, referrals). We may begin to see how teachers understand the social, intellectual, and political implications of language use and how they influence meaning in the classroom and the school community when we read the newsletters, letters, and flyers. We can start to uncover how a teacher understands the importance of audience and purpose when selecting ways to communicate ideas only after we read the transcripts of staff meetings and the contents of day books and/or parent-teacher meeting minutes.

Ideally, teachers model communicative activities as they put forward accurate, effective communications. Teachers are constantly conveying ideas and information. When teachers ask questions and respond to students they are modelling communicative behavior. To capture such evidence requires a focused eye and ear. It is possible to record by hand some of what is said yet an observer is overwhelmed by the non-verbal information. Using video allows us to review material repeatedly yet the video camera with its one eye and ear often distorts the reality and this is a limitation.

One action research study involved reflecting upon how we, as teachers, use effective questioning techniques to stimulate discussion in different ways for specific instructional purposes. This action research effort required not only a good memory (reflection) but also a number of sources of data in order to corroborate claims and assertions within the action research. The study made use of student products, teachers' plans (written evidence), and an action research diary (reflections) to broaden and deepen the findings. Luckily, most teachers create varied opportunities for all students to use effective written, verbal, nonverbal, and visual communication in the classroom and this can become the evidence within an action research effort.

Most teachers challenge students in a supportive manner and this provides students with constructive feedback. The problem for the action researcher is capturing these efforts in a manner that is efficient and useful. We have mentioned video and we can add tape-recording to the list yet we can also enlist other recorders to help us collect data. You may want to have other action researchers become part of your study and each of you can observe (privileged observer) in another's classroom. Of course you may need release time and failing this, you may need to donate your preparation period for the cause. All teachers use a variety of communication modes to effectively communicate with a diverse student population and it follows that all action researchers must use a variety of teacher communications to investigate diverse research interests.

As you move forward within your action research effort, you are supported by the fact that most teachers already practice effective listening, conflict resolution, and group-facilitation skills. These skills are essential for all action research projects and the fact that all teachers communicate using a variety of tools allows researchers to utilize these.

Narrative Writing

Narrative is a form of communication that, if written well, allows readers to view the lived experience as the writer does. Narrative writing includes the life stories found in both biographies and autobiographies. The biographer tells a story of another and we can sense via the writing the perceptions of the writer. The autobiography, on the other hand, is a window into the personal story of a person who has elected to make public the perceptions and lived experiences as they themselves sensed it. Traditional narrative involves one of the oldest forms of knowledge construction (storytelling). When we write, we reconstruct. We address a series of events and their causes. In addition, narrative also can involve the interpretation of stories that reveal past experiences, actions, opinions, and happenings.

A narrative is built upon language and text, and it is naturally seamless if it is well written. Most of us however think in terms of feelings and emotions and these seem to obscure and color the conscious collection of events, the discernment of actions, and the intellectual processes required to understanding what is going on around us. Our thought mechanisms filter the incidents and our sense perceptions color the sensations.

In the biography mode, we rely on others' information of what they sensed (heard, saw, etc.). We compare it with the composite network of information stored in our memory. We compare it to what we think or know. Some biographers may add or misinterpret due to a lack of similar composite memories, which leads to misinformation or errors within the biography. I recently required a graduate class to construct a biography of a classmate assigned to them at random. The resultant tensions and frustrations during the process were tangible and at times quite stressful. The biographers wanted to "get it right"; however, the telling of one's life story is often not a convenient linear experience that can be assembled neatly. In conversation, events surface and themes emerge which can confuse and distance the biographer. Narrative requires people to prepare to speak or write. It requires deep thinking, reflection, and broad communicative (writing) skills.

Narrative is most often built upon some type of organized deliberation. Narrative is about positioning what we reckon to be the most significant features of our thoughts within or upon a particular shape (linear or otherwise), and we are usually able to suspend the proof upon the sides of such a shape. Annotation, from within the story, is likely suspended from the shape in a complimentary manner. This approach is an orderly technique as bits of the supporting evidence can be skillfully interlaced. An exemplary narrative can present more than one voice, however this is quite difficult to maintain in the narrative form except by the most skillful of writers. I would encourage readers to read beyond this text and to look for more images and exemplars of narration. Look to biographies, autobiographies, ethnographies, and the work of researchers such as Connelly and Clandinin (2000) who have, quite capably, detailed this mode of inquiry for many years.

Journalling

For educators the word *journal* is not a mysterious thing. however, when confronted with the task of constructing your own journal a number of questions can emerge. For instance, what does an action research journal contain?

Usually, an action research journal will have a *form* that is maintained and your senses enlighten this form or shape. *Shape* can be the area of concern, the problem, a set of questions, an action research model, or your topic as it filters through your perceived thoughts, feelings, ideas, and activities. Recording your experience allows you to capture interpretations and lay out a chronicle.

Journalling can offer the writer a means to a greater sense of clarity about who you are, what you are doing, and how it is going. Your journal may contain reflections upon the past, present, and intuitive suggestions concerning the future. Journalling can be a method of finding your way, locating solutions to problems, organizing thoughts, setting goals, and recording a means to reach them. Journalling improves your writing skills and documents your progress in many areas.

Getting started requires some discipline and time. You may like to select a bound book with blank pages or purchase a loose-leaf notebook with colored, lined, or fine-looking ornamental paper. I have used spiral notebooks that fit nicely in my palm or slip into a pocket. Write in something that compels you to write, or type on a palmtop, a laptop, or desktop computer system. You could even purchase "Dragon Speaking Naturally," a software program that can record your spoken word and commit this to paper via the computer. I have used pocket recorders while teaching and then later transcribed this information to paper.

Traditionally, we journal while sitting down and reconstructing what has just happened. Do not throw up obstacles while writing, pay no notice to sentence structure or spelling, and do not criticize or stifle yourself. Let yourself write and develop a flow, a feel for writing just as a swimmer develops a feel for the water. Write anytime, anywhere, about anything, and do it often. However, we need to remember that the underpinnings of action research involve systematic and strategic actions that you design and nurture. I found that I would write anywhere, preferably a quiet, private place. Writing is a portable activity that you can do anywhere. Writing calmed my soul, provided perspective, and an outlet for emotion. Sometimes I logged my activities, other times I focused on my thoughts, perceptions, and ideas concerning my action research project. For example, I noted this in my journal on 17 October 1997:

> Pat is really working at getting all the information she can quickly in order to get ahead. However, I did this too when I started teaching and discovered years later that teaching can never be mastered. Every day is a new challenge and a chance to add to our resource base. Change happens to you when you are least aware of it. It could be a decision to question differently or apply resources differently that reflects a shift in beliefs. (p. 6)

My note was a reaction to a small group discussion that occurred regularly in our action research group. Another member of our group wrote,

> I have a lot of experience in different areas and the thought of getting involved in more reflection, since I didn't like it in the Fac. of Ed., makes me think it will be different this time since teachers are doing it and not people who want/might be teachers. (8 October 1997, p 1)

A much later journal entry by Pat:

> After months of talking and teaching, I think its time for some kind of a break. It has been a tough year but we've pulled together and I feel we are better for it. I just hope I'll have a job next year with Bill 160 and enrolment. Anyway, I'll use what I have learned and it will help. (10 April 1998, p. 43)

These journal entries are candid, honest, informative, and help action researchers to pull together their thoughts for further consideration. Journal entries can create pictures in the minds of readers and if you cannot find the words, possibly a drawing may be appropriate within your journal to capture a moment.

Test Results

Tests, which are nothing more than a series of tasks completed by students, can illuminate student or class achievement, needs, and assessment error. Test results allow us to rank, group, and attach a value to results. Grades and achievement can be related to the completion of tests and can provide the evidence for researcher claims. Tests indirectly illuminate the quality of instruction and even the quality of the test can be called into question. We can examine test construction, application, and marking practices. We can reflect on the progress of students and question the assessment and evaluation scheme. Testing within a classroom is a tradition that often includes formative and summative tasks as well as objective (multiple-choice, matching, true/false, etc.) and non-objective tasks (essay, student constructed responses) which can provide credible sources of data.

Recent innovations in classroom measurement has allowed for the use of authentic tests that permit students to apply skills and abilities as they would in real life. Authentic tasks such as the development of a new product or process, or improving an existing one, provides a wealth of data. Students who have a chance to exhibit their skills and abilities (performance) often believe the process of performance and the embedded evaluation scheme is more logical and more fair than traditional means of assessment and evaluation. Indeed, the area of authentic assessment and evaluation is fertile ground for action researchers. Teachers today, faced with authentic performance tasks, exhibitions, and portfolios are grappling with questions of reliability, validity, and equity when in fact the new assessment and evaluation innovations, just as in action research, are predominately non-generalizable and are rooted in the qualitative experiences valued on a case-by-case basis. This is what makes authentic assessment and evaluation so appealing. Authentic tasks do not easily lend themselves to tradition assessment and evaluation practices such as ranking and comparative analysis. Gathering this type of data can be time-consuming; however, with the use of multimedia tools, data collection is less frustrating.

Multimedia

If we had to characterize our current living environment, we would eventually use the word *digital* at some point in our description. The digital information age is more precise, expedient, and demands that the user be informed. Most teachers and researchers today could use a digital camera, a digital video camera, and a compact disc at some point in their day. Armed with a digital camera an action researcher can produce complete mobile files on compact discs that can later be re-examined. Innovations in education often require new modes of high-tech record keeping. 'Shop' classes today involve computer assisted design software and secondary classes in videography are common where students construct original video works and edit the same on computers. Teacher researchers can make use of these classes, or develop courses (units) to gather evidence. For instance, evidence can be captured via digital camera and transmitted via the internet to remote sites where it can be archived and examined later. Digital cameras provide picture and sound therefore we can examine both nonverbal and verbal behaviors. We can create a record of physical activity and use this to show human behavior in various milieus.

Questionnaires

Questionnaires help researchers by providing answers to specific questions. Sometimes statements are used to solicit information. The challenge for researchers is to develop each question or statement on the questionnaire that will extract accurate, useful information from respondents. The questionnaire provides insight, illuminating, and often revealing themes that can be further examined. A questionnaire can be an opportunity to use numbers as responses can be ranked (likert scale 1-5), summed, and averaged. The mix of quantitative and qualitative data is a good one for action research as you can gain support for your claims via each method.

Developing a new questionnaire is not always necessary since there have been many good (and not so good) questionnaires constructed in past studies. I recommend you attempt to locate a questionnaire that is already out there, and modify it to suit your needs. Another strategy to alert you to the pitfalls and successes inherent in questioning, is to begin developing questions and have people respond to these probes. For instance, at your next meeting, ask people to write down answers to two simple questions. Ask for no more than a paragraph and collect this data.

This preliminary work will allow you to see how difficult it is to simplify questions and get the data you might expect. Your goal is to diminish misinterpretation, encourage responses, and do both efficiently. For example, consider the following:

How often do you exercise?

Daily __________

Weekly _________

Monthly ________

Is this a simple question, or do you need more context? For instance, during the summer I exercise more than I do in the winter so I may average my response. Another possible reaction to this question is to ask, what do you mean by exercise? What about exercise duration, intensity, and the type of exercise as this will factor in somehow, so the question needs some work. Often while questioning in our classrooms, we refine our questions during the first one or two responses in order to zone in on the information we are attempting to elicit from respondents. We realize that closed-ended questions are more uniform as the responses are predictable. For instance, do you like hockey? The responses likely include yes or no. Open-ended questions leave room for the respondent to provide a more varied answer. For example, how does rainy weather make you feel? Even if we could provide an exhaustive list of possible responses to assist respondents, the issue of bias would appear and, therefore, would need to be addressed.

We try to avoid ambiguous questions, vague terms, jargon, slang, or technical words that throw up barriers for respondents. The topic needs to be examined from various levels, as some statements/questions can be politically, professionally, or personally objectionable. Sensitive topics include private issues and other areas that respondents believe are not for public viewing. Each item needs to be phrased positively to avoid misinterpretation. For instance, the statement, "Teacher unions should not include principals" creates confusion as respondents may agree in some respects but may want principals recognized as members of the unions for other reasons. Review your questions to address prejudice and bias.

I suggest a questionnaire be no more than a page in length and easily read so that respondents can complete the task without too much trouble. The next time you are in a restaurant take home a questionnaire that asks patrons about the service, quality of food, and overall experience.

Organizing the Data as You Collect It

One of my earlier action research efforts involved a group of Secondary science teachers. I opted to use this approach and described the data collection mode in this manner:

Over a period of eight months, data were collected via supportive weekly tape-recorded discussion groups, individual interviews, classroom visitations, daily journals, and randomly collected documentation. Data collection through reflection, was, in itself, a systematic and strategic process. The reflection process, carried out by all participants, was the analysis, which led to theorizing and the transformation of understandings of assessment praxes. (Stinger, 1996) Within the transcripts and journal notes, evidence that supported changes in assessment thoughts and practice was identified and described. Winter (1996) explains that "action research is seen as a way of investigating professional experience which links practice and the analysis of practice into a single, continuously developing sequence" (p. 13). Thus, data collection and analysis were not separate acts; they occurred simultaneously. Some early action researchers (Corey, 1949, Lewin, 1946) have treated the *act* of data collection and *analysis* as separate entities. Barnsley and Ellis (1987) suggest an acceptable contrast in method as they explain: "data analysis can begin while the research is in progress as well as after the data has been gathered" (Part V, p. 24).

As the data were mounting, I began to skim the collection and commence the task of reflecting on what I had sensed. Further reflection brought to mind key concepts and words that supported these concepts. I use the word *concept* to describe something that, to my mind, is unambiguous. The key concepts were used to assemble a matrix. I believed the conception of data analysis articulated by Sagor (1992) suited me best:

> Data analysis can be most simply described as a process of sifting, sorting, discarding, and cataloguing in an attempt to answer two basic questions: What are the important themes in this data and . . . how much data support each of these themes? (p. 48)

My assessment themes became key terms and were used on the horizontal axis of the matrix. These included:

What, Why, Who, How, Time, Isolation, and Views.

- **What** meant *What do you assess?*
- **Why** meant *Why do you assess?*

- **Who** meant *Who completes or develops the assessment?*
- **How** meant *How do you assess?*
- **Time** indicated that *some mention or inference was made to time as a constraining feature of assessment praxes.*
- **Isolation** indicated that *some mention or inference was made to teacher isolation as a feature of assessment praxes.*
- **Views** indicated that *a view had been expressed repeatedly and strongly.*

On the vertical axis, I had sources of data (group discussion, one-to-one discussion, journal, classroom visit, informal communications, and documentation). Each key concept was given a color code. As the data were skimmed, sifted, sorted, and a linkage to the key concept was found, the data were highlighted in the corresponding color. As well, in each box of the matrix, coordinates were noted, such as the date and page number. So, if I were looking for data concerning the 'what' (key concept – horizontal axis) of assessment praxes, I could go down the column to locate the source: group, 1:1, journal, document, visitation, informal note. Located in a specific matrix box would be the source's location by date and page number, thus enabling rapid location and recovery of the information.

In this short example, you can begin to see how we proceeded. Today, action researchers can do the same, or can opt to use a computer and the accompanying software to accomplish the same ends. However, unless you have free access to qualitative analysis software, it can be an expensive undertaking.

A Case Study

Our study was entitled: *The assessment praxes of a first year Secondary Science Teacher* and I began with this introduction.

Introduction

The following descriptions and interpretations concern the actions of a first year secondary science teacher. Pat (pseudonym) was a novice teacher who participated in our action research study in order to help us illuminate the assessment praxes of a first-year Secondary science teacher. Central to our research was the term *praxis*, which is henceforth understood as an established teaching practice, and *praxes* indicating several established teaching practices. To illuminate teaching praxes required a non-evaluative mode of collaboration, often referred to as participatory action research.

Pat was part of a group who were collectively participating in this practical action research effort in order to bridge the gap between theory and practice. Each of the participants "in participatory action research are joined by a thematic concern, that is, a commitment to inform and improve a particular practice" (McTaggart, 1997, p. 30). Hence, this examination of assessment praxes was linked thematically to a commitment to inform and improve assessment praxes.

Pat: Past and Present

Several images of Pat, as a participant and first year teacher, are described herein. Pat's images create an identity for her as she strives to increase her knowledge and understanding of assessment. It is through these images that rationales are connected to emerging themes. The themes and rationales were generated via our data collection and analysis. Our bouts of reflection served as a means of professional learning and much of our work culminates in the final sections where the images of Pat's assessment praxes are described as a search for competency and identity as a first year teacher.

Assessment Praxes: Pre-service Experience

Pat and I usually met for one-to-one sessions in one of three science laboratories at the school. Since Pat had a copy of the meeting schedule she was ready when she needed to be. I would arrive on time with tape-recorder in hand and we would commence our discussion focused on some aspect of assessment. This scene played out for most of our meetings, yet on a few occasions we were momentarily interrupted by some other staff member who came into the lab to get supplies. I would usually meet her during a preparation period, before class or after class, which meant that the room was quiet enough, or empty enough, so that our tape-recorder could pick up our conversation without interference. We never had technical difficulties with our tape-recorder and each of us became comfortable with the format. Pat wrote in her journal.

> I was not too crazy about the recording of what I said at first but since I will be hidden behind some pseudonym as well as the school then I guess that's good enough. It makes me feel what I say is important and I don't know if I'm ready for that. (30 October 1997, p. 17)

This entry struck me as honest and assured me that the data recorded would also be honest, sincere, and heartfelt. On most occasions our discussions seemed to go beyond the allotted time because we were both engrossed in our conversation. This always left me with the impression that we didn't have enough time, yet it was probably due to the fact that we had so much to discuss in the area of classroom assessment.

We discussed pre-service training and its aim to expose students to theory, methods, and skills. We reflected on our school placement experiences, which provided opportunities to apply pre-service learning. We discussed the amount of effort a first year teacher requires (Wideen, et al., 1998). We also discussed the alternative-based pre-service program modes, which might include action research (Carr & Kemmis, 1986; Sagor, 1992) and reflective practice (Schon, 1983). As we reflected, it became apparent that Pat had experienced a mix of both alternative and traditional pre-service training. I wondered to myself: Was it a consequence of this pre-service experience that certain opinions and beliefs developed within Pat? It seemed as though Pat's beliefs had come from an earlier stage of her life. If so, this supports the assertion of Wideen et al. (1998) who point out that beginning teachers enter pre-service teacher education with firmly held views about teaching (p. 168).

The notion that graduates of pre-service programs may enter the workforce with previously developed beliefs and values concerning teaching is useful to veteran teachers, teacher educators, and researchers who might try to work with first year teachers. The pre-service experience can then be viewed, by participants, from a highly critical stance. It can be perceived as a less than valuable experience. Indeed, beginning teachers are little influenced by the interventions that occur in pre-service teacher education (Wideen et al., 1998, p.168). This may be because the teacher in training often devalues pre-service and puts forward critical images of the experience when reflecting upon it, just as Pat noted in her journal early on:

> The Faculty 'process' of training teachers is not really valid. It is too subjective; it takes you down a path and asks you what you think along the way during the journey, or asks you to reflect at certain endpoints. I didn't have an answer; it was too much reflection and not enough reality. I knew what teaching was and what it wasn't. At the Fac. of Ed. we talked about what if, and why, and most people turned off. I woke up when I worked in classrooms and had to perform. (14 October 1997, p. 12)

Pat wanted more practice teaching in pre-service. She valued it more than the theory she was exposed to in pre-service. According to her, reflection in alternative based pre-service programs is an overused practice. This seemed to be a frequent theme for Pat as she reflected on her days as a student at the Faculty of Education at the University of Toronto. During a 1 October 1997, group discussion, in response to my question about assessment while in her pre-service year, Pat recalled what assessment was like for her.

> A lot of it has been very cognitive, very little creativity and, well, group work – I'd say a lot of people assess group work very superficially. I mean, did you work? Great there you go, you got an 'A.' I mean, if you didn't break any windows, there you go, you got an 'A' in group work. Assessing group work might be very, very subjective and it depends on how people work. Together, some people can do that and other people can't, I don't know. I just find it fairly subjective in class group work. I found I wasn't assessed that way in University at all. There is no creativity part at all. It was how you communicate and how you can write. It's hard to focus on the assessment. The assessment this year has been interesting because how to word a question and what they comprehend from the question . . . just from the assessment you can tell how the person thinks. I mean, yeah, they wrote something, here's an 'A.' And if you give them less than 60 percent, everyone complains. I'm not very happy with the grade 9 assessment; it's very different than the grade 10. You go from one step to the other so quickly. (p. 1)

I matched Pat's critical responses to the insights of researchers such as Wideen et al. (1998), who suggest that:

> Future work [in the area of preservice program development] must systematically challenge myths that underpin most current programs of teacher education and focus on the structures and the ethos that must be created to assist beginning teachers to examine their beliefs and to understand how to support new practices that are consistent with their changed beliefs. (p. 169)

I thought the points made in this quote were essential to our discussion and I shared these with Pat, who laughed at their accuracy. Secondly, we thought that until these changes are made pre-service teachers might consistently graduate with similar beliefs. For instance, Pat decided that the year invested at her Faculty of Education had not paid dividends.

Clearly, not all in our group shared her opinion. However, I found a means to understand not only Pat's position on this question, but others' as well. My understanding became clearer once I had made attempts to decode Wideen, et al. (1998), who astutely point out that "preservice teachers do not typically develop new perspectives, [they] simply become more skillful at defending the perspectives they already possess" (p 142). So, Pat was in a defensive and highly critical stance, as she suggested her pre-service program required only "breathing and running around," as criteria for passing. This opinion of Pat's was probably related to the views of some pre-service teachers who suggest that "teaching [is] something one does, not something one ponders" (Wideen, et al. 1998, p. 153). Therefore, sitting idle in a Faculty of Education classroom, quite removed from the *front lines of teaching*, caused Pat to be uneasy about her teacher training and some aspects of teaching in general.

In spite of her pre-service experiences, reactions, and impressions, Pat was at this time, confident, yet frustrated in most areas of teaching – including assessment. Within the group setting Pat often vented and seemed to be somewhat annoyed.

> Give me something concrete and I'll run with it. I'm not a cadaver. I did self-assessment and I did peer-assessment and the group said I got a 100%, everyone got 100%. I had just as many discipline problems. So, to say the old way is, I'm not saying all is good, there are a lot of problems. But a lot of people are incorporating a lot of things. I think the new method is very illogical in a lot of areas. Whereas the sheet of paper saying do A, do this, here's a handout, be quiet, boom, I mean until I can get some of that, I mean content is very important. (22 January 1998, p. 4)

Obviously there was tension in the air as Pat addressed some of the frustrations she faced in her classroom. I asked myself if she was just making a case for giving up her ideals in favor of traditional practices (content-based program), as noted by Rosaen and Schram (1997) in their study of first-year teachers. Clearly, Pat supported a content-based program. Content-based programs offer a series of lessons that are regimented and cause students to follow a predetermined course of learning (Griffin, 1998). Pat viewed herself as a transmitter, there to deliver a body of knowledge. She wrote:

> In order to lay down the law in class you have to know your course of studies inside and out. Because I do I find it easier to take care of the behaviour of the students. Both

> of these areas are of interest to me. If I control their behaviour then we can deal with the content. If I can take control of the content then I can deal with their behaviour. (19 November 1997, p. 21)

This preoccupation with control (discipline) is well documented in the pre-service literature (Rosaen & Schram, 1997;Schoonmaker, 1998). This insight may also be applicable to first-year (novice) teachers; it certainly seemed to be so for Pat. Later, during one of our many group discussions, Pat explained, "I'm the boss, I can make the rules and if you don't like it too bad, ha, ha, ha" (12 November 1997, p. 3). Pat then complained that grade 9 assessment was not ideal, but rather too subjective, or easy, and grade 10 was too difficult, too large a step from grade 9. It could be that Pat might be experiencing challenges to some of the idealism created in pre-service, or even before pre-service, while Pat was a student. Her current dilemma created serious problems and confusion for her (Wideen, et al. 1998).

Pat thought her Faculty of Education experience was enriched by her practicum. However, she felt that away from the practicum, in the areas of study that are more theoretical, there was less value for some teachers, who view it as too detached from practice. Indeed, Schoonmaker (1998) suggests,

> The literature tells us that if . . . [a person's] development as a teacher is typical, she will leave the university with the conviction that theory is abstract and unrelated to the realities of teaching (p. 562).

The merits of this observation were explored in our group. Pat offered this insight concerning the development of assessment literacy at her Faculty of Education.

> **T.R.** Did classes in assessment help you?
>
> **Pat** Nothing was good. Science was not bad and they did some assessment. Math was a total waste of time. Special Education was eight hours of 'there are special kids out there and don't worry about programming because the special education department will look after that.' Obviously they don't, because I had to do it. Discipline, we played with pom-poms and found out what type of personality we are. Law was not bad: This is the law-bang-bang-bang. That was half-decent. The psychology was useless. He told us stories about how he grew up on the prairies. He was about 80 years old. The TSS course was off the wall; she didn't open her mouth the whole time.

> She told us her life. It was a really a huge waste of time.
>
> **T.R.** So, how would you change the year at the Faculty of Education to make it more useful?
>
> **Pat** More practical exercises, such as making tests for grade 10 science. Stuff the reflection; we had reflection right out the wazoo.
>
> **T.R.** OK, the assessment classes were not useful, so your practicum was time well spent?
>
> **Pat** I've got a strong science background and fairly strong math background, so they let me walk in and do things by myself because I was confident. It was teacher-to-teacher level and not teacher-to-student.
>
> **T.R.** During your placements, did you use any alternative assessments?
>
> **Pat** Not portfolios, but self and peer-assessments.
>
> (7 January 1998, p. 3)

Pat, in fact, saw most of the pre-service year as a waste of time, with the exceptions of her practicum, and one or two of her professors. This highly critical stance towards the Faculty of Education can be linked to the striking contrast between what is done in pre-service and what a teacher's needs are inservice. Therefore, the hindsight becomes quite cynical and some may say that "all is lost if teachers succumb to pessimism and cynicism" (Hargreaves & Fullan, 1998, p. 58). Yet, Pat was determined to overcome this pessimism. One means to overcome it was to be forthcoming, and I supported this virtue as best I could, as did our group. I noted in my journal early in our study:

> Pat stands out because her insights seem so much out of 'sync' with what the other veteran teachers are saying. I include myself as part of the veteran group. The established view versus Pat who brings in the alternative. I don't quite know how to describe it – I guess I could just say she is a first-year teacher who has yet to become accustomed to certain ways and means in education. (10 October 1997, p. 2)

Pat reflected on her experience of being assessed and came to the conclusion that it was mostly cognitive and narrow. By this she meant traditional content-based assessment, with paper and pencil methods. Assessment, as she experienced it, did not involve the application of skills or varied tasks from each of the three domains (psychomotor, cognitive, and affective).

Pat viewed self- and peer-assessment as less than adequate and not a valid way to assess either in the Faculty of Education, or the classes she now teaches. Therefore, her assessment praxes involved many of the tools she was most familiar with and coincidentally believed in, such as multiple-choice, fill-ins, and short-answer objective style questions. Pat's assessment praxes seemed to be a perpetuation of what has been done traditionally in assessment. Her influences have been her experiences as a student. Smith (1988) explains:

> Professors in faculties of education have told me that student teachers are not 'ready' for theory – and that most practicing teachers are not either. These professors argue that student teachers must be given 'survival skills' to get through the day and that they must be prepared for the way schools are, not for the way schools ought to be. Teachers, like students, behave in ways that reflect how they have been taught. (p. 126-127)

If this insight had been available to her, Pat would possibly have graduated with a better impression of the faculty and its educational program. Pat's assessment praxes closely matched those of her predecessors. However, as mentioned, Pat had been hired close to the beginning of the school year. Consequently, she felt under siege and was attempting to "ground herself" by doing what was easiest, given the multiple demands of the job.

Search for Competence

Pat, as the newest staff member, had interesting perspectives on the role of a secondary science teacher and possible indicators of good teaching. On 3 December 1997, we had the following conversation.

> **T.R.** What criteria would you have that makes a good teacher?
>
> **Pat** One – competent in their field, two – industrious, three – creative, four – energy, and five –patience. I think that's it.
>
> **T.R.** If I said to you, "A good teacher is one that wears a blue shirt," would you wear one?
>
> **Pat** Yes, I would. (p. 3)

Pat was the kind of staff member principals look for because of her enthusiasm, dedication, and innumerable skills suited to the job. I was not the only member of our group to appreciate Pat's efforts. Jan, another veteran teacher, stated in a 9 April 1998 group discussion that although Jan had trouble transcending routines, Pat seemed less constrained.

> I found that with a couple of courses I've taught, it has served as a limitation – I'm teaching a new course, and to learn the content was impossible. I follow the plans I've inherited. That's what impressed me with Pat this year. As a first year teacher she has a binder. She is just not getting through the stuff as I did. She is making a lot of changes, and including computers. She is using some of the same labs, but I found that she is kind of a breath of fresh air for this particular Biology course. I think that's great. It might encourage me to do some new things. There have been other courses where I have been limited by the binder. I just kind of use it to get through the day and the semester. (p. 4)

Pat was willing to do whatever it took to develop her professional expertise and comments like Jan's helped Pat establish her professional identity. Beginning teachers can choose to follow many paths that are influenced by any number of people. The choice to follow a certain path is ultimately due to their own beliefs concerning notions of competency (Rosaen & Schram, 1997).

Assessment Praxes: Perspective Transformation

For Pat, our efforts to examine, act, and reflect caused her, over the course of eight months, to behave in a manner that demonstrated a change in philosophy. She began our study, I believed, in a defensive mode. I saw it more as an issue of trust. Yet, as time passed she began to see our efforts as a *bottom-up* rather than a *top-down* approach to the development of assessment praxes. By the end of the project, she seemed to be quite proactive and open. Her transformation may have been due to our cultivation of an atmosphere of mutual respect and tolerance of others' views (Elliott, 1991). For example, by 3 April 1998, Pat reflected:

> Getting together with other teachers has been something I usually do after hours. It was a time to relax. I find I am more able to do the same during school because our group lets me do this. I can lean on Jan or someone else while I get rid of my feelings, it's like being married and I'm not yet, but I guess I'm right. In the future I'll try to do more of this, it's been helpful. (p. 40)

From the onset of our study, Pat made it clear that although she was in her first year of teaching and had a basic understanding and appreciation of assessment, she wanted more. Pat understood that our discussions and interactions would impact her perspective and on-going transformation during this study. Our attention came in many forms. For instance, on several occasions I watched her in the classroom while she made changes in her praxes. My attention was general, yet I did have a specific concern: assessment. Pat did not always assess when I visited, hence my observations could be labelled 'general' (Hopkins, 1993) on some occasions. I followed some good advice as I was careful not to move too quickly to judge; I used my interpersonal skills when "invading another person's space," and I tried to follow my aide-memoir (Hopkins, 1993). On 10 December 1997, I visited Pat's class and came away with these impressions.

> I was the first person in the class, which was the same one used by Cal, Bob and Jan. As the students began to enter the room I noted the different types of clothing and where each one sat. It was funny, how girls tended to sit with girls and boys with boys, yet it was grade 10. Everyone came prepared to work but as soon as Pat stepped into the room everyone seemed to increase their level of activity, becoming more active and louder. Pat started to talk to various students about different issues such as work not done and poor grades, absences, and work without a name. I saw some students start to cross that behavioral line. I felt my own brow start to furrow. Pat turned, looked at the offenders, and made a quick comment about grades and turned back to the blackboard. The three students did become quiet, but as I was unaware of their past, I don't think I understood exactly what was going on. Pat handed out a worksheet and assigned text pages to read for homework. The remaining time was spent working from overheads (copied the ecosphere drawing). The class in general seemed to settle once the tasks were assigned and I left with a good impression of the period. Pat had only a few minutes before the next class so I told her we would talk later. (p. 33)

Following the advice of Hopkins (1993), I gave Pat her feedback within 24 hours, using facts, and welcomed a two-way discussion. After this class observation Pat suggested that this was her good class and they seemed to handle most tasks well. Later in the term, in this same class, she would experiment with more student assessment input. The decision to use this class was, in part, due to her perception that this class was easy to control. I knew what she meant, since I had visited her other two classes and seen that they were behaviorally more challenging. In her 'good' class, I think she appreciated the respect they showed her. They responded well to her behavioral prompts and cues. While in our group, Pat listened carefully and brought forward timely insights as we voiced our individual "ways of looking at and thinking about events and interactions of the classroom as a basis for improvement" (Rudduck, 1991, p.18). For instance, Pat added, "Assessment – well we have two choices, either go back to what we were doing, or come up with applications to replace past practices" (4 March 1998, p.3).

Pat's straightforward approach was refreshing and, to some extent, a beacon for our group. She was eager to change (to engage in action) and mentioned that if someone would "give her the tools" she would "run with it." Pat felt she needed to have someone else provide the assessment tools. I understood this stance to mean that until this happened, little, if any, change was possible. For Pat, being able to find that 'time' to change assessment praxis tended to dictate what was possible and what was not. A lack of time meant her tests were like those of her colleagues, mostly content-based, traditional, and narrow. Yet upon closer examination, Pat's assessment praxes were a curious mix of tradition and alternative modes. On 4 February 1998, I asked her about her assessment activities.

> **T.R.** What assessment means are you using in the second term that are new or refashioned from the first term?
>
> **Pat** Well the way they work, independently, is not good. So, I'm setting up more group work, seminars, and I have them making web pages that are much more interactive. Because, that's what they want to do, so, that's what I want to do.
>
> **T.R.** To what extent will peer or self-assessment play a role?
>
> **Pat** About the same as first term, but they are more involved.

She explained that she thought her use of many modes, such as peer-assessment and the Web (Internet), allowed students more opportunity to demonstrate achievement through involvement. This effort to involve students in assessment demonstrates a change in values, compared to a point early in our study, where Pat mentioned that most students were incapable of completing these types of assessment. As a group we agreed with Pat's initial position, yet the group movement was towards these alternative and varied assessment modes, which indicated to me a shift in preconceptions. Pat noted early in our study:

> I use a lot of different methods and I don't have time to make my own assessments, so I need to borrow and beg from others. This is, after all, my first year and I'm just organising. (Journal, 15 October 1997, p. 3)

Pat was, in the early stages of our study, establishing standards and sorting out targets. This pursuit of self-awareness meant a movement from decisions based on theory to critical descriptions of practice. Her practice now became a place to theorize. Part of that development included her realization that students could complete more self- and peer-assessments. I noted this in my journal on 17 October 1997:

> Pat is really working at getting all the information she can quickly in order to get ahead. However, I did this too when I started teaching and discovered years later that teaching can never be mastered. Every day is a new challenge and a chance to add to our resource base. Change happens to you when you are least aware of it. It could be a decision to question differently or apply resources differently that reflects a shift in beliefs. (p. 6)

Pat always wanted to be viewed as the participant who was either already doing what we discussed, or had already done it in her class. Eventually, she let us see another side of her and admitted that she, too, needed to collaborate with others more often and involve the students to a greater degree in assessment efforts. Pat added:

> I am just saying that if you need it you get it, I have stuff from Bob and others – or you find it yourself. I need to get a lot more information on assessment but I like to do this informally. It gets pretty sticky if it's formal. It's the same with the students. If you work with them informally then you get a lot more done. (4 March 1998, p. 1)

This sentiment contrasts with statements made by Pat earlier in our study, which were less open and more protective. Pat's transformation was mostly interpersonal, as she seemed to trust our group more as the relationship aged. Professionally, Pat became more collegial. Near the end of our study, 4 March 1998, I asked Pat about her readiness to share.

> **T.R.** Do you exchange resources?
>
> **Pat** I have stuff from Bob and others. I'm very independent, if I need it I go and find the answer. I don't like it forced on me. I don't like it because it's not my style.

> **T.R.** What do you mean forced?
>
> **Pat** I am just saying, when someone says you have to do it this way or this person will help you, well, you may not be able to work with that person. I'd rather have it informal, rather than formal. Things that get official get sticky. I get more work done unofficially, and, I'll go get assessment tools. If I have a question and I want an answer, this is who I'll go talk to.

I hoped that our individual and group discussions had caused her actions (change). However, it could be that even our mere presence (peer-pressure) was the cause of her growth. During another visit to her class, I noted several changes,

> Pat was busy setting up a lab (limewater test for carbon dioxide) for her grade 9 advanced class when I walked in Room 123. I helped her make sure all the groups had the right materials. The task within the lab was to observe chemical change using commonly available substances. A few minutes later several students came in to help. These were her assessors from her grade 11 class. Pat gave them clipboards with pencils and asked them to note who did what. *Great,* I thought, *Pat is delegating and empowering.* I asked if these assessors were being graded and Pat said, "No, next time." As the students arrived they seemed very serious (test faces) yet Pat was quick to explain and show (exemplars) in great detail that they would have several chances to do well. I noted that this seemed to be evidence of an outcomes-based program and not content-based. I was happy for Pat as she moved around the room making suggestions and reminding assessors to help out. The 70 odd minutes flew by even for me and as the buzzer sounded, indicating the end of the period, some students seemed frustrated that the period was so short. Pat remarked "You couldn't please them all" (25 March 1998, p. 47).

Pat was, for this class anyway, more of a facilitator then in her usual practice. Pat was looking for students who could not only apply skills but also explain it to an assessor. It was very open-ended and each student had opportunities to demonstrate an outcome. I believe our efforts helped Pat validate her perspectives and solve problems that faced her. Pat explained in her journal,

> Listening to other teachers complain is good. It lets me know that I'm feeling the same as others and this gives me

> a boost that I can run with for days. Meeting is a source of power; a refuelling that gets me over the next hump. (12 March 1998, p. 39)

In sum, our experiences led to a collegial mode of communication from one that was less so. Our group's ability to mesh allowed the examination of beliefs and dilemmas concerning assessment praxes and eventually led to the limited use of alternative and varied assessment tools. Sometimes our actions remained theoretical and other times they became part of a practice. If the research had continued we would have been able to more fully put into practice the modes we discussed and reviewed. Admittedly, we did not overcome the "constraints of overload, isolation, and compartalization that are endemic to schools" (Earl and Cousins, 1995, p. 42). To do so entails fundamental change at the system level.

Note: Our Action research data was extensive, and within this excerpt, much of the information is missing due to the need to make this text more easily manageable. A case study is usually descriptively thick, and deep in scope.

Ethical Considerations

We know that every teacher has the right to improve his/her own practice. Yet, the method of improvement, in this case action research, needs to heed ethical boundaries. We need to consider several critical issues within the data-collection process. Data are something we require to complete our research. Informed researchers are obligated to evaluate data and describe, explain, predict, propose theory, construct summaries, or offer conclusions. Data are synonymous with many words including, but not limited to *information*, *facts*, and *record*. As researchers (scientists), we make observations in a methodical manner. Our methods are controlled in some manner and this data collection evidence needs to be protected. We need to be reminded that it is privileged information. When you move forward with your research, you must explain to potential participants, and understand for yourself, that all data (records) are kept confidential and secure. We do this to ensure that data are treated in an ethical manner and in confidence. Afterall, researchers often make personal facts public, or gain access to the private lives of participants. Each of our lives has personal, political, and professional elements that need to respected and secured. Most of us do not want our personal lives published or otherwise aired within a public domain. Sometimes this is not the case as action researchers and others deliberately choose to air the often very personal elements in their research for various personal, professional, and possibly political reasons.

Data are not always completely anonymous no matter what steps are taken. Data collected anonymously can sometimes be traced to the participants. Some research efforts may require that further information be collected that can be linked to the previous information. Most, if not all universities have ethical reviews that must be complete before permission is granted to move forwards with any of the intended research. Ultimately, ethics approvals seek to ensure that no harm is done to anyone during the research.

Researchers ultimately need to be able to identify where the data came from. A coding system can be set up by labelling elements such as students (S1, S2, S3), classrooms (C1, C2, C3), teachers (T1, T2, T3), or schools. Further suggestions will be offered in the data analysis section. We seek to keep data anonymous yet organized, structured, and within a framework that is confidential and secure, and our sources are never revealed to the public.

We now know that data are privileged pieces of information that are collected for a purpose. The manner in which we collect data can be described in lengthy detail with the aim of ensuring that our data collection efforts are both effective and ethical. As a researcher collecting data we attempt to illuminate a particular set of circumstances, an answer, provide a solution, or make an improvement. Some may view your efforts to improve as solutions or answers, and others may interpret your actions as an effort to professionally develop. For instance, a teacher-researcher might want to poise this research question: How can I improve my classroom management? This seems like a common question, at least in education, and one that is worthy of research effort. Asking how you can improve your classroom management is a general research question that requires thoughtful research planning. You need to have a roadmap in order to find your way through the data collection jungle in an effective, prudent, and ethical manner. *Ethical research* is informative and one essential element is to inform all participants, which usually means a letter to parents that action research will be undertaken. The following sample letter illustrates one example of a letter to administrators.

Principal Sample Letter

Principal ______________________________

School ______________________________

September 4th, 1997

Dear Principal: __________________

I am inviting your school and four science staff to participate in an Action Research project. My project is being conducted within the Department of Curriculum, Teaching, and Learning at the Ontario Institute for Studies in Education from September 1997 to April 1998. My research project will be submitted as partial fulfillment of the requirements of the degree of Doctor of Education at the University of Toronto. By agreeing to participate in the Action Research project we will be able to explore issues and practices in assessment within science while working collaboratively as an Action Research group.

The Project

Each of the four participants of the project will be invited to discuss and plan meetings, critically reflect on practices, plan and design alternative curriculum materials and practices within this supportive group. We can implement developed materials in class, evaluate these in action, and share with others, our experiences, feelings, and ideas as a way of informing and guiding our group's professional development.

Data Collection

Data will be collected by tape-recording group meetings and field notes. Individual interviews will be held during the year with each participant. The recorded information will be transcribed and copies made available to the same teacher. I will be visiting participant's classrooms upon their agreement. Information collected will be shared with that teacher only. Visits are necessary to promote understanding and promote professional development.

Participants will be encouraged to keep a journal. Teachers are asked to note assessment reflections, decisions, practices, habits, and rituals that they use in classes. Beliefs about assessment can be written, as can general thoughts concerning assessment theory and practice in science. I will be keeping a journal, also. The information collected in the journals is important to the action research process.

Ethics

All work will be anonymous and confidential. All names will be changed, as will details that may reveal the identity of the participant. Only the field notes, interview transcripts, and journals will be seen by my thesis committee. All tapes and journals will be secured once the project is completed. Your consent will be necessary if any publication of this data is possible.

The project seeks to study teachers as they collaborate while participating in an Action Research Project in science. The actions of non-participants may appear only for background context. If student input is necessary administration, teachers, and parents will give permission first.

Findings and conclusions will be shared with participants and careful interpretations will be recorded as the project moves forward. An editing process will be used which is helpful and important. Our aim is to present an accurate, fair, and agreed upon account of experiences. If agreement is not reached, both accounts will be written into the data. Participants may delete any text and a final summary will be provided.

Note: All have the right to withdraw at any point without reason.

If you are willing to participate in this research project, please complete the attached form. Thank-you for your support and co-operation in this Action Research Professional Development Process.

Respectfully,

Thom Ryan

Department of Curriculum, Teaching, and Learning (CTL)

OISE/UT

Principal Consent Form

I, ______________________________________ agree to allow my staff to participate in the study entitled: An Action Research Study of Secondary Science Assessment Praxes, as outlined in the attached letter.

Signature ____

Date _______________________________

Researcher ____

In another research study, I had to ask the parents for permission and the following permission letter was used.

Parental Sample Letter

Dear Parent/Guardian:

I am a researcher from Nipissing University, investigating students' perceptions of the nature and impact of the new curriculum: curriculum, teaching strategies, integration of technology, student evaluation and reporting, and teacher advisory program (TAP). Results and recommendations from this study will assist teachers in designing their curricula and adapting exemplar teaching strategies and quality assessment strategies for their courses. This study is conducted in accordance with the ethical standards for research at Nipissing University.

Your son/daughter has been randomly selected to take part in this study. The survey your son/daughter is asked to complete in class should take 10 minutes. It contains questions pertaining to teaching and evaluation methods used by each teacher, difficulty of the courses, classroom atmosphere, approximate course grades, and the TAP program.

You can be assured that all information collected will be strictly confidential. In fact, students are asked not to put their names on the questionnaire. Please indicate below whether you would permit your son/daughter to take part in the study. Your cooperation will be sincerely appreciated. Please contact us at Nipissing University if you have any further questions.

Sincerely,

Thomas Ryan, Ed.D.

Note: Completion of this survey is voluntary and your child can choose to withdraw without penalty.

I agree to allow ______________________ taking part in this study.
(Son/daughter's name)

I do not wish ______________________ to take part in this study.
(Son/daughter's name)

Parent Signature __________________________
Date ____________________
Please return this form to the Home Room Teacher

Chapter 3

Analyzing Action Research Data

Critical Elements of Action Research

In the last section, I addressed data collecting opportunities available to the action researcher within the education milieu. Once you begin to collect the evidence, multiple questions emerge. For instance, you may ask, how should I look at the evidence? Is there a guide that will tell me how to proceed so that I can avoid making errors? What do I look for, and how do I know when I have found something? I recall the sense of excitement, concern, and caution I experienced as I moved forward within my first action research inquiry. What I learned, and have yet to learn, is illuminated in the following sections. I consider how researchers can analyze data within their own action inquiry.

How to Analyze Data

Action research data are best analyzed as they are gathered. Understanding the depth, breadth, and context of the collected data can be transitory in the course of a research project and this is why I like to deconstruct, examine, and order data as they are gathered. Data and their analyses do not have to be separate activities or events. However, analyzing as you collect the data is not always possible, especially when you work in the hectic world of education. Yet, if you have joined fellow teacher researchers, you may be able to share the analysis tasks. One member of the group could look at, or for, one theme, and another member could sift through data while attending to a different theme. The process is one of discovery, investigation, and presence of mind. The recursive review of data can cause elements to surface that may have gone unnoticed previously.

Most action researchers, whether working alone or with others, are involved with a project that is based on lengthy transcripts (in-person, audio, and video) from recording sessions or detailed notes made during and after the interviews, and/or the thorough examination of school and classroom documentation. All of these activities take time and traditionally, in the absence of technological data analysis aids, it is almost impossible to mix both data gathering with data analysis. The process of data analysis is most often conducted in a semi-ordered fashion (systematic), to allow for researcher brainstorming within an action research mode (model/framework). High-quality action researchers consider the wider social contexts influencing the areas they are studying. An engaged researcher seems to be continuously reflecting, examining, and making use of what some might describe as an analytic perspective. The events and activities within your research project will cause you to break down what you perceive into elements that appear to address your question(s) or complement your themes.

The data I scrutinize are frequently quite different than the actual lived experience. We experience life in three dimensions; it is dynamic and relatively fast paced. Your data will often be the opposite. It is largely static, two-dimensional, and we can revisit it whenever we choose at any pace we choose. For example, the typical classroom context is a rich source of data as the furniture, arranged in a strategic manner, can be documented via a drawing, photograph, or videotape. The drawing and the photograph capture a context and make it static. The videotape record is more life-like than the other forms yet it does only extract a slice of life as it has a start and end point. The video camera has only one eye (lens) and one ear (recording device), therefore the video has limitations and tends to skew the observation. I once undertook a creative writing course where I was asked to capture the view of a child less than five years of age. I spent several hours about one metre from the ground and I tried to write about this experience as best I could. Data needs to have meaning in order to use it effectively. The point is that in the land of children the person who can reach the highest can open many doors and even be deemed a leader because of this ability.

Predicting Results

Predictions, prophecy, forecasting, and guessing are all words that can be used to describe, to some extent, the abilities of people to look forward into the future and tell us what may happen. In research, we can write about the future and create a hypothesis. If we were to roll a die, as we do in grade 5 math (probability), we would learn that you have a one-in-six chance of getting one of six numbers. If I predicted or hypothesized that I could roll a five once out of every six rolls, then I would possibly realize this prediction since that is precisely the odds of rolling a particular number on a die. A hypothesis is a prediction of what specific results or outcomes are expected to occur. We could hypothesize that increasing student numbers in classes decreases a teacher's free time. We could also hypothesize that test scores will decrease as student numbers increase in classes due to a lack of time to work individually with students. Both hypotheses are useful as frameworks to undertake and direct research, predict results, and direct the analysis of data.

An action research study is built upon routine and probability in a sense since routines and predictability seem to share a relationship. The more predictable you are as a teacher the more likely you are to follow a routine closely. Similarly, the more predictable the student, the more knowledge the teacher may have concerning their routine behavior. This is especially true for students in special education whose program (routine) is often related to their predictable behavior. To illustrate, consider that a researcher predicts a score someone (the subject) will obtain. A prediction, in research, can only occur *after* a result is known or measured on a variable. For example, if the researcher knows the result a person achieves on a multiplication test, the researcher may be able to predict the subject's performance on a math achievement test because multiplication achievement is related to math achievement.

As a researcher you have many opportunities to use your ability to predict, hypothesize, and forecast what may be, in the course of completing your research. The key is to know when and where these revelations need to placed to better communicate and illuminate your work.

Looking for Patterns

Looking for patterns is currently a task within most mathematics programs at the elementary level, however within action research projects the task of patterning means something else. Action research is about unpacking your lived experience in a manner that makes things easier to see, sort, and analyze. It is as if your life were spread out across a field, perhaps following a tornado. It is up to you to walk through and identify, organize, and examine items for meaning and significance. Action research becomes part of your life for a period of time. It sometimes felt as if I were in the eye of a tornado since it was calm yet the events of each day seemed to accelerate past and through me. During your research you spend a great deal of time looking at the data in order to locate themes, patterns, relationships, connections, frequencies, and the like. In one study I completed, I kept coming across the word 'time' and I highlighted this term each time it presented itself on a transcript. Following this highlighting I counted over 350 references to time in our transcripts. I then looked at the context of each sentence that contained the word and affixed meaning to each occurrence. Ultimately, I discovered that every instance when we talked about change, time was introduced as a negative factor that made even the slightest notion of change in classroom program difficult, if not impossible, at any point during a school year. Searching deeper I also discovered that Secondary teachers were not totally opposed to change; however, they believed the best time for devising new plans was during the summer so changes could be implemented at the start of September. By reviewing the transcripts in this way, I was able realize several useful conclusions in my study.

You could review your data in a low-tech manner as I did in the previous paragraph, or, if you have your data on a computer, you can use a word-processing program and choose the 'find option' on the edit drop-down menu. Explore the usefulness of the highlighting option which allows you to count the number of times a term is used. More recently, with the proliferation of software, there are many high-tech approaches to the identification of patterns in data, many of which can be researched on the Internet.

Quantitative Analysis

Quantitative analysis involves math; it requires us to classify and count, and usually demands that we build results via an often intricate arithmetic process or model. For instance, if we want to describe data we first identify it as *ordinal*, *nominal,* or *interval* (ratio data). For *ordinal data* we calculate the median, or midpoint, of the data. For *nominal data* we would calculate the mode and for the *interval data* we can calculate mean, median, and mode as well as variance. Sometimes we may use a survey so we can assign a number to the responses and from these numbers we can attempt to explain what was observed. Findings can then be generalized to a larger population and compared to other studies or findings and results. To compare your findings with others requires valid sampling and the application of standards associated with that particular quantitative research mode.

Surveys frequently are used as tools to consider group differences. We could simply look at percentage, choosing one option from others, or we could compare item choices based on various characteristics we may be interested in looking at such as gender or age groups to further the data analysis. To go deeper into quantitative analysis for survey data you would do some type of test for correlated samples if it involved interval data. To better understand the quantitative worlds, visit the sites listed at the back of this book.

The allure of qualitative research for many people relates to the potential for side-stepping the above to create a more complete, holistic representation of their research. Quantitative research traditionally has been accused of supplying a resulting image that is largely an abstraction of the research. Put another way, the data which emerges from quantitative analysis is less rich than that obtained from qualitative analysis. For instance, a survey may uncover that an item either belongs to class b, or it doesn't. The quantitative mode is an efficient way to rank, discriminate, and judge things or people. It is largely indirect and distant. For instance, consider provincial testing and its merit. Quantitative analysis is a glorification of the data in most instances. To use both qualitative and quantitative modes within research is to make use of a mixed method approach. When I have used a qualitative approach I have depended upon the advice of other qualitative researchers to some extent. When I turn to quantitative research I again seek out guidance from others. One source of quantitative guidance comes from Mertens (1998) *Research Methods in Education and Psychology*. In her book she has constructed a chart on page 338 that details how to choose the statistical method for each type of quantitative research effort.

Qualitative Analysis

Coding

Education is ripe with codes – just look at any funding model, or peer into special education services. We tend to label, code, and identify students in countless ways and our employer uses a system of identification that digitizes us. Even your union has a system to order its members (seniority). Humans seem to gravitate towards order yet some seem to work against the order to some extent. In my classrooms I have coded reading groups, math groups, and physical education activities according to level of difficulty, identity of the student (Special Education), and time of year. Coding is not new to educators and this helps as we venture forward in our action inquiry. I like to use colors, numbers, letters, or symbols to identify elements within my research data.

In action research efforts, coding usually occurs after we have read something. We decide to note down a type of identifying information. Often the evidence is identified as a symbol or short note in the margin of the item we are reading. We might code the categories or properties contained within, or decide to highlight what is implied in a sentence by coding it. Some researchers prefer to code manually; however, software is also available.

Definitions

The importance of defining words, terms, and phrases in research is rooted in efforts to promote shared meaning and understanding. The English language can be confusing since words, terms, and phrases usually have several possible meanings. Open a dictionary and you will see multiple meanings attached to most words which can contribute to misunderstandings. Educators speak in a manner that embraces educational acronyms, yet shares words (prep period, detention), common ground, and phrases (long-term occasional teacher) within the profession. Once we leave the direct face-to-face arena of communication, we are left with avenues that are even more challenging. For instance, with books we are disadvantaged as we are not able to use the nonverbal channel. Clear writing is a necessity. Even the tape recorder only captures sounds and written transcripts usually do not contain evidence of the audio communication signs and symbols.

In all research we need a common ground. Even within action research there are many ways to define the mode. I suggest action research is disciplined inquiry by practitioners working to investigate issues related to improvement. Action research causes teachers to be more reflective. They develop their own knowledge and understanding, thereby enhancing their professionalism. Many researchers have defined action research in various ways. For instance Kurt Lewin (1947) defined action research as a three step spiral process of *planning* (which involves reconnaissance), *taking action,* and *fact-finding* about the results of action. Stephen Corey (1949) suggested action research was the process by which practitioners attempt to study their problems scientifically in order to guide, correct, and evaluate their decisions and actions. John Elliott (1991) described action research as a process through which teachers collaborate in evaluating their practice jointly, raise awareness of their personal theories, articulate a shared concept of values, and try out new strategies to render consistency between the values expressed in their practice and educational values they espouse. Based on their results, teachers record their work in a form readily understandable by other teachers and thus develop a shared theory of teaching. Finally, it was Emily Calhoun (1994) who simply told us that action research is a fancy way of saying let's study what's happening at our school and decide how to make it a better place. Choose whatever definition appeals to you and your research endeavor. You will discover that sharing an understanding is a powerful force in research and some believe we must build on the shared understanding of words and terms as they have evolved in the literature.

Data collection and analysis involves terms and words that need to be detailed within a study via definitions. For instance, researchers commonly refer to anecdotal records yet some fail to define these terms. In each research effort we need to supply a list of terms. I define an **anecdotal record** as *an account of observed behaviors which are written down in the form of anecdotes*. I also believe the best anecdotes inform us accurately and explain what the participant did or said without making evaluative statements in the course of reporting these data.

Clearly defining the terms is a necessary step to ensure that the research question or problem is sharply focused. It also increases the ability of individuals outside the field of study to understand the work.

Memos

At home a memorandum, list, note, or message is used to remind you of something. Often this list of items jogs your memory and makes your travels more efficient. The use of memos in action research is similar but is a little more involved and demanding. Memo use in action research is more systematic, disciplined, rigorous, and strategic than your at-home memos. Action researchers write each day (systematic) and record their feelings, thoughts, intuitions, concerns, and anxieties (strategic) in order to help themselves cope, grow, and realize new notions that are often embedded in their research. Memos can involve storytelling within lengthy essays that are both analytic and a means to release tensions onto paper. Memos can be short comments within data sources and they can be highly theoretical offerings.

Memos come upon researchers at all times of the day and it is necessary to seize the moment as the ideas and feelings are very often short-lived. The act of creating memos can be the 'glue' that draws together the pieces of your puzzle. This adhesion in action research is mandatory as it is usually a piece-meal process where it can be easy to lose oneself. The hectic, often chaotic pace of everyday life can overstimulate and cause us to reassess. One mode of reassessment can be through memo-writing where we can be reflective and reconstruct what has happened in order to slow it down, reexamine, and evaluate.

Validation

Within the tradition of quantitative research we would address validation as a means to test a hypothesis, to prove it acceptable or unacceptable, based on the evidence gathered. We would then go on to look at three aspects of validity such as internal, external, and construct validity. However, action research (qualitative) accomplishes the above by employing different strategies to check the accuracy of the findings (results). The strategies include triangulation and the use of a critical friend CF, or critical team/panel (CT).

Triangulation

Triangulation (A-B-C) triggers memories of geometry for some and to some extent this mathematical image is a useful one. Imagine the mixing of three or more data sources or methods – survey, interview, and journal – into one study that unite on a single characteristic or theme. This is triangulation. We do this to nurture and seek out validity, truthfulness, and accuracy. Data triangulation involves multiple data sources with similar foci; for example, individuals (students), groups (clubs), or collectives (schools), and the eventual data, can be triangulated around a single term, word, theme, or construct (for instance, anger). We do this to validate our findings, conclusions, results, and the entire research effort.

Consider the triangulation within the methods whereby more than one research method or data collection technique is utilized because each taps a diverse facet of a problem. Triangulating is utilized to supply proof and ensure comprehensiveness. It also is an attempt to relate sources to neutralize the threats to validity in each and captures an inclusive and contextual illustration. Triangulation often reveals the speckled proportions of the given observable fact and the sources contribute additional pieces to the problem. Pursuing triangulation in research reduces bias and improves validity. Data analysis via triangulation coupled with the mixing of qualitative and quantitative modes is really a numerical and linguistic intersection. This mixing, if you choose to employ it, involves both qualitative and quantitative modes; however, proceed carefully by observing the research standards, norms, and traditions.

In an action inquiry it is best to gather data in three ways and search for the intersecting point that emerges once you begin the process of sifting through the data. The following figure illustrates three modes that could be used to gather data. Two of these modes, *journalling* and *interviewing*, have roots in qualitative research whereas the *survey*, depending upon how it is used, is usually seen as a quantitative research mode. The mixing of these modes gives rise to the label of a *mixed method action inquiry*.

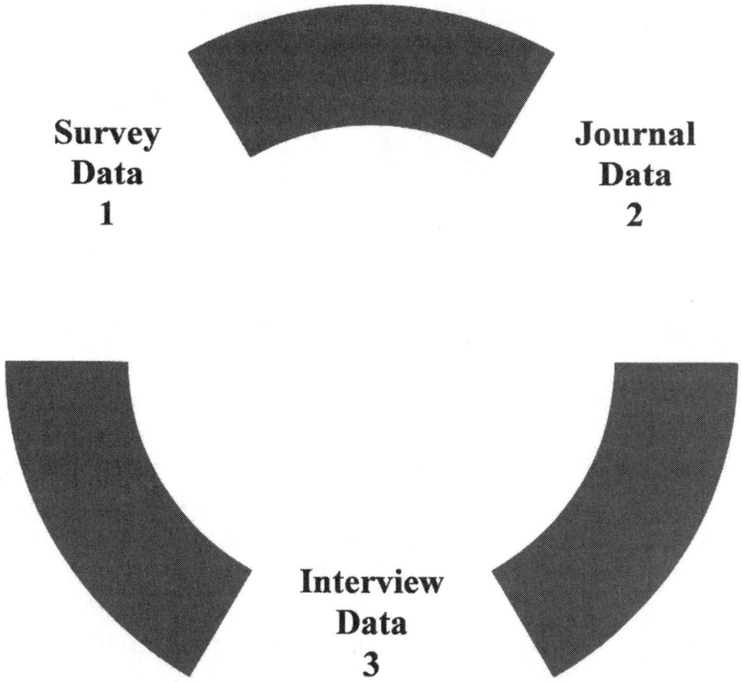

Figure 3. Critical Friend (CF) or Critical Group (CG) (Team – Panel)

A validation friend/panel/team supports you and guides you in many ways. They clear up confusion and defog the research effort by making sense of the data you have collected. As a researcher you are much too close to the data to examine it entirely in an impartial, objective, or accurate manner all of the time. Recall your singular efforts to hang a picture on the wall only to find out, upon stepping back, that the picture is too high, low, or crooked. Hanging a picture, as I have learned, is at least a two-person task and even more help may be required for unique wall hangings. The CF or CG members are helpers who engage you in vigorous debates about all aspects of your research. They ask firm, penetrating questions. CF/CG probes awaken the researcher causing accelerated and concentrated thought. Try the approach outlined below. Meet with the CF/CG to explore:

A. The orientation/stance of the research and selected pathway;
B. The notion of sensible steps such as methods, discussion, conclusions, summative/formative statements, etc.;
C. The need to change course or alter data collection modes to gather or consider other elements; and
D. Float alternative thoughts for data collection, analysis, and stance in your writing.

You may want to begin this process early by presenting your earliest data which might include a survey, results from assessment or evaluation efforts, documentation from staff, students, administration (quotes), your personal notes from observations, transcribed interviews, or journal data. Ensure you have the approval to share this data from all who supply it.

My validation panel asked if the data were useful and necessary. At first, I responded defensively but later warmed up to their good intentions. They further asked me why I collected these data. Be careful not to take these lines of questioning personally – it is in the interest of creating a solid research project. My panel then asked if the data helped or actually got in the way of my question. Some asked simple questions like, "What does this data mean?" By enduring these questions I was forced to consider critical issues. My direction became much more obvious to me as I knew what I should do with the information I was collecting and I could see the potential impact of my research more clearly.

Formative Analysis

From the onset of any action inquiry there is an orientation period where the researchers take time to build an understanding and awareness of their project. They agree on route, modes, criteria, and language. This process allows the inquiry to develop an identity and during this break-in period (early formative stage), the participants distill goals to build up strategies for the road ahead. The analysis within the formative stage (quality control) is often a means to monitor, improve, identify, sort, and react to data as it is gathered. The process is somewhat akin to life itself in that you know what you are doing, where you are going, and that it may cost money, yet you are never sure of what you might or might not find. What we theorize and what we discover are often dissimilar.

Often, formative analysis allows researchers to realize a deeper understanding of the inquiry as they may witness the realization of goals, obstacles, and the outright failure of certain efforts. I have experienced such events. For instance, I did complete my action research inquiry (realization of my goal) but along the way, participants missed interviews or cancelled meetings (obstacles) and at one point, the necessary data I wanted was deemed confidential and so denied (failure). I then made decisions to use other data; I rescheduled interviews and worked longer hours to ensure I could realize my research goal.

Goal-setting is a reflexive dynamic procedure that continues all through the life of an inquiry and this impacts the analysis of your data. Your action inquiry is a time to formatively discover, to reconsider original plans, and to make adjustments, as obstacles and failure present themselves. Researchers, in the formative stages of analysis, regularly realize there is a gap amid their espoused goals and the goals emerging (tacit knowledge) from within their research. The formative analysis provides a means to compare intentions with what is actually happening. It is not a control apparatus for keeping the inquiry on the correct pathway, however, it does allow for new discoveries, change, and contradictions. These discoveries can then be used as tools to reshape and enhance the action inquiry. The formative analysis is an opportunity to improve the inquiry as stakeholders reflect on the up-and-coming data and compare this to project goals, aims, theory, and expectations.

Summative Analysis

Traditionally, summative analysis is a time to consider the end product. It is a test drive to see if what you built performs as expected and you decide if it is what you wanted. The test drive may bring with it new discoveries. We consider elements such as the design of the product, the quality, and the elements that are lacking. The finale, or end-point, of an inquiry considers original aims, goals, and the newer emergent ones that appeared throughout the inquiry. We do this to create a reflective or retrospective assessment and evaluation. Researchers often realize new assumptions and means to reexamine their understandings. I found myself asking, "Did I reach my specified targets, objectives?" I then considered the degree to which I had or had not, and asked myself if I had made errors. I fixated on questions concerning how, and what could have been done another way, or better. The summative analysis is a means to value, appraise, and uncover elements that only the completed inquiry can illuminate. Our illuminated knowledge, collection of beliefs, and understanding is, at this point in time, cumulative yet evolving and dynamic. From this vantage point we can look back at our footprints and we can look forward to choose a path that will allow us to grow as researchers.

Case Study

Data Analysis Effort Within an Inquiry

Over a period of eight months data were collected via supportive weekly tape-recorded discussion groups, individual interviews, classroom visitations (notes), daily participant journals, and randomly collected documentation. The result of these efforts included over 18 hours of audio-tape, two observation binders that contained over 200 pages of notes and five 150-page journals completed by participants.

Data collected through reflection was in itself an orderly and intentional process. The reflection process, carried out by all participants, made up part of the analysis, which led to theorizing and the transformation of understandings of *assessment praxes*. (Stinger, 1996) Within the tapes (transcripts) and participant journal notes, evidence that supported changes in assessment thoughts and practice were identified and described as I happened upon them. It was a matter of decoding the transcripts and uncovering evidence. The evidence was emergent and surfaced due to my careful analysis and critical reading of the transcripts. I began to see patterns and themes as certain words, terms, and phrases became commonplace.

Winter (1996) explains that "action research is seen as a way of investigating professional experience which links practice and the analysis of practice into a single, continuously developing sequence" (p. 13). Thus, data collection and analysis were not separate acts; they occurred simultaneously. Some early action researchers (Corey, 1949; Lewin, 1946) have treated the act of data collection and analysis as separate entities. Barnsley and Ellis (1987) suggest an acceptable contrast in method as they explain, "data analysis can begin while the research is in progress as well as after the data has been gathered " (Part V, p. 24). I embraced the latter analysis approach and moved forward.

From the onset of our inquiry, as the data were mounting, I began to skim the growing collection and commenced the task of reflecting on what I had sensed during face-to-ace meetings, classroom observations, and while reading participant journals. Further reflection brought to mind key assessment concepts and assessment words that supported these concepts. I use the word **concept** to describe something that, to my mind, is *unambiguous*. The key concepts were used to assemble a matrix. I believed that the conception of data analysis articulated by Sagor (1992) suited me best:

> Data analysis can be most simply described as a process of sifting, sorting, discarding, and cataloguing in an attempt to answer two basic questions: [1] What are the important themes in this data . . . and [2] how much data support each of these themes? (p. 48)

My assessment themes became key terms and were used on the horizontal axis of the matrix. These included: What, Why, Who, How, Time, Isolation, and Views. The *What* meant: What do you assess? The *Why* asked: Why do you assess? The *Who* meant: Who completes or develops the assessment? The *How* referred to: How do you assess? The *Time* indicated that some mention or inference was made to time as a constraining feature of assessment praxes. *Isolation* indicated that some mention or inference was made to teacher isolation as a feature of assessment praxes. The *Views* term indicated that a view had been expressed repeatedly and strongly.

On the vertical axis, I had sources of data (group discussion, one-to-one discussion, journal, classroom visits, informal communications, and documentation). Each key concept was given a color code. As the data were skimmed, sifted, sorted, and linkages to the key concept were found, the data were highlighted in the corresponding color. As well, in each cell of the matrix, co-ordinates were noted, such as the date and page number. So, if I were looking for data concerning the 'what' (key concept – horizontal axis) of assessment praxes, I could go down the column to locate the source (group, 1:1, journal, document, visitation, informal note). Located in a specific matrix cell would be the source's location (GD, 1:1, J, CV, IC, D) by date (eg., GD Jan 15) and page number (GD Jan15, p. 02), thus enabling rapid location and recovery of the information. View the following example and note the cells have not been filled.

Data Matrix	What	Why	How	Time	Isolation	Views
Group Discussion (GD)						
1 to 1 (1:1)						
Journal (J)						
Class Visit (CV)						
Informal Communication (IC)						
Documentation						

Summary

Part II has moved quickly through critical areas in order to prompt thought, flesh out reader positions, and promote understanding. We learned that action research data are best analyzed as they are gathered. Doing this actually helps researchers to appreciate the depth, breadth, and context of the collected data as it can be transitory in the course of a research project. Admittedly, the data are frequently quite different than the actual lived experience. We experience life in three dimensions; it is dynamic and relatively fast paced while our data is not.

At many points during the research process predictions are made as a means to forecast what may happen. In research we can write about the future via hypotheses. The eventual data may yield predictable evidence in the form of patterns. In fact, looking for patterns is currently a task within most action research projects. It has been said that action research is about unpacking your lived experience in a manner that makes things easier to see, sort, analyze, and understand. Understanding could require a quantitative analysis as we examine, classify, and count certain word frequencies or theme occurrences in our data, and then apply various qualitative techniques to arrive at conclusions.

Within Part II it was noted that education is seasoned with codes as elements have been labelled, coded, and identified in countless ways. Most systems currently employ a means of identification that digitizes. In view of this digital world it is even more important that we understand what is said. We touched on the importance of defining words, terms, and phrases in research efforts to promote shared meaning and understanding. In an effort to increase communicative evidence in research we considered the use of memos in action research. We discovered that memo use in action research is more systematic, disciplined, rigorous, and strategic than your at-home memos. Indeed, action research as a qualitative research effort employs different strategies in order to check the accuracy of the findings (results). The strategies highlighted included both *triangulation,* and the use of a *critical friend* (CF) or *critical team/panel/group* (CG).

We learned that the CF or CG members are helpers as they engage you (researchers) in vigorous debates about all aspects of your research. They ask firm, penetrating questions. CF/CG probes awaken the researcher causing accelerated and concentrated thought. These thoughts and ideas cause researchers to stop, start, or continue various actions. The process is known as Stop, Start, Continue (SSC) strategy and has improved many research efforts. The SSC strategy as a formative analysis tool allows researchers to realize a deeper understanding of the inquiry as they witness the realization of goals, obstacles, and the outright failure of certain efforts. To use SSC at the summative point allows researchers to consider the end product in a way that influences future research efforts.

Chapter 4

Elementary Reflections

Introduction

We know that pre-service education programs involve practicum sessions and it is during these sessions students acquire teaching experience that is informative, rewarding, and memorable. At the onset of the year, pre-service-teachers are usually required to visit an assigned school and complete a classroom orientation. This offers the pre-service students an opportunity to observe, reflect, and enter into discussions with practicing teachers. Upon return to their Faculties of Education, students can be heard discussing their experiences formally and informally in university classrooms and hallways. The second practicum in the field often lasts two weeks and it is during this session that pre-service teachers begin to teach partial days. This session, in many cases, is their first opportunity to teach in a school and many feel compelled to share their experience. Realizing this, most Faculty of Education institutions build in a reflective (journal, log, task) requirement that supports and facilitates the sharing process.

A common task in numerous pre-service programs is to have student teachers write about their *actions* (ACT), write about their *thoughts*, and communicate in writing their *feelings* concerning their teaching actions (reflect). An additional step involves documenting what they plan to do to improve their teaching (revisions). This task – ACT - REFLECT - REVISE – is but one means of collecting evidence and documenting the beginning of their long journey in education. The task is systematic, strategic (action research) in that it must meet certain criteria as noted, and it must be constructed from within the repetitive rounds of practicum. The Act-Reflect-Revise (ARR) sequence, also the model of action research used herein, is a tool to improve teaching, classroom management, advance teacher professional skills, professionalize the practice, and make findings public. "Action research is a mechanism for teachers to improve their own effectiveness. Action research is a mechanism for teachers to improve their own practice and focus on positive changes within the classroom" (Cantrell & Cantrell, 2003, p. 119).

Faculty of Education practicums vary in length and duration, and during each one there is an opportunity to complete the ARR cycle again. We can then say that the practicums make for a recursive experience that allows students to revisit, modify, and improve their praxis. The pre-service year is a developmental model that supports and invites the use of action research. However, this type of action research enterprise is difficult to judge, therefore, many professors will simply provide feedback with a checkmark on a task-list, indicating that the task has been completed to a certain standard. For example, one might look within reflection for the following elements:

1. Action – plot-expectations, setting-environment, character profiles;
2. Reflections – your perceptions of your teaching; and
3. Revisions – plans to change teaching praxis.

An Opportunity to Use Action Research

Within a course such as Classroom Management, and during each practice teaching session, pre-service teachers are required to write about their classroom management actions; write about the memories, context, and feelings concerning their actions; and then write about what they plan to do to improve their classroom management abilities.

The ARR task is an opportunity to utilize the action research mode in order to improve their classroom management. As an action research effort, the pre-service student is asking: How can I improve my classroom management? To what extent have I improved? What do I plan to do to improve and how will I achieve this?

Typically, the recursive task includes earning marks for key elements and a checkmark for task completion. For instance,

1. ACT – Actions I undertook to manage my classroom – plot, expectations, setting, environment, characters, profile – 3 points.
2. REFLECT – Evaluation of myself as a classroom manager – 3 points.
3. REVISE – What I plan or need to do now – 4 points.

This task has caused many students to illuminate various elements of classroom management that are now *documented* and made public (with permission) for all to use. For instance, consider the following pre-service teacher experiences:

1. Jamie Bradburn – "Give Me 5"

Jamie Bradburn is a pre-service student searching to make sense of new classroom management experiences.

During my October practicum at an Elementary school I used a few different classroom management actions, some were learned from my Associate Teacher and others were my own. I found that in a practicum situation where I am teaching in another teacher's classroom, it was necessary to use some of the management strategies already in place. My Associate Teacher (AT) had a few management actions in place that the students were used to and therefore proved effective.

The first strategy in place was called **"give me five."** This was what I or my Associate Teacher would call out if we needed the class's attention. What this meant was that all students need to [1] *stop* what they're doing, [2] put their *hand up*, [3] be *silent*, [4] have *eyes on the teacher*, and [5] *listen* to what the teacher is about to say. There were five things for the students to do so we'd say, "Give me five," and there was a sign up in the classroom explaining it to the students as a reminder.

This strategy was very effective as students all knew what it was and what was expected of them when they heard us say it. It was even to the point where we would say it and students who were quiet and listening would tell the other students who were not, to do the same. It almost became a form of self-discipline for the students, as they would instruct each other and themselves because the action was so familiar to them.

I would use this in my classroom because it is a simple idea that is not demeaning to the students and it really worked. It was also good because it was a constant in the classroom environment and the students felt comfortable following it. It was also a nice thing to have in place as a teacher; it was a management tool that was always there to use. It was part of the daily routine, and it was not negative, so the students did not see it as punishment or yelling.

The second thing that was in place in the classroom when I got there, that I used, was the strategy of **consequence and excel slips**. This was a team-wide action that has been used in the school before. Students who *misbehaved* in the classroom could receive a **consequence slip** indicating what they did to receive one. After three consequence slips, a call was placed home, by the teacher to the parent(s). Students who did *something nice or positive* in the classroom would be rewarded with an **excel slip**. After three excel slips the students could trade them in for a slice of pizza on pizza day, or a drink or snack from the classroom tuck shop.

This strategy is effective as all students know about these slips and most of them do not want a consequence slip. It is also a form of self-government. The students know that it is in their control whether they get a consequence slip or an excel slip so it does give them a sense of power over their own actions. Also, having given out quite a few excel slips it is nice to reward good behavior and not just the bad. Students who receive an excel slip feel extremely proud, honored, and happy. As a teacher it was nice to see a student experience that.

I would use this strategy as it shows students what is good and bad behavior, and that there are both negative repercussions and positive rewards to bad and good behaviors respectively. One modification that I made during my placement to this strategy was that once a student received a consequence slip I gave them the rest of the day to show me good behavior and if they did I would rip up their consequence slip. I found this to be an effective modification because it became another management strategy since I had a student who was now trying to behave well to get rid of their consequence slip. I felt it to be very important to allow the students to redeem themselves after making a mistake. Everyone makes mistakes and deserves a second chance and I know students were grateful for this opportunity. In my placement, students told me that I was a very fair teacher and that meant a lot to me because as part of my classroom management I tried to listen to all students, give all students the benefit of the doubt, a chance to be good students, and a second chance if they made a mistake.

I found that the most effective actions I can take as a teacher in classroom management are to *get to know my students*, *respect them* for who they are, *treat them fairly*, and *as individuals*. I found that showing my students fairness and respect resulted in them respecting me in the classroom by behaving appropriately.

As a teacher, I realize these strategies will not work for all students. I find these strategies to be useful to me and have given me ideas for how I will set up my own classroom in the future. I know that whatever management strategies I decide to implement in my classroom, I will make my students aware of them from the beginning and I will not keep changing them throughout the year. I recognize the *importance of routine strategies* in place in the classroom as a management tool so that *students know what is expected* of them and can get in the habit of doing them.

If I was going to make any changes to what I have seen and done in my October placement it would be to place less focus on the negative things students do and put more emphasis on the positive. Every student knows when someone in the class does something bad but good behaviors often go unnoticed. It is important to support positive behavior and publicly endorse good deeds. I think this is a huge problem in the world and what better place to model the opposite than in a classroom. In November, I plan to make an effort to promote positive behavior and perhaps this will make other students want to do good things as they see others being recognized.

I have learned a lot about management from my experiences in the classroom, from my Associate Teacher, and other staff members in the school. This experience is helping me to shape my own ideas and feelings about classroom management. I have seen many good ideas and I have been able to reflect and form my own opinions as to what I will expect from my students. Respect is the most important thing to me in a classroom as well as modelling and recognizing good behavior, fairness, and positive treatment of all students by the teacher and students. I believe that with these things in place in my classroom, management will become easier and the enjoyment of education will be experienced by all.

***Question*: What did Jaime learn about classroom management during his first practicum? Also, remember that reflection is a means to examine what is working, what needs work, and what is missing.**

2. My Grade 7 Practicum – ADHD and Me

Another pre-service-student teaching in a grade 7 classroom wrote,

After speaking with many teachers in Elementary Schools, most agree that the most difficult grade to handle behaviorally is grade 7. Their maturity levels are low, attention spans still short after years in the primary and junior divisions, and attitudes are rising and developing. My practicum for session one is in a grade 7 class in a Roman Catholic elementary school in Southern Ontario.

The class is very talkative, a trait that my AT does not like, so he is quite militant about their volume and talking in general. A particular area of problem for this class is behavior during morning exercises (during these exercises the French teacher has the grade 7 class, so I just observe her). Certain students felt the need to talk and fool around during the praying of the rosary. During normal class time, when work is to be done quietly, some students felt the need to continue talking and being disruptive. I also have two students who are identified as having Attention Deficit Hyperactive Disorder (ADHD), which of course makes it more difficult for them to stay on task and focus on the work at hand. One of these students literally does no work. His desk is an absolute disaster area. Even if he wanted to do work there is no way that he would be able to find the books which he is looking for. He sits there, doodles, plays with his ruler, doing just about anything except the work assigned.

In terms of their general talking, my AT has no issue with using the dreaded "ssssshhhhh." When I felt the class was getting off track, I chose to raise my voice in an authoritative manner in order to get my point across (i.e., to be quiet and resume doing quiet work, or listen to the teacher). At the end of certain days, my throat was dry and my head hurt. If there were students who still did not follow directions and quiet down, I addressed them specifically, asking them in an authoritative voice to settle down and get back to work. Morning exercises are very important in a Catholic school, as it is a time for reflection and prayer, so as a teacher, I emphasize their value. Unfortunately, the French teacher does not have the best classroom management skills, so I took it upon myself to walk around during these exercises and observe the students. If I found a student to be disruptive or talking, I simply put my index finger to my mouth, motioning for silence. If I found them playing with something, I would take it away from them. I brought one student into the hallway to discuss their unruly behavior and unwillingness to take part in Morning Prayer.

In terms of my ADHD students, I do try to make special considerations for them in terms of the workload or answers that I expect. When it is clear to me that the students cannot handle sitting with the other students and still do work, I move them to a solitary desk at the back of the room. This is never done in a mean or malicious manner, yet both [ADHD students] see this as a punishment. If both are acting up, then one sits at that desk while the other sits at my worktable with me, so I can keep a closer eye on the work they are doing and that they are not being distracted. The unorganized, unwilling to work student is a little more difficult student to deal with. By my second last day, I was so tired of his excuse of not being able to find certain books when they were needed, I went to his desk at the afternoon recess, dumped it and told him to organize his workspace.

Upon reflection, I realize that raising my voice is not a viable option for long or for everyone. Students will become immune to it and I felt that the more I raised my voice, the more I showed my frustration with the class. A sign of weakness that any student would exploit, much like a lion picking off the slowest of the herd. A technique I hope to use this time out, is to be quiet and wait for them to snap to attention. An incentive to this may be that for every minute of my time in class that is wasted for talking, I will take two of their minutes at recess. This applies for the whole class, even if it is a select few talking. I feel that this will establish a real sense of teamwork amongst the students and perhaps encourage those rowdier students to consider the consequences of their behavior and how it affects all the class, not just for recess time but at learning time as well. In terms of the prayer issues during morning exercises, instead of reprimanding the student time after time, I will be keeping them in at recess and having them write out selected bible passages, and then have them signed by their parents/guardian. The passages will be relevant to the importance of prayer so that the punishment can serve a purpose, unlike the old-fashioned way of giving out lines. With my identified students, I need to explain to them why they are being put at the back of the room and take a more active effort in seeing that they stay on task. I also know that I need to show more patience in my tone of voice and mannerisms with this student. In hindsight, dumping the students' desk was probably a bit harsh. In retrospect, I should have offered to help him organize it in a kinder fashion. I will try to be more positive with this student when I go back, attempting to use positive re-enforcement to try and motivate him to do some work.

This experience has helped me realize that although my AT is a fabulous teacher with lots to teach me, I do not care to mimic his classroom management style. I plan to allow some quiet talking amongst clusters of desks and be more patient with the students. At the end of the day, if I am yelling and screaming at my students, I will have a very short life span in this career. I also noticed that I paid a lot of attention to the "trouble makers" and not enough attention to the students who have listened and done their work. Positive re-enforcement for these students is definitely a goal that I need to work on during the next round of practicum.

***Questions*: How can you support your AT and at the same time explore you own classroom management philosophy, actions, and skills? Teaching requires personal, professional, and political stances that require informed awareness and tactful deployment. List several ideas concerning the personal, professional, and political you, then share these.**

3. Amy Post – Token Economy

Amy detailed her elementary classroom management throughout her practicum and comments on the use of the token economy. Amy explained:

Act

Most of the management actions that I took were adapted from the strategies already existing in my AT's classroom. I fully agreed with the reward strategies that were in place in the classroom and had no difficulty following through with them. Although I did not fully agree with some of the punishment strategies and ensuing actions that I had to take as management, I did give some detentions after school in accordance with my AT's management plan.

The classroom rules have been established with this class since September. They were told that the same rules apply when I am teaching. Before I would activate any management of negative behavior, I would remind the students of the rules. For example, "Johnny has blurted out. I want to remind everyone that you must raise your hand in the classroom and wait to be called on before you speak."

The strategies I employed to reward good behavior were mostly in place in the classroom when I arrived. There is a **ticket individual reward system**, where a child receives a **ticket** each time they are *working quietly or are very polite*. They then put their name on the ticket and place the ticket in a box for a weekly draw. Prizes for the draw include candy, a coupon that gives the bearer a right to chew gum in one designated class period, or the right to choose what games are played in gym during the 'students choice' gym period. Additionally, coupons are given out in conjunction with a **marble challenge**.

Marbles are given to *reward the class as a whole*. A marble must be earned on behalf of the entire class. Each marble is worth two points and the points go toward activities in which the entire class participates. Marbles are earned for an all green day on the green machine, for every student in the class having their homework done, for catching a mistake (made by a teacher) on the board, and for completing the detectives challenge on Fridays. The first level is a half class period of free time. The music goes on and the students are allowed to draw, read, or play with a quiet activity. The next level is an entire class period; the third an entire class period with snacks provided by the teacher, and the fourth and most coveted prize, a 'G' movie, or party with snacks provided by the teacher. As each level is reached the class votes on whether to continue on for a larger prize or use their marbles now and start again from zero.

In addition to tangible rewards, I created a positive classroom environment through verbal encouragement and recognition. Positive reinforcement was given when students were working quietly, cooperatively, and when they mastered a difficult task. If a reward was lost due to behavioral difficulties, I attempted to let them earn that reward in another way, such as passing out tickets during quiet reading time or by issuing a marble challenge.

As much as the rewards were varied, the punishments were varied as well and were often included with the reward program. If a rule was broken it could lead to the loss of a potential marble. For instance, if one student neglects to complete their homework the entire class fails to earn a marble. If one rule is broken, such as blurting out in class without raising your hand, the name of the student is written up on the board. The second time the student breaks a rule a checkmark goes up beside their name, their green machine card turns to yellow, and the good behavior marble for the class is gone for the day. If another rule is broken by the same student their card goes to red in the green machine and they are asked to leave the classroom. Although I never had to turn any of the cards to red, I did on two occasions turn one student's card to yellow. Both instances followed a direct challenge to my authority in the classroom; they specifically did something I had just asked the student not to do in front of the entire class.

In addition to the loss of a marble and the green machine, I used cues to allow the students to understand that I was ready to teach. A simple phrase such as "I am ready to teach, are you ready to listen?" often quieted the sometimes boisterous grade 6 class, especially when paired with the timing method that this teacher employed. We often gave the children 30 seconds to 1 minute to get ready for a lesson. After the designated time ran out, timing started until all of the students had finished the required task; the seconds accrued were then put up into the penalty box. The students served all of the time at the end of the day, after the bell, sitting quietly at their desks.

Reflect

I was very pleased overall with my classroom management at my placement. Most of the strategies were in place when I arrived and I found them to be very useful as a beginning teacher. However, I did find myself to be uncomfortable with several things. Unless it is an extreme case of endangerment to the children or the student themselves, I dislike sending students into the hall. More often than not some of their friends wander along, or they continue to exhibit negative behavior out in the hall. They are also missing valuable teaching time as they sit outside and concepts that are taught during that time often need to be re-taught to the student later. I was sent out in the hall once as a student and I remember the utter mortification as teachers and students walked past imagining my misdeeds – did she hit someone, swear? No – just talked too much! This type of discipline either rewards bad behavior by allowing them to continue their misdeeds in the hall, or causes anxiety, mortification, and tears in some cases.

In addition, I would like to modify the amount of times students are required to stay after school. Often, if their infraction was first thing in the morning they have either forgotten what they have done wrong or have anxiously awaited their meeting with the teacher after school which affects their work during the day. Reinforcement for breaking the rule should be done as immediately as possible. This way the students will remember what negative behavior led to their consequences and hopefully work to modify it.

I require work on my management in the gym. My first gym class degenerated into chaos by the end. I was shocked at how quickly the class can get out of control. Without the safe tried and true methods of management utilized in the classroom, I felt adrift in the gym, overused my whistle, and ended up talking over the students. One of the students was hit in the head with an indoor soccer ball; this jolted me into an authoritative stance. I quickly got the class sitting in their squads and sent the child to the office for ice. After reestablishing control the class proceeded well. I only regret that it took an injury to get me started on effective gym management. The next gym class was much better. Control was quickly re-established with either the whistle (used *much* less frequently) or stopping the ball in play and having everyone sit down. I realize the revision of my management methods in my second gym class made it more enjoyable for the students and myself, however, I still have a ways to go before I am comfortable in the gym.

I also need to work on realizing what misbehavior to let go, such as quietly fiddling with something while I am teaching versus talking quietly when I am teaching which should not be allowed to continue. In addition, I need to employ more strategies such as “Put your pencils down and look up here," when I am teaching to ensure all of the students are paying attention and less needless questions are asked after I have finished.

Revise

Instead of sending a child into the hall, I would employ a quiet spot in the classroom, such as a study carrel or a desk up at the front against the board, as an area for errant students.

Instead of having after school detentions, I could employ the children to clean the erasers or boards in the morning during the announcements.

During gym, I will have to employ a little more authority and use the squad idea more as a management tool, rather than just a strictly organizational one. I will also wait to explain the rules of the game until I am sure that I have the attention of all of the students. While I am waiting for them to settle at the beginning, I will, under my supervision, have one or two students get out all of the equipment. I will use the natural breaks in the game such as after a goal is scored, as a teaching moment to get the game under control and clarify any questions. I will always think of the safety of the students first and foremost in the gym to avoid injury.

I will add an extra incentive for getting homework done, such as a class treat if all of the homework is done six days in a row.

In general, the management strategies already in place at my AT's class work well for me. The students respond well to me, especially in the classroom setting. I have adopted many of my AT's strategies but do realize that I will have some different ideas when I have my own classroom. I understand that it is important to have clear and defined rules for behavior, conduct, and academic expectations in place at the beginning of the year. The students do not hesitate to challenge you if they think you are being unfair, thus it is important to have *back-up* for your actions in their eyes and clearly defined expectations stated verbally and shown visually in order to give them acceptable guidelines for behavior.

Questions: **Would you be tempted to use these classroom management systems and if so, what would you add or avoid? Why?**

4. Danielle Thompson – Surprise

Another pre-service student, Danielle Thompson, was assigned to a grade 8 class and was surprised frequently by many elements within the classroom. Danielle reflected:

Act

I am placed in a grade 8 classroom environment. There are 30 students in the class, five of which are identified with extreme behavioral and emotional problems. Three of the students are identified with having learning disabilities. Students are seated in rows of two or three. Overall, the students behaved very well for my associate as she has a good rapport and mutual respect with the students. She is direct, organized, and demands a lot of them in their work.

Going into my placement, I expected that classroom management was not something I would have to address right away because my Associate Teacher was with me at all times. I figured the students would probably behave very well for me considering the teacher was in the room while I was teaching a lesson. As I found out, classroom management does not only involve behavioral issues. It also includes organizational issues. I expected that students would know how to take notes and follow instructions without me having to be too specific. After all, this class was in grade 8. Were they not reaching young adulthood,taking on more responsibility for their actions?

My expectations quickly changed after my very first lesson. Yes, the students behaved very well. However, there were many little things I had assumed the students would automatically do. For instance, I had asked the students to copy down a note, and half of them did not have out the correct books or writing tools. I quickly realized that for my next lesson, before I began talking, I would have to ask the students to take out their specified notebook and writing tools. I would not start the lesson until every student in the class had followed the instructions properly. Once this was done, I could start the lesson and know that everyone was prepared to take the note.

After the first day of teaching, I made the mistake of asking the question, "Does everyone have this handout?" I did not receive any responses. I learned to rephrase the question; "Put up your hand if you have not received this handout." Instead of asking an open-ended question, I rephrased it as an instruction. Those students who did not have the sheet, readily put up their hand to indicate they needed the worksheet.

One incident that should be mentioned, was an encounter with a grade 7 student. My Associate Teacher teaches grade 7 science and I was observing this particular class. This student has severe oppositional defiant disorder. He thrives on confrontation. I happened to be sitting in his assigned seat that day. He came right up to me and demanded, "Get out of my seat." I looked up at him and replied, "Pardon?" He looked up and down at me and repeated, "Get out of my seat!" I could not believe this student was so rude. I knew that he enjoyed confrontation and I wanted to avoid this at all costs. I calmly and quietly said, "If you ask me nicely, I will move out of your seat." He looked, sighed, and finally asked, "Can you please get out of my seat?" I told him that sounded better and went into a different seat. This student was difficult to deal with because he could have reacted in a confrontational way. I knew that if I used the same tone with him as he did with me that would have provoked him to get confrontational.

Throughout my placement there were many little things that occurred similar to what I have mentioned so far that made me revaluate my thoughts and feelings on classroom management.

Reflect

From my experience with classroom management thus far, I have been fortunate to be with a class who respects their homeroom teacher. This has worked in my favor, because they give me the same respect they would give my associate. They know she is in the room watching how they behave. This has been a positive factor, because I can practice other aspects of classroom management with the students, the organizational part of things. I have not had to worry about students acting out because they understand that is not done while a teacher is delivering a lesson.

I think that having my associate in the classroom is a helpful tool in assisting classroom management but it can also hinder me. If I rely upon her presence, it will reflect upon my management skills when I have my own classroom. I feel I began to recognize this during my placement. I knew there were times when I was delivering a lesson where students might have got off task. Those times were during transition, going from homeroom to a rotary subject.

I did not realize how important it was to give directions for everything. I thought this was true for younger grades, but older students also need this guidance. They need to be reminded of routines. As a teacher, I feel that being consistent with routines will help to have the classroom run smoothly. There is less confusion from the students if there are specific routines for note taking and entering the classroom.

The only time I was really placed in a position where I did not know if I was reacting correctly, was during the situation with the grade 7 student with oppositional defiant disorder. Looking back, I felt that I handled myself quite well. I think I did the right thing in using a calm voice. The only thing I am unsure about was whether I should have given him the seat. I think if a teacher was sitting there, they probably would have had him choose another place to sit. It is hard to know what the right way was. I was successful in having him ask me politely rather than his rude demands, but he should not address any adult with that tone.

Overall, I was pleased with my ability to adapt my classroom management skills. I feel that I acknowledged when something did not work and then tried to adjust it so that it would be effective the next time. The best place to learn was from my own mistakes. It is one thing for people to suggest what works, but the right way is not known until I encounter it head on. These experiences provided me with several points to reflect and improve upon.

Revise

I know I have a lot to learn when it comes to the area of classroom management. In the past, I have never been in the position where I am in charge of 30 people. The teaching is the easy part. I believe there are many things I can do in order to correct my presence in the classroom. Even in the short time I was at my placement, I began to realize which strategies would be effective. I decided that I did not want to be one of those teachers who constantly had their voice raised. Not only did I find this unsuccessful, but it also eliminated options for the teacher as students began to tune out a teacher who is constantly yelling. This becomes a waste of energy for that teacher and they have lost the students in the process. A teacher who rarely raises her voice, gets the students' attention and this becomes effective.

On reviewing my classroom management notes, they suggested that teachers need to be aware of the emotional, societal, and psychological state of students. In order for me to begin to understand why students might behave in a certain manner, I need to understand what is going on in their lives. Many things influence the way they act. I believe I have done a good job in trying to get to know the students and their family situations. I think this will help me acknowledge problems ahead of time.

I will also try to clarify all my lessons and be sure the content I am teaching is understood by the students. Students are unhappy with teachers who have difficulty explaining things. They do not like to be left confused. I cannot control a student's family background or psychological state, but I can control my instructional skills. In order for me to become successful in this area, I believe I should try to plan my lessons very thoroughly. This way, I can go over the content and anticipate any problems the students may have. Appearing unprepared allows students to see me as someone who is unorganized. How can they become organized if their own teacher does not display this in his/her own practices?

Another way that I can improve my classroom management for my next placement is to be more direct with my instructions. This may be the area where I am weakest. I had mentioned previously that I adapted the way I asked questions. I need to be more direct and consistent with this procedure. For example, asking, "Can everyone take out their math book?" may create some sarcastic remarks, such as someone simply saying "no." A better approach might be to say, "Everyone needs their math notebook on their desk." Students do not have the option to give an answer.

Finally, another area I may need to improve on is when students get off task. There will be times where they might finish assigned work early. I have to have a backup plan for students. There must be always something for them to do. If students are not given other options for work to be completed, then they will freely socialize. This would cause students to start talking aloud, causing other students to get off task.

I can now see why classroom management plays such a crucial role in the success of a teacher. There are so many issues a teacher needs to consider when organizing their classroom. I need to establish what type of teacher I want to be and build from there. All these experiences from my October practicum have contributed to how I perceive classroom management. I am hoping that by implementing some of the ideas suggested in my "revise" section, I will become stronger in the management side of teaching.

***Questions*: Has Danielle been too critical of herself, or is this just a necessary stance to take if you want to grow as a teacher? How can you prepare to deal with inclusion from a classroom management perspective? Please comment.**

5. Wendy Runions – My Style!

Wendy, a pre-service teacher assigned to a grade 5/6 split observed several necessary elements within the well-managed classroom.

My placement is in a very well-managed grade 5/6 class within a small school of 117 students. My Associate Teacher, an experienced and very capable woman, is teaching this same group of students for the third year. She has firmly established routines, of which the students are very cognizant. Another important part of the classroom environment that affects classroom management, is my associate's well developed rapport with the students. It is obvious she knows a great deal about each of her students and cares about them as individuals. She also has a very relaxed and unhurried persona. The children reflect this; they are very relaxed, unstressed, and tend to cause few problems. There are 27 students in the class; eight of them have identified learning disabilities.

Before I started to teach, I was a little concerned because my teaching style tends to be extremely dynamic and exciting. The groups I teach tend to reflect my style and become very involved and excited too. However, if I am not careful about making sure that students know where the boundaries are, this has the potential to cause behavior problems. One of the things that I wanted to do in this placement was incorporate some of my associate's style so that I could become a calming influence on the class as well as initiating excitement.

I cannot say that I witnessed many management problems while I was teaching. In all honesty, I would not say this is due to my incredible classroom management skills. It was a result of my Associate Teacher, who has firmly established routines. They know what is expected of them and what will happen if they do not meet her expectations. During the first lesson that I taught on Thursday, I noticed that after we completed an activity and I started to speak, the students did not come to the dead silence and focus on me as quickly as they did with my AT. What I realized was that my Associate Teacher does not begin to speak until she has total silence and all students are focusing on her. I tried waiting just those extra few seconds and it worked beautifully. Another thing that I noted was that my Associate Teacher usually flicks the lights to get everyone's attention when they are in the middle of an activity and the class noise level is a little high. I had been reluctant to do this during my first lesson because it is not what I usually do and it just does not feel natural to me. I decided that during my next lesson, I would use the lights to bring the students' focus back on to me, since that is what they were used to. It worked perfectly and I used it several times over the course of the week. Normally, I would think this is one of those things that would lose effectiveness over time, but apparently it is what my associate always does. The students recognize it as a signal, just like when the school bell rings.

On the Friday before Thanksgiving, there was a lot of activity in the school. There was a Thanksgiving celebration in the gym in the morning and a "Stone Soup" meal in the afternoon. In addition, our class was busily trying to finish a major Thanksgiving art project by the end of the day. I had a lesson planned about Ancient Greek myths. We had been working on Ancient Greece in Social Studies and I thought I would do a little curriculum integration in Language Arts. I came in dressed as the Greek playwright Euripides, wrapped in a bed sheet toga, leaves in my hair, and the whole bit. You should have seen the students' faces when I entered the room. Their jaws dropped, they were wide-eyed, and you could have heard a pin drop. I called them all barbarians for speaking "no Greek" and talked to them about the beauty of the Greek tongue and then, in my best oratory style, told several Greek myths. At the end, I commanded them to write their own myth in the Greek style and swept out of the room. When I came back in the room sans costume, the students were trying to pretend nothing happened, but they couldn't keep up the pretence. They were giggling as they told me about the Ancient Greek who had come to visit. I played dumb, but said that I thought this Greek person had a good idea. We started the process for writing a Greek myth. It seems that this lesson was as smooth as silk, so why bring it up for classroom management? When I reflected on this lesson, I realized that this could have been a disaster. This was an extremely exciting day with lots of things happening and it was the last day before the long weekend. The students were keyed up enough and this was probably not a good choice for a very exciting lesson. I should have probably stuck with something a little more routine and saved this lesson for another day. Another thing that I realized is that I have to bear in mind where the students are going after an exciting lesson. If they are going out to recess or if I am going to have them for the next period, that is probably fine, but if they are going to go to the Music teacher or the French teacher, it might not be such a good idea.

Another thing I learned during the practicum was about deadlines. Since I was not sure of the speed with which students would be able to complete something, unless it was a science experiment, I was reluctant to set deadlines. The class was working on developing posters on a

Greek god and when the students asked when they had to be finished, I said that we would see how far along they were at the end of the period and then I would set a deadline. This was a big mistake. The students who are very motivated see how quickly they can get it done, but the others consider it permission to waste time and procrastinate. I learned my lesson. When it came time to work on the Greek myths, I let the students know that the rough drafts must be completed by the end of the period, or they go home for homework. I would be looking at them tomorrow. The procrastination disappeared and students were on task.

There were many little things I noticed that students did because I was new and they wanted to see if they could take advantage. The biggest thing seemed to be about washroom breaks. The Associate Teacher is pretty strict that, except in cases of dire emergency, washroom breaks are to be taken at lunch and recess times. I have a daughter who has had four surgeries to correct problems with her urinary tract and she needs special consideration with regard to washroom breaks, so I have a bit of sensitivity on this topic. I granted a few students permission to use the washroom and although I didn't have a huge problem, I noticed the same couple of students always asked, and by the second or third day, I noticed they always asked about five minutes before recess or lunch. They were not going to the washrooms, but to their lockers to get stuff for recess. After that, I always asked, "It will be recess in five minutes, can you wait?"They always said yes. The other way they tried to take advantage of my being new, was extra help. When students were working on math problems or writing their myths, I always circulated and looked for students who needed my help. My associate pointed out that two of the students who were asking for help, did not actually need it. They were faking a problem with the math to get me to spend time with them. My associate and I thought this was quite humorous. I reflected on this and realized that when I was working with them, I was not available to help others, but if a child was in so much need of attention that they were willing to fake problems, maybe I should spend a little time with them. However, it was important to give them attention for doing something positive and so I started looking for things the students had done well so I could give them attention for that instead.

I also have a young lady in my class who was a bit of a mystery to me at first. She has been shifted from foster home to foster home for years and is new to the school because she is with a new family and in a new community. This young lady is personable, intelligent, and seems eager to please, yet she always seemed to get herself into problems in the past. We had been warned not to leave her alone for a moment in the class, as she tended to steal when left unattended. When I met her on the first week of placement in September, it seemed difficult to believe some of the things in her OSR (Ontario Student Record). I firmly believed that she had decided to turn over a new leaf and was going to do very well.

When I got back in October, I found she had not turned in a single assignment. She started everything with miles of enthusiasm and stopped at about 95% completion. Social Services were sending a social worker to assist her in trying to catch up once a week. This seemed wrong; there is no reason that this child could not complete the assignments. She has the brains, talent, and ability. Why wasn't she completing the work? I am sorry to say that I did not find a solution before I left, but I could not stop thinking about her. In one of my classes, someone talked about having a student with a fear of failure and I thought, "Could that be it?" Is she afraid to fail so she doesn't finish so she won't face evaluation? "Maybe," I thought. When I went to see my Faculty Advisor (FA) on another matter, I ended up bringing her up. When I described this student, several times I said "She likes to be the centre of attention." When we talked about her personality, it became clear that the need for attention was her motivating drive. My FA asked, "What happens when she doesn't complete her work?" My associate and I did what any responsible teachers would do; we had her stay in on some recesses and lunches to catch up. As well, she now has this social worker who devotes all her time to her for an hour every Tuesday. "That's her payoff," said my FA. This really struck a cord for me and I knew that she was right. We had to find a way of giving her the attention she was seeking when she finished something, not when she didn't.

Together we came up with some ideas. If the students were assigned to write a short story for the grade 1 students in the school and read their stories to them, she might be motivated to finish so that she could be the centre of attention in that grade 1 class. I am also going to try to break her work into smaller chunks and praise her when each small chunk is accomplished. If I can give her the attention she needs for positive things, it might mean she doesn't need to seek it for negative things. In the end she may start getting her homework done and we might prevent some disruptive classroom behavior as she seeks more attention. This young lady may not be a classic classroom management problem. Unfinished assignments don't really interfere with the teaching act, student learning, or student safety, and they cause no damage to school property. However, other students may emulate her behavior and I have noticed that she uses attention seeking behaviors at other times. She asks questions, makes interjections unnecessarily and frequently, and she attempts to gain my attention at inappropriate times, such as when the associate is speaking or a video is playing. Unless this problem is dealt with, she could become a disruptive influence. I am hoping that I will be a positive influence on her when I get back in November.

There is one last behavior issue that I would like to bring up. At the end of the day, all of the students pick up their chairs and put them with the back two chair legs in their desk. This means that the custodian can clean the floor a little easier. One of our grade 6 students, the self-declared "class clown", always puts her chair with only one chair leg in the desk. She then tries to sneak out of the class without my associate noticing. She is successful about 80% of the time. It drives my associate crazy, although it doesn't really bother me. The chair is still quite stable and unlikely to fall on anyone as my associate fears. The young lady in question knows this irritates my associate. When the students were asked to write a paragraph on "How to drive your teacher crazy," she included this as one of the tips. Frankly, I think the student just likes the attention and the thrill of seeing if she can get away with it again. When she gets caught, she gets attention, when she doesn't she gets the reward of "beating the teacher." I think this is one of those behaviors that would just go away if the teacher stopped noticing it. I am not trying to criticize my associate here. She is amazing and I could learn so much from her about classroom management. I just think in this case, she has a blind spot and has ended up in a head-butting contest with this student. I think in classroom management, we have to choose our battles and this one might not be worth fighting. Each teacher is different, though, and what one teacher can tolerate another can't.

As you can probably see, my practicum was pretty uneventful when it came to classroom management, but I still think I learned a lot. I will continue to carefully observe my Associate Teacher when she is teaching, because one day I would like a class as well managed as hers. At the beginning, I said that my goal was to incorporate some of my Associate Teacher's calm, relaxed, and unhurried style of teaching. Was I successful? Maybe not just yet. I really want to find a balance between creating an exciting and dynamic classroom when appropriate and a relaxed, low stress atmosphere. At this point, I am looking forward to my November practicum and to learning more about classroom management.

***Question*: How would you handle the negative attention-getting student who likes to stay in for recess? Share your ideas.**

6. Dan Coutu – 1, 2, 3 Magic!

Dan provides this glimpse inside both his head and his practicum.

During my two weeks of practice teaching, I got a chance to observe a great deal of management strategies, as well as put some of them into practice. I received a great deal of information just from my observations. My associate had me observe just about every class in the school. I also sat in on a section 20 and LAC class. What an interesting experience. It is interesting to see what management techniques work for some teachers and not for others. The only thing I found difficult was observing some of these classes for such a short period.

The school in which I am practicing has a high number of behavioral students. I am very fortunate to have been assigned such a challenging school. I feel that the experience that I will gain from this placement will only help my career in the future. It has also given me a new-found respect for the educational assistant. Without them, the classroom environment would be even more chaotic than what it already is at times. The class that I teach is a grade 4/5 split with 24 students. Out of that number, there are about 15 identified students and one educational assistant. Occasionally, I teach the grade 5/6 split their religion component. There are about the same amount of students as the 4/5 split, but with about 20 identified students and one educational assistant. Talk about a challenging group to work with.

It is interesting how it is just one or two in a group that are the catalysts for the disruption of the entire class. Sometimes it is best to remove these individuals when they are not contributing anything to the class. Chances are they are affecting the learning of others.

My grade 4/5's are generally a good group. One of the things with this group of students is that it is very difficult to keep their attention for any length of time; therefore, they get off task very easily. One of the management strategies that I use is called **1, 2, 3, magic**. This is the same strategy that my associate uses with them and it seems to be very effective. Sometimes when the students are getting off task, I will just simply stand and wait until everyone's attention is focused on me. It does not usually take them very long before they realize the message that I am trying to get across. The overall classroom management is based on accumulating points to earn rewards. Very rarely do the students lose points during the course of the day. I like this because it emphasizes more on the positive and less on the negative. Children at that age need to see something tangible as a means of motivation. They do not yet appreciate the importance of a good education and the intangible rewards that it brings.

One of the systems that I had not really thought about was how to control students leaving class for washroom or drink breaks. The school has a policy that does not allow students to leave class without a hall pass. In my class, we have one pass for each [gender]. If someone in the class requests to leave the room and there is no hall pass, that person must wait until one is available. This is a great way to help eliminate some of the useless wandering. In my classroom, I would only have one hall pass. I would not allow any student to leave the class in the middle of the lesson. I would encourage them to use their recess time wisely or wait until the lesson is complete. This will help discourage students from abusing the privilege.

Overall, my practice teaching experience was a positive one. I look forward to going back and applying the new knowledge that I have obtained. From a management standpoint, I believe that with more practice my comfort zone will broaden along with my ability to educate my students.

***Question*: Does age play a role in maturity or is it possible to have very mature self-managed young students?**

7. Catherine Ann Shisko – John

Catherine Ann Shisko revisits her Grade 7 practicum and constructs several admissions. She begins by stating,

It really is true what people say about teaching: it is 5% teaching and 95% classroom management. No matter how interesting and rock solid my lesson plans are I must be aware that students are not all going to sit quietly and hang onto my every word while lapping up all of the information I present. Even though I knew all of this before I started my lessons, I did not enter class with a deliberate management plan. I thought the solutions were in my back pocket; that I had enough teaching experience that I would know exactly what steps I had to take to keep the students on task and immersed in a positive learning environment. I was wrong.

I still want the students to like me. I do believe it is possible to maintain professionalism as a teacher and still have the students genuinely like me. However, in this case I approached it in the wrong way. Instead of setting the ground rules for our interactions right from the beginning of my practicum I played more of a support role in my Associate Teacher's (AT's) classroom. I wanted to be a fresh pair of eyes that would give all students a chance to be seen in a different light. I heard the talk in the staff room and warnings from my AT about the 'problem' students and I wanted to avoid making judgments about these kids based on preconceived notions.

There is a student, "John," who is repeating his grade 7 year. Apparently, he did very little work last year even though his mother monitors his progress due to the high number of phone calls and notes home from the school. The word about the staff room was that John was simply not the favored child in the home. John is labeled as "behavioral" and has an Educational Assistant (EA) assigned to him for a part of each class. From what I could see, the EA did not spend a significant amount of time with John and moved around the classroom too much to have much effect on the student's minute-to-minute behavior patterns.

The class had been working on a self-directed "Special Interest" project for the last few classes and John had chosen to do his project on Tupac Shakur (the slain rapper). He was working well and I was pleased with his progress and obvious passion for the project. John talked to me at length about it. I responded positively in hopes that he would feel I was a teacher he could have a fresh start with and that there would be a payoff with some good behavior. When it came time to present my first full poetry lesson, John tried to take control throughout the class discussion. I struggled because John's input stayed in the realm of poetry but was off task in terms of the assignment we were discussing. I did my best to integrate his input but refused to stray from the path of my lesson. His attempt to take control averted, John started to interrupt and offer silly answers to straightforward questions. I asked him to stay on task, but the damage had been done and others in the class hopped on John's train of thought.

Once we got into the interactive part of the lesson, John was feeling a bit more confident, buoyed by the fact that he was a bit of a silly hero to his classmates. While he was participating in the assigned task (writing descriptive words on various pieces of chart paper around the room), he kept bringing attention to himself by signing his name every time he wrote something. I noticed and informed the whole class that signing your name was not required. John, however, continued to sign his name and was encouraging other students to do the same. There was a lot going on in the classroom and I had an overwhelming need for John to stop his behavior right then and there. After I explained the rules again, he engaged me in an argument and then he shut down. There was nothing we could do to get back on solid ground. While the event wasn't catastrophic, it had gone far enough that John was sent to the office with his EA.

The next day, John was asked by my AT to apologize to me before entering the classroom (which he did). I decided to simply accept his apology and not harp on the subject because I felt that enough adults had reprimanded him for his behavior. I didn't want to overwhelm him and, I suppose, I still wanted him to like me.

The first thing I would do differently would be to verbally acknowledge the fact that John's input was valued but that he had to stay on task right at the beginning of the lesson. If the wager to gain power over the class continued, I would ask the EA to sit with John to help him focus. Considering the behavioral challenges in this particular class, I would change the structure of my lesson and have them work independently or with only one other person at their desks instead of moving around the classroom to finish the activity. Most importantly, I would avoid being sucked into an argument with the student. Instead of trying to change his behavior, I would give him some options: ask him to take his seat; sit quietly; write in his journal; doodle something in relation to the task at hand (something he likes to do), or; brainstorm about the task with either his EA or myself.

In relation to the situation I've just mentioned, I said I didn't have a concrete management plan. I mistakenly thought I could handle any situation without having to resort to sending students to study hall or detention. These are school-wide initiatives that have been in place for a very long time. Whether or not I agree with them is not the point. The point is they have been proven to work for this school and I have to respect that. As a teacher, I must follow through in a predictable manner so it is fair for all. The procedures are there as a tool for each and every teacher at the school. I didn't want to be seen as the "heavy" and thought a different approach would be refreshing and, ultimately, more effective than the plan already put into place. At the very beginning of my next practicum I am going to sit down with my AT to review the procedures for discipline and then use them in a way that I am comfortable.

As I mentioned before, the lesson I taught worked well with the morning class. There are, however, very few exceptional or behavioral students in there and I was able to 'hook' them much more easily. In the future, I am going to tailor each lesson to individual classes so that I can meet the same expectations and provide similar experiences that serve individual classes. For example, I will pinpoint the exceptional or behavioral students and make sure I meet with them right after I finish the lesson to answer any additional questions privately and also reinforce the task.

Generally, my lessons were all activity-based and used a variety of activities to reach the end product. I taught poetry and constantly had students crowding around me asking for my feedback on their assignments. I'm not totally convinced it would make things more manageable, but I may try situating myself in a specific location and limit my visitors to one person at a time. I could set up "appointments" and call each student when I was ready. The students in line would either get a peer to evaluate their work or re-read their rough copy and make decisions for improvement on their own.

While I was helping the crowd of students around me, I found it difficult to monitor the rest of the class while giving enough attention to the student in front of me. I have yet to earn my "eyes on the back of my head." I'm hoping we get them before graduation in May. When I had trouble monitoring, the volume tended to get louder and louder as the students went off task. I don't like yelling or threatening and am going to experiment with a visual signal that lets the students know when the volume is too high.

I may have made my experience sound like a complete nightmare, but it really wasn't. The students respect me and are comfortable with me leading the class in everyday routines and lessons. Having said that, I look forward to more practical experience in classroom management. These reflections have forced me to set up an action plan for my next placement and I intend to follow through.

***Questions*: Do our feelings about what happened color and blur the reality we experience and if they do how can teachers cope? Would it help to have an objective mentor give you their view as you teach?**

8. Jason Glassford – Shock and Awe

Jason used strong words to convey his feelings and created a vivid analogy of his grade 6/7 classroom for us to follow.

Management Situation

Being able to partake in real classroom experiences, such as the first day of school, is something I will not soon forget. During my first two practicum experiences, I was thrilled with my Associate Teacher (AT) and the students of his grade 6/7 class. I found myself bragging about their educational desires and their excellent behaviors. My AT was well in control of this finely tuned super-car of education. His classroom was arranged in continuous horizontal rows, which allowed for easy access to all eyes in the room. While completing my October practice teaching I was elated with every lesson and left feeling confident in my skills.

When I returned to class in *November*, I was *shocked* to see that he had rearranged his classroom into four groups of seven students. The seven grade 6 students were the group at the front of the class. As I observed my AT teaching the students I could not help but notice how chatty the groups were, even when the assignments were individual. As I took the wheel and started this awesome vehicle, I was not prepared to be thrown out the door. Standing in front of the class, prepared to start a lesson, I could not help but notice that I only had half of my audience looking at me. I would raise my hand in the air in an effort to flex some classroom management muscle, but only the half that could see me would respond. The others continued to be chatty. I slugged my way through several days of instruction but left each day a little more frustrated and disappointed in my abilities. I had planned a fun game in Language Arts called *Spello*, a knockoff of Bingo but with weekly spelling words. The experience was horrible. My students continued to be chatty and their comments were inappropriate. Students that had always been superb were out of control. This seemed to be the proverbial straw that broke the camel's back in my teaching practicum. I could feel my internal temperature rising and my patience was at its end. However, I continued on and completed the lesson, knowing that it was a complete flop.

Following my lesson, my Associate and I sat for our daily reflection and he inquired about my feelings for the day. He and I both commented that my lesson on Spello was a disaster. He stated that my level of patience was incredible. We talked about my practicum to date and that we were both frustrated with the group environment. My AT commented that he has been a little lax in his classroom management, letting behaviors exist that he would normally not stand for. He apologized for not setting a better example in this area.

Analysis of Event

Where did I go wrong? At what point did I lose control? Do I continue, or should I stop right now? During my lesson on Spello, these questions ran through my head constantly. It was at this point I began to question my desire to teach for a living. However, the lesson itself was not the problem, but the students had been given so much leeway to chat and be irresponsible that my lesson acted as the catalyst to the loss of control. I do not believe the students were completely aware of my loss of control, or that their behavior was over the top. In between my October and November placements, my Associate Teacher had major surgery and was off school for three weeks. When I returned for my November placement and walked through the door, it was also his first day back into the classroom. We were both excited to be back and were motivated by our eagerness to teach. Reading the notes of the supply teacher should have tipped us off that the group environment was not a productive one for this class. Her comments included: "hard to focus," "off-task chatting," and "inappropriate actions and comments." Then the realization hit me – the awesome students that I was bragging about after my first two placements had changed. I had noticed several times over the first two weeks of my placement that I had to take steps to control the class that I had never taken before. At first I was emotionally shocked that my students were behaving this way, then as my placement continued, I found the group environment offensive to me as a teacher. When group assignments where administered the environment was acceptable, given the nature of the work. However, it was the daily routine of lessons involving math, reading, French, and social studies that were greatly affected by the group environment. In an effort to control chatter I threatened additional homework and delayed time for recess (which only really affects my 15 minutes of tranquility, not theirs).

In speaking with my AT about the group atmosphere, he stated that he was not thrilled with groups but that the principal herself had requested the change. We talked about what might have happened during his time off and what the supply teachers' expectations were from the groups. It could be we had different expectations of the students than she did and, therefore, needed to address what is appropriate behavior in groups. My AT has utilized group environments in his past teaching, but never really enjoyed the experience. I commented to my AT that it seemed as though the students were inexperienced in the expectations of group work. We both concluded that the group environment should be eased into, taking one lesson or subject at a time. During a science unit the students could arrange their desks into the groups for each lesson, then back again for the next subject. I realize the importance of group work and group dynamics development in children, however, I also believe in the development of each student and their individuality. The next day during prep time, we created a new classroom-seating plan, going back to the original horizontal rows. We moved the desks during last period and the students where excited about the process. For the final week of my practicum, I taught the students in this environment and excelled in my role as teacher. I captivated every student's attention when I instructed and they remained on task during work time. I had no idea that class management of excellent students could be so affected by classroom setup.

Personal and Professional Learnings Derived from the Event

The most profound learning that I experienced was that classroom environment has a great . . . no huge, affect on classroom management. I was also surprised that even good students will act out if given the appropriate environment. As teachers, we must be willing to try new things and accommodate our teaching environment to meet the learning needs of our students. It is also my opinion that students need conformity in the classroom. They need to know what is expected of them at all times. I can appreciate my AT's Principal's requesting that he change his class environment to provide various learning opportunities for all the students, even though he has fantastic success with his horizontal rows environment.

Classroom Environment

In September of 2004, when I walk into my own classroom how am I going to arrange the learning environment? Where do I begin? How often do I change things?

During my week of observation in October, I was fortunate to observe teachers utilizing groups, pairs, combinations, and other shapes for their classroom environment. For each teacher, I found their own set-up effective for their teaching style. I understand the advantages of group environments but also the disadvantages. As the main adult figure in the majority of students' lives, the teacher is seen as the role model; the person that sets the norms by which others will follow. This is so for a number of years; however, as students grow older they rely more on their peers for information regarding attitude, values, skills, and other information unobtainable from adults. The group environment also provides a frame of reference for the development of self-perception. Peer relationships exert tremendous influence on social and cognitive development and student socialization. Peers influence productivity and educational aspirations. The goal of the group environment is to promote prosocial behavior in students which in turn lead to increased self-esteem. Therefore, the group environment must be carefully arranged as to not alienate any one student placed in the wrong group. They must all be well balanced with strong and weak, chatty and quiet, extrovert and introvert, hard working and lazy students. This combination ensures that no one student can bring the group to a halt and it allows for the development of prosocial behavior in a culturally diverse population.

Why Were My Good Students Acting Out?

Looking at the prosocial behavior mentioned above, I believe that the groups in my classroom were not evenly balanced. The groups lacked harmony. My one table of exemplar students that misbehaved had me stumped at first but then I researched how groups should function and I realized they were missing key components to make their group work well together. It might have been the extrovert student that usually acted out; consequently, the group as a whole modeled this behavior in an attempt to create harmony. As I experienced, the results were catastrophic. What if the situation were more serious and the students of the group were members of a gang and one student was not? What would happen to the lone student? Would they be tormented? What social peer pressures would be placed on the lone student? What if the group was all boys or all girls except for one member of the opposite sex? What effect would this situation have on a student's prosocial behaviorism for the rest of their lives? It is a simple question; groups or rows? But the effects could be everlasting.

Try New Things

As educators we must realize that children are easily distracted and all have unique learning styles. What does this mean? I believe that the ideal classroom will have numerous learning opportunities for all students. The classroom will have a row of single desks for independent learners, a row of pairs for students that require an "enabling other," and two large group areas for others that work better in team environments. My classroom will have numerous stations set up around the room, for various learning opportunities. As I mentioned earlier I believe the key to the group environment is balance. Creating balance is knowing your students and knowing takes time. Reading OSRs and having discussions with previous teachers helps to provide the information necessary regarding our new students, therefore, better preparing ourselves for how we will arrange our classroom environment.

Student Expectations

In reflecting on my practicum experience with my AT, we both realized that the students were inexperienced in the expectations of group work and working in a group environment. As I struggled through my first few days of my placement, I found myself needing to express how I wanted the students to behave and how to act in their groups. This action seemed to help control the inappropriate or off-task behavior but only shortly. As the students had already been in the group environment for three weeks their actions were already ingrained and as we all know, it is difficult to teach an old dog new tricks. During each practicum we are guests in someone else's classroom. I would like to think that I could walk in on day one and arrange the students how I would like to teach but this behavior is unfitting of a guest. I can see the advantages to throwing off the classroom vibe by rearranging the classroom environment, thereby creating a complete imbalance with a new teacher and new environment. I could lay down the law of expectations and move forward while they are still trying to figure out what has happened and what they can and can't get away with.

***Questions*: Should you change and arrange things in your practicum? What things or changes are out of bounds during a practicum and why?**

9. Grade 7 – Where Do I Fit?

Grade 7 is a pivotal year for many students and to align yourself with a group is to identify who you are. It seems in this reflection there is tension concerning where the student teacher should position herself.

Act

The class that I have been assigned to, to do my practice teaching, is a grade 7 class made up of 15 girls and six boys. In light of this, the dynamics of the classroom are shifted toward the interpersonal relations between the female members of the classroom which in the past have been hostile at best. As a female practice teacher and after my initial encounter with the students, the female members of the class saw me more as a colleague to one of the three cliques in the classroom and thus the other girls of the classroom were somewhat offended. Although no particular incident occurred that would have created this dynamic, as my AT pointed out the girls align themselves with authorities around the school in hopes of gaining advantage over the other groups. She made sure I was aware of the potential for difficulty that this imagined favor might have.

For instance, the AT is also a relation to one member of one of the three cliques in the classroom and as a result, this clique feels that the AT is on "their side." The groups that chose to align with me were opposing to that group and thus felt that I was a valuable ally. However, the third clique in the classroom, which was made up of three of the more rebellious female members of the classroom, were now demonstrating open hostility toward me over the alleged allegiance. I realized that these three girls, despite my best efforts to remain neutral in the classroom, had interpreted my assisting another group in an assignment as a taking-of-sides in an incident that occurred outside of the classroom, and of which I was unaware. Because these three girls could not hear what I was saying to the other girls about the assignment, they assumed I was speaking to these girls about the incident. The AT had not informed me of the issue (appropriately so) but in my ignorance, I did not consider that my attention to one group over the other would have an impact. Because the girls assumed that I knew of the incident, they felt that when I was speaking to the AT later on that day, that I was "tattling" and that I had taken sides on the incident. When the AT left the classroom during my instruction of an art lesson, I realized the extent to which these female members of the class resented my presence in the classroom and their attempts to intimidate me. The girls began by speaking loudly after being told to speak quietly and they began passing notes in my direct view. When these attempts at classroom disruption failed, they began to openly defy the classroom routine of using hand signals to leave their seats or talk to a classmate that was not close by. They went further then, to directing "dirty looks" in my direction and calling me over to answer questions, then using a disrespectful tone to respond to me. The action that warranted my direct address however was the subtle accusation, made loud enough for me to hear but not made directly at me, was that I was just "sucking up" to the AT and that I was a "crappy" teacher. Because of the word choice and the obvious attack, I felt it necessary to address the disrespectful behavior in an authoritative but quiet manner.

Because I felt that to make a public display of the incident would just invite further attacks by other students and thus challenge my authority in the classroom, I approached the three girls as the rest of the class was involved in group work and informed them that I had in fact overheard the comment and that it was inappropriate and unnecessary. Furthermore, I informed them that despite the fact that I was a visiting member in the classroom, my authority in the room was not conditional on their liking me, but that their respect of me was necessary based on the school code of conduct. To this, the girls began to increase the openness of their disregard of my authority by refusing to participate in the classroom, using negative body language directed at me, and increasing the intensity of their "dirty looks" which now included loud sighing, groaning at my instructions, and mumbling under their breath.

Reflect

Later when I was speaking to the AT about the events that had transpired in the classroom, she mentioned the incident that had occurred and I realized that the incident of the girls behavior towards me in the classroom in her absence was related to her (the AT's) dealing with the event. Because the AT is also the Vice Principle of the school it is sometimes difficult for her to not be seen as VP in her classroom as well as the classroom teacher and as such I was seen as the "soft touch" in the room. When I challenged the girls on their behavior, they realized that I was not an ally, a soft touch, or a subordinate to the AT in terms of my authority in the classroom and as such, I was from then on given the respect of the students in the classroom.

On this day, I realized that in my classroom I am not going to be liked nor am I a friend to my students. Because of my youth and my gender, the female members of my classroom had interpreted my kindness for overtures of friendship and thus my response to their inappropriate behavior offended them. I must then be concerned with the fact that I will not necessarily be liked by my students, but I will be respected in terms of my authority and position. This is a difficult realization because I find myself desiring to be liked and wanting the approval of my students but I realized that the students want only to get as much past me as possible and are not concerned as much with my liking of them as they are concerned with the approval of their classmates. The approval of classmates comes from their ability to control the classroom and thus their challenges of my authority are central to that goal. Therefore, it is necessary to be the authority in the room and not concerned with my overall approval rating in the classroom. Furthermore, I have come to the realization that I should not take personally the attacks my students direct at me; rather, I should accept that they are at a stage that challenging any authority and is part of their development. It is not my person that they necessarily dislike, but the fact that I have authority in the classroom that they want. It is difficult to conceptualize the idea that the students are not attacking me, but I believe they would do this to whomever represented an authority and that although I am the target of their hostilities it is my position that challenges them, not me personally. The difficulty then lies in the altering of my perception of myself as fellow student to teacher and in this transition, I must be aware of the new responsibilities and obligations that I have in a classroom. No longer do my activities in the classroom occur independent of the members of the room. Although I may intend these activities to be neutral or I am oblivious to their impact in the room, it is my obligation to be seen in the room as above reproach and outside of them as students.

Revise

I intended to demonstrate more awareness of my role and impact in the classroom in the sense that I will more definitely establish myself in the room as an authority and not as a student seeking approval. I will demonstrate this transition in thinking and behavior by working on my overall confidence as a practice soon-to-become teacher. I attribute my taking personally the attacks of my students to my very human desire to seek approval but I realize that it is not student approval that I seek. Therefore, I attempt to use the classroom management strategy of identifying that it is my "role of instructional leader" (Levin and Nolan, 1) and not assume that "some forms of verbal intervention defuse confrontation and reduce misbehavior" but can actually, "escalate misbehavior and confrontation" (Levin and Nolan, 11). To demonstrate the awareness of this potentiality, I plan to incorporate these members of the classroom into my instruction and increase my eye contact with all members of the classroom and not just directed at those students who behave positively towards me. Further, I plan to more clearly define that when I am in the classroom and instructing, that I am in authority; and when the AT is in the classroom and instructing, she is the authority. In this way I feel it will build trust with the students that any interaction they have with me as practice teacher will not necessarily be intervened upon by the Vice Principle AT. I will always discuss the events with the AT but with her permission, will more definitely separate myself from those interactions which occur between herself and the class. In this way I feel students will come to trust that the AT and I work as a team and that the expectations of behavior that the AT has for the class are the same for the expectations I have for the class. Lastly, I intend to make a concerted effort to avoid the appearance of favoritism in the classroom. To do this, I will attempt to be more aware of the cliques and their operation in the classroom and not be seen to align with any particular members. To do this I will direct instructs or assistance to the whole group instead of focusing on one group and I will attempt to make the classroom more cohesive by choosing activities that address the interests of the class more wholly.

Because it is apparent to me that the nature of favoritism in the classroom can create unnecessary classroom disruption, I intend to be more watchful of how other teachers handle the issue in their classrooms and attempt to discover methods of teacher behavior that reduce the possibility of the perception of favoritism. Although in this incident, no behavior was evident, it was still apparent to this practice teacher that the girls thought enough of the incident to think I had chosen to align myself with other members of the classroom and as a result I realize there might have been techniques of classroom control I could incorporate into my teaching that might reduce the chances of this event occurring in the future. Although I realize that despite my best efforts, students may see my behavior as favoring one student over another. Being aware of the possibility will improve my chances of reducing its impact in my classroom.

***Question*: What can we learn from the turbulence within this practicum?**

10. Joel Beaupre – Too Tolerant

Joel's grade 6 classroom was the scene of too much tolerance and students who tested his limits. Joel wrote,

During my two weeks of teaching practice in October, I used my time in the grade 6 classroom to develop and observe effective strategies that help keep students on-task and engaged in everyday lessons and activities. Although some of these strategies proved to be more effective than others, the overall experience of leading a classroom helped develop my ability to recognize, address, and subdue common disruptions from students. Before having the opportunity to teach my own lessons to the students, my Associate Teacher encouraged me to implement those systems that were already in place to help manage the children. Knowing that the students were already fully aware of what criteria was expected for each of these commonly used systems, I could see that they would become an important element in my everyday teaching routines. Although the Student Teacher is not the party responsible for creating these systems, I believe that he/she should feel obligated to acknowledge and respect the strategies that have already been developed by the Associate Teacher, so that the students develop a sense of consistency and fairness. Without question, using established routines might have been the best way to exercise control over the students in the class.

When I was presenting a lesson, however, these were not the only techniques I used to maintain an appropriate environment. For distractions such as talking, giggling, or whispering, I found it effective to simply pause in my speech and wait for the children to regain their composure. After the noise level had declined, I reminded the students that they were wasting their own time for completing activities and that incomplete assignments were to be finished at home. A second method that also proved to be effective was to frequently review the classroom rules and expectations. Because the students had taken part in establishing these behavioral "Do's and Don'ts," they felt more obligated to follow them. By implementing this democratic process at the beginning of the year, the teacher essentially placed responsibility on the children themselves, making misbehavior not only an act of disrespect, but also an act of hypocrisy. I believe students should always be given an opportunity to identify their own behavioral expectations, so they recognize the reasons for which a teacher will suppress these actions in the classroom. Students *know* what it means to respect others. By identifying those acts that are considered disrespectful, most children will attempt to correct their own behavior.

Reflect

Looking back at the different methods that I used to establish order and control in the classroom, I realize that some of my actions could have been more effective with a few important changes. One of the first things that I noticed while overseeing the classroom was the manner in which some children would respond aggressively to those teachers who take a passive approach to instruction. Regardless of whether or not a teacher is merely attempting to be courteous and polite, some students will target this behavior as a weakness and exploit the teacher by pushing the boundaries of his/her tolerance against misbehavior. This, I believe, poses as a problem for many student teachers, because they wish to befriend the students as opposed to control them. Furthermore, many of these teachers in training, including myself, possess only limited experience within the classroom setting, thereby making it an intimidating environment to work in. With this, student teachers lack more confidence than experienced educators and seek to avoid being labelled as 'a bad guy' by the class. In some cases, the feeling of being disliked by the student body can be detrimental for a student teacher's experience during his/her placement, as it might cause feelings of inadequacy or disappointment towards one's performance. This assumption, however, is one that should be ignored and/or overcome by young teachers, as their primary objective is not to be liked, but instead, to be respected. Those teachers who are most effective at their jobs, I believe, are the same ones who are well respected by their students. Knowing this, young teachers should strive to gain confidence while applying those methods that are intended to keep students on task and focused on the lesson that is being presented to the class. By learning how to overcome the fear of being disliked and concentrating on classroom management techniques, teachers will earn more respect from his/her students and, consequently, create a learning environment in which children are dedicated to meeting their educational needs. Upon my return to the classroom in November, I intend to improve my ability to uphold a more respectful environment.

Revise

One mistake that I was guilty of committing during my practicum was that of exercising too much tolerance with the students. My Associate Teacher pointed this out to me after noticing that the children were taking advantage of my reserved approach to teaching by chatting, or becoming overly-excited during my instruction. In order to correct the disruptions more effectively, she recommended that I should make it clear within the classroom that I would no longer tolerate any disruptions when attempting to address the class. To do this, I knew that yelling and threatening would be exaggerated methods that would perpetuate negative feelings among both the teachers and students. Instead of resorting to these methods, I decided to identify those practices that were allowing the students to expose my inexperience in classroom management. After holding a discussion with my Associate Teacher, I realized that I was using *polite* words, such as "please" far too often while addressing the students. Because of this, the children were taking my requests lightly and neglecting to follow the expectations applicable to the whole class. After noticing that this improper vocabulary was the cause behind some of management failures, I sought to change the way that I would phrase my requests and demands in succeeding lessons. The day after I reached this decision, I noticed that the students, although still restless and easily excited, were more attentive and composed than in previous lessons. I also realized that by using the word *respect* when reminding the students that interruptions and distractions were unacceptable while I was teaching, the children were more likely to identify their own wrongful actions. After implementing these new strategies, many of my troubles in managing the class were reconciled. Because I had succeeded in making the students aware of why disruptions are disrespectful against the teacher, they had taken it upon themselves to exercise more self-control and corrected their own misbehaviors before I was given an opportunity to address the issue. In retrospect, I am grateful that I revised this element of my classroom management philosophy.

***Questions*: Is it really possible to be too tolerant, too proactive, too aggressive, or too assertive and if so, how do you know?**

11. Homework – R E S P E C T !

Act

On my November practicum, I was responsible for teaching an entire Math unit on Geometry and Polygons. The students loved the activities and lessons I had planned and all-in-all each student seemed to be learning what I wanted them to learn. Before each lesson ended, I would assign homework and give a brief explanation of what was expected. The next morning, I would find a handful of assignments done and would expect those students who had not finished their homework to remain in at recess to complete it. Some would, some would not. I was getting the impression these students did not take me seriously.

One of the problems I faced by letting students stay in to complete their work was math was taught before recess. This meant I would review the work from the previous night and take up any questions students had. Those students staying in at recess now had the answers to complete their homework. I finally clued in that some (not all) were deliberately staying in so they could turn in a perfect homework assignment. I responded by giving all students a surprise test. It confirmed my suspicions of who understood the concepts and who didn't. I was worried that good homework results, on account of staying in, would someday come to haunt me. I could envision parents being very concerned, yet confused by great homework results versus test results. I was getting more and more frustrated as time went on as I felt students were taking advantage of me. My problem boiled down to this: I perceived students did not respect me and that I failed to cultivate enough classroom discipline.

Reflect

Analyzing this situation, I have concluded that my Associate Teacher and I have different opinions and styles when it comes to discipline, lesson planning, homework, assessment, and evaluation. Her assessment and evaluation techniques seem to focus more on drill and test results and less on whether assignments/homework get done. Many students took advantage of this and would consistently come in each morning with none of the assigned homework done. Most were "A" students who felt they did not need to do the work, however, a handful were struggling students.

There were a number of things that bothered me about the situation. First, students felt they could get away with not doing homework and why wouldn't they? Besides staying in, there were no other consequences. Secondly, there seemed to be no reward system in place to acknowledge the work of students who did complete the work. I felt there was injustice. Thirdly, there seemed to be a lack of respect for both my Associate Teacher and myself. I was feeling horrible. Lastly, I was worried about students who were using this as an opportunity to get good homework results, but really did not understand the concepts being taught.

I needed to put an end to this lack of respect and homework misconception. I asked my Associate Teacher how she weighted assignments, tests, homework, et cetera, to determine a grade level, but did not get a satisfactory answer. I determined grading is very subjective. There are no formal rubrics. Students don't understand how they are assessed and nothing is documented. Student profiles don't exist and information about each student is retained in my Associate's head. I knew I had to do something. I was getting more and more frustrated. I was feeling angry, or perhaps jealous towards students who were not doing the work, but also felt compassion for those students who were. I wanted to show students they couldn't get away with not doing the work. In a way, I felt betrayed. I wanted every student to show me respect.

I responded by doing a lot of thinking and brainstorming about the problem and possible solutions. I wanted to put the responsibility back onto the students shoulders for doing (or not doing) their homework. Although it's my job to assign homework, ultimately it is the students' job to actually attempt or do the assigned problems. I decided to first, talk to the students about respect and what it means; and secondly, introduce a weighting system that placed more emphasis on getting their homework done and less on tests or quizzes. In this way there would be an obvious consequence for not getting their work done and I would be rewarding those students, struggling and not struggling, who did get their work done on time. I felt it was a fair system and began to communicate it to all students.

I spent half of the next session talking about respect and explaining this new weighting system. I was very firm in my explanations and expectations and told them that late or unfinished homework would not be accepted after math class, unless they had come to me before class with an explanation. There would be no need for students to stay in at recess. The next week produced marvelous results. Every student now took me seriously and without exception, each one had their homework done before math class. I now felt I had the respect of every student. It was a very rewarding experience and the final quiz showed spectacular results. I was very proud of everyone.

Revise

On returning to my next practicum, I plan to improve my classroom management by doing the following:

1. Sit down with my Associate Teacher to discuss assessment and evaluation techniques that are used. Discuss how I can incorporate these techniques into my teaching.
2. Before starting a unit, establish the expectations right up front, so students know how they will be assessed and evaluate.
3. Continue to greet students at the door when they arrive. Remind them what they should be doing.
4. Be consistent. Make students responsible for their actions and hold them to the consequences as much as possible.
5. Deal with problems quickly, firmly, and consistently.
6. Be sincere.
7. Continue working with students who shout-out or are off-task. Use the strategies above that worked and continue to learn new strategies.

***Questions*: When you are disappointed in your practicum what can you do to refresh yourself? What is your classroom management plan going to look like?**

12. Shawn Keown – Time-Out is not the answer!

Shawn Keown discovered just how needy identified students can be.

Shawn reflected, "During my time at the middle school, I was immediately faced with several Classroom Management issues which I was forced to address. Within my Associate Teacher's (AT's) classroom there were several distinct management issues including students with identified exceptionalities. These exceptionalities included a student with Turrets Syndrome (Student A) and a student that has been identified as a Behavioral Exceptionality (Student H). Also, several of the students within my AT's classroom were easily distracted by any disturbances within the classroom. I had to address all of these issues.

During the initial lessons I was teaching, several of the students began to exhibit off-task behavior. Students were observed turning to talk to their classmates, leaving their desks to receive materials from their classmates, and interrupting the instructional sessions with inappropriate comments. Most of the students in the class could be brought back to task via a slight verbal reprimand. However, there were several students who would not respond to sight cues and more forceful verbal reprimands were required. In the case of Student A, who was also observed displaying all of the off-task behaviors described above, an increased degree of latitude was afforded due to his exceptionality. However, some verbal prompting was required to limit the disruption to the rest of the class. Student H was by far the most disruptive of all the students in the classroom. This student, who as stated above has been identified as a behavioral exceptionality, displayed a number of off-task behaviors including a refusal to do his work, resistance to instruction, and defiance of authority. Student H was also observed interacting with his fellow students encouraging off-task behavior, being verbally abusive, and encouraging other students to display unacceptable behaviors. Student H was also suspended during the initial observation for fighting with other students when placed in the hallway for a "timeout." Therefore, this was not a management strategy that could be employed to deal with his behavioral actions. Students within the classroom environment who displayed off-task behavior on several occasions, and who did not respond to verbal reprimands, were kept after school in a remedial detention.

Another management difficulty that was encountered initially was the evaluation of the students' level of understanding of the material which was being covered. An attempt to guage the level of understanding was made through a simple question and answer process ("Does everyone understand how we got this answer?"). However, this process was further complicated by several students who consistently answered "No," whenever this question was posed; whether they understood the material or not. I found that I had begun to ignore the students whose default answer was always no.

Reflect

During my initial lessons, I was extremely discouraged with the student's preponderance for off-task behavior. As stated above many of the students within the class were easily distracted; so as one student would begin to exhibit off-task behaviors others would follow. I was reluctant as a teacher, to reprimand the students within my AT's classroom. However, I had witnessed my AT using such a management strategy. Therefore, I decided that such a strategy would be appropriate to employ. Initially when this strategy was employed, the students would react and begin to refocus on task. This initial success was encouraging, but the off-task behavior would begin again as the various students began to disturb the class. I found that my frustration would increase as the same students were constantly getting off task. I also observed that one student in particular was more likely then most to simply deviate from the designated tasks.

I found that Student H served as a catalyst within the classroom. As this student's off-task behaviors would surface he would, to put it simply, take others with him. This student acts as a leader within the class and I found that it was a constant struggle to maintain order within the classroom while Student H was present. As I witnessed this dynamic forming within the classroom, I found my level of frustration with Student H growing. I was also extremely frustrated with what I perceived as a lack of useful management strategies that could be implemented in order to control this student's behavior exceptionalities. I admit that this frustration stems most from my inability to control this young student and the feelings of inadequacy; then the apparent "failure" to maintain a properly disciplined classroom; then the actions of the student in question. Upon reflection, I considered many options in an attempt to curtail this student's disruptive tendencies. I first considered changing the student's position within the classroom; however, I could not bring myself to do this as Student H is verbally abusive with several of the other students within the classroom and is currently placed as far away as possible from these students. I also considered placing Student H in the hallway for a "timeout," but this practice was one that I was particularly hesitant to employ as this student had already been suspended for fighting in the hallway during one such "timeout." Finally, I determined that sending this student to the office for disrupting the class, which would occur every day, was not an option. I therefore came to a decision concerning what my actions would be if this student was in my own classroom that I believe would be in both his best interests and in the best interest of the other students in the class. This decision was based partially upon observations of classes dedicated to behavioral classes within my host school.

Also, during such reflections I was faced with the difficulty of assessing the level of understanding that the students within the class possess without formal evaluation. Because my instructional time with the students is very limited I attempted to guage their reaction to the material given to them by simply asking them if they understood the material presented and by watching their facial expressions. However, as mentioned above I was faced with students who would answer that they did not understand the material even if that was not the case. Therefore, I unconsciously began to develop a tendency to ignore these particular students when they stated that they did not understand the material. However, as time went on, I noticed that several of these students wore looks on their faces that displayed an increasing level of frustration. I surmised that these students were indeed having difficulty with the concepts being taught, therefore, a change to my approach was required.

Revise

As my time in the classroom was limited I found that many small changes had to be made in my teaching approach and that I have several ideas that I hope to implement upon my return to the classroom. However, I am limited as a teaching candidate as to the extent of the actions I can take. In fact, one management strategy that I may wish to implement in my own classroom is a drastic measure that is not feasible given my current position.

As mentioned above "off task behavior" is consistently a problem within the classroom in which I was placed, as is evaluating the level of understanding that is exhibited by the students. In an attempt to address both issues, a series of interactive questions and brainstorming activities were chosen to be used during language arts lessons. These exercises allowed the students to offer input and express thoughts that could be considered higher-level thinking. These activities appeared to keep the students on task though several of the students did not participate in the dialogue. This lack of participation will have to be addressed in subsequent lessons.

An attempt was made during a math lesson to address both the off-task behavior and the apparent lack of understanding displayed by the students. The students were led through a series of problems with many of the solutions to these problems being placed on the front board by myself. The students were initially challenged to find the solutions to the problems on their own and student volunteers were asked to come up and present their answers to the class. While this method appeared to work for a time, the students soon became restless and the off-task behavior returned. Concurrently, several students appeared to have difficulty understanding the topics no matter how step-by-step the answers were presented. It was apparent that these students needed more individual attention than was possible within a full classroom. Therefore, I offered to provide additional instruction for these students after school during the remedial work period. Several of the students attended this help session which lasted for almost an hour and a half. I fully intend to once again instigate this after school program upon my return to the school, though the issue of *alone time* with the students will have to be addressed.

Finally, the case of Student H was one of the final classroom management issues that I feel needs to be addressed. During my time at the school, I was lucky enough to observe several special education classes dedicated to students with a wide range of exceptionalities including ones that were behavioral in nature. The dynamic in these classrooms, though "energetic," was far more conducive to learning. This conducive learning environment is due greatly in part to the presence of full-time Educational Assistants who often spend their time moving through the classroom and providing additional help to students in need. I do believe that Student H would benefit from such an environment, as would the other students in his class. This theory was somewhat borne out during my last day of in-class instruction during which time my Associate Teacher sat with Student H for a short time to offer him assistance. During this time he stayed on task and was able to solve rather complex problems with a minimal amount of prompting. It should be noted that when I left the practicum, steps were already underway to relocate Student H into a special education classroom equipped to handle his exceptionality.

***Questions*: How do you deal with the fact that you are not teaching in your own classroom? Does this arrangement undermine your classroom management?**

Chapter 5

Secondary Reflections

1. Matt Bonisteel – Proactive

Matt, a pre-service ***Secondary Teacher****, reflected on his proactive teaching efforts in the gymnasium and discovered that he needed to give students more time to respond. He also found that when he participated he was watched closely by students as he modeled skills.*

Act

During my placement in October, I felt as though I did an excellent job managing the two different types of classes I taught. The first class I was responsible for teaching was a grade 9 geography class in which I used proactive measures to prevent disciplinary issues from escalating. I did various things to accomplish this goal: when someone spoke out of turn, I quickly corrected the problem before it got out of hand. Simply saying the student's name with a firm tone of voice allowed me to combat the problem.

The amount of confidence I had in what I was saying also had an impact on how the students responded. When I was able to deal with disciplinary problems with *confidence* they were easily managed; on the other hand if confidence was lacking, the students would walk all over me. Another tactic that relates to the issue of confidence is giving students enough time to respond. Obviously, as I grow as a teacher, my confidence will grow and I will feel comfortable just simply giving the children **wait time** to respond to questions asked or to copy notes from the board. As a teacher it is was important that I give students this time to avoid responses such as, "I don't know," and "I wasn't paying attention."

Allowing students the right amount of *time to answer* questions or to copy notes gives the students confidence as well in the subject matter. Use caution when using this technique, however, as allowing the students too much time to copy the notes and respond to certain questions can also be a danger as students who comprehend and complete the task faster will be bored and more apt to misbehave. In this standard geography classroom setting, I experienced a great deal of class management success; however, my experience in the physical education gymnasium was a little more challenging.

In the gymnasium, I found it difficult to manage a large class. My Associate Teacher thought I did a great job and for the class it was a great job, but I think I have some areas to improve upon. This class contained 35 students, 11 of whom were making it difficult not only for me to manage but for my Associate Teacher to manage. During my observations of this class, I noticed the teacher was having significant difficulties controlling the class, forcing him to make the decision to sit certain children out of this physical education class. Personally, I myself was forced to make the same decision as my Associate Teacher did and have certain students sit out of the activities. I found it nearly impossible to teach the class effectively with some of the students present. However, I found that *making connection* or forming a common bond with some of the children who would normally misbehave, made a huge difference in the attitudes of these students. Some of those students who would not normally participate were in fact participating under my leadership.

The routines I established for this particular physical education class were an asset to class management for me. Having the students sit in their squads directly after the whistle blew contributed to the sense of control I had over the class. Another class management tactic I used in the physical education environment was having the students put away their basketball or volleyball into the bins provided before I started talking. This was extremely useful; in fact, if I had not done this during my practice teaching, I feel as though chaos would have resulted.

During the placement I found that *participating with the students* during the drills and scrimmage games helped the students to focus, learn by observing what I was doing, and it acted as a *motivating factor* as students wanted to participate because I was doing the task as well. It also allowed me a chance to use the *proximity rule* with students who were not staying on task.

I used wait time in my physical education class, also pausing until all students were either paying attention or until they understood the instructions. This strategy was important to me as a teacher as I had no desire to repeat the same instruction or to talk over students' voices.

Reflect

I feel that simply stating the names of the students who were misbehaving was an effective method of causing a change in the behavior of the students. Perhaps, during my next practice teaching placement, I should use caution with this strategy as it does, in fact, centre out certain students on a regular basis. This strategy also caused me to pay too much attention to the child who was misbehaving and too little to the other children who were behaving. Also, I found that wait time calmed students down and made them accountable for their actions.

I also believe that ignoring some minute whispering in the class may be more effective to me as a teacher then disallowing students to make any sound whatsoever. However, complete silence is what my Associate Teacher likes to have in his classroom so I almost feel as though I should be waiting until I have my own class in order to allow the students a little bit more freedom within the context of the class.

With regards to the physical education class, I feel as though I did a great job as some of the students who would normally misbehave during his class were paying complete attention to me simply based on the premise that I was able to get them interested in the subject manner. Perhaps this is, in fact, the best management strategy I have for the classroom – get the students interested in the task. When the students were interested and engaged in the subject manner, they were less likely to act out. I really do not enjoy sitting students out during physical education class but sometimes it has to be done. This is something that I have difficulty with as I have always felt that physical education was one of those subjects in which everyone could participate, even those students who may not perform well at all in other subject areas. I particularly enjoyed that while I was teaching, the students who may have otherwise caused trouble were experiencing some degree of success in my class.

Revise

In the future, during my November placement, I hope to build upon the foundation of class management skills I have developed during my last practice teaching placement. I will go to great lengths to learn the names of all the students as I still feel as though there are some invisible children in my classes. I really feel as though this is a shame and that it takes away from my ability to manage the class. By not being able to say the names of the students, I think it prevents me from forming the connections necessary to have effective class management skills within the entire class. During my next placement, however, I will make an effort to learn all the students' names as this would definitely aid in the class management process. I find that if you just say the child's name usually that will be enough for the child to relax and get back on task.

I plan to use wait time more frequently during my next placement rather then having me point out particular students, making them feel like they have done something wrong. By simply pausing, I find it does not disrupt the class to the same degree as if I were to stop, point out a particular student, and deal with what it is they are doing that is disruptive.

I also plan during my next placement to go with the flow more often. My Associate Teacher was impressed with the fact that the student who had been out of uniform for six weeks managed to bring that uniform while I was teaching the class. I like to think that my teaching style and philosophy had something to do with this individual really wishing to participate. By going with the flow and what worked, or the *teachable moments,* I was able to get these students, who were otherwise not interested in school, to participate and act as a part of a team; it was really a wonderful thing.

***Questions*: Was Matt content with his performance or do you believe he is unhappy with his classroom management? Secondly, what classroom management techniques did Matt use and what do you think of these management efforts?**

2. Lianne Cuillerier – A Typology

Lianne illuminated her grade 9 classroom management as follows,

Act

An explanation of my classroom management strategies first necessitates a description of my students and their learning environment. I am working with a grade 9 Core class, meaning the students remain in the same room with the same group for the afternoon, with a two minute break between periods alternating between Math/Science and English/Geography. You may well imagine that they get antsy after an hour of math. It is with this in mind that I say they are an excellent group, although undoubtedly *conversational* and *exuberant*. They are bright, out-going, and friendly, with at least four of the boys vying for the most esteemed position of "Clown." They have shown remarkable initiative and drive in the relentless pursuit of this objective – it's really quite impressive. Their behavior calls forth images of small woodland creatures: you know, the shy little things with wide-set, staring eyes gleaming with curiosity- impossible not to love, right? Well, that *curious gleam* often veils another persona. However, it is this aspect of their personalities that adds an important dimension to the class: this is what builds relationships. The livelier their personalities, the more tangible they become. The other students do a nice job of judging the clown acts and supporting new material; it's really something! There are also other personalities: the *Wallflowers*, the *Sensitives,* the *Know-it-All's* (self-explanatory), the *Russian Girls* (who have no interest whatsoever in anything other than my make-up/hair/clothing), the *Ambitious*, the *Sleepers*, and lastly, the *Easy-Going* (fairly straightforward). The variety of personalities makes for an interesting group that requires some creative management.

The classroom atmosphere is bright, open, and conducive to both discussion and activity. My Associate Teacher (AT) is outgoing and caring – the kids adore her. The walls, literally covered with creative visuals, keep the students engaged and the class work is often activity-based and student-focused. The students are grouped in roundtable arrangements of 3-4. My AT has encouraged me to try new strategies, her only request that the students not be seated in forward-facing rows. She does not use behavioral tactics (i.e., turning off the lights) but rather uses her voice as a means of management. The variety and youthful exuberance of the students necessitated I create an overall strategy as a means of management – the most successful tactic I could envision was to develop my own relationship with the students and to give them active roles to play in every class, with a special focus on the recruitment of the clowns.

Reflections

My first lesson – I'm delivering my rendition of *A Guide to Proper Essay Format in the Social Sciences* – and it's all going smoothly . . . I'm a hit, they're getting it, they're having fun . . . I'm okay (sigh of relief). Self-satisfied, I reflect on my most excellent performance and prepare for the consolidation exercise. It's important to note here that I've worked all night preparing this little bit of brilliance and it has even been copied onto golden-hued paper, sorted and hole-punched – We are "good to go" as they say. I'm feeling so confident at this point that I think I am actually strutting. I say, again with great confidence, "Okay class.

That was fun, but we're going to work on the format we've just learned. Don't worry, we'll go through it together." I smile as I pick-up my ***stack*** of carefully sorted handouts and decide, magnanimously, to give an eager student a role. In my infinite wisdom I say "Go ahead X, just make sure everyone gets a copy." I have my back turned for all of about a minute when I realize . . . and then it's too late. There she is – 'X' – standing perfectly still while the room explodes. She is about to cry, there are papers everywhere, some kids are confused, others are delighted, the clowns are having a field day, everyone is yelling to see who has which bit of this, and why do they have two page #2's, and how many are there supposed to be, and I have to go to the bathroom . . . and my AT is sitting at the back smiling! "B" decides to alert the room that two bees have come in through the window – apparently they must be killer bees, a logical conclusion. Then, "P" (clown hopeful) finds a diorama at the back of the class. In science, we have just studied the planets and this diorama is a model of them – I will leave the ensuing jokes ("P" finds these so hilarious he feels the need to repeat them relentlessly) to your imagination. I had forgotten how funny Uranus was to a 14-year-old (to his credit, he had some fairly good material).

The Strategy: Stay calm, employ the students, time to use my method . . .

"Stay calm, keep it light," I say to myself. "Split-second decision time . . ." Instinct kicks-in and I crack a few jokes to get the clowns on board (if you can't beat 'em . . .). I've given "P" the sign to cease and desist – I let him know, loud enough for all to hear, that he's very clever/funny but he's going to make a poor class clown if he relies on old material (humor works well with this group). He thinks about it, decides that it makes sense, agrees about the "old material" bit and stops – it worked. I call him up to the front and get him to draw the class's attention by quietly talking to him. I tell him I need his help and I'd like him to tell them to listen-up, but to do it in a creative way. They are all very curious at this point as they do not like to be left out of anything and "P" delivers an excellent performance. The kids have now been given jobs – clown A, I have dispatched to the front of the room. I use my *more interested* voice to get the students to listen (I will not yell, but it works anyway). I hold up the first sheet, while hanging on to "X" and ask everyone to find that one and put it down in front of them. I ask two other students to help out at the tables. The room is starting to calm down – I tell them: "It's no big deal, let's go through the pages together and make sense of them so we can start the activity" (I'm shutting the window and letting them know the bees aren't of the *killer* variety). I pause and think to myself, "What kind of an idiot does that to her own lesson?" Despite this, the kids had some fun and I remained calm. The relationship is beginning to be established, the roles/jobs really work, and . . . I hope I will never make a mistake like that again – they were so attentive prior to my arrogance. It's interesting how management issues don't always originate with the kids!

Reflections and Final Thoughts

Although I learned a great deal from my practice teaching experience, I feel it required nothing more than low-level management, mostly to bring the students back to task. My classes were not integrated and, as such, I was not faced with the added challenge of working with behavioral or identified students; this is not to say that I would have minded working with more challenging students, I am simply making the point that I could have been faced with much graver management issues. On the whole, my students were well-behaved. At their worst, they behaved as any normal, healthy teenagers would have. I found, in working with them, that the best strategy was to stay flexible and relaxed, but in control. The strategies required for this group were never related to serious discipline problems, but rather were used to calm over-anxious kids who had been sitting still for too long – one can hardly blame them. In my limited experience, I have come to believe that successful classroom management is rooted in the establishment of an honest rapport with one's students. This is not to say that the teacher must be overly lenient or try to befriend the students; rather, the teacher simply be friendly, accessible, and open. Kids are intuitive and are also highly sensitive. They require a great deal of patience and understanding. If they feel you will help them, respect their questions, and will at least attempt to understand their point of view, they will most likely afford you the same treatment. I have had some great discussions with my kids and have often asked them for input. This group responds to understanding and respect; it's not as threatening as an authoritarian stance.

My teaching style was informal and I tried to keep the atmosphere light and the lessons flexible; my philosophy is that the kids need to be 'on board' or they aren't going to get anything out of school. Although our strategies differed, I feel my AT's rapport with her students helped pave the way for my own successful management. I felt at ease and the kids, I think, picked-up on this. I learned that a teacher's instructional strategies can result in situations where management is required – both students and teachers have a hand in classroom dynamics.

I found the most effective strategies were to a) establish an honest rapport with the students, and b) keep them as actively involved as possible in each class. I tried to assess the differing needs/personality traits of each student and to use these accordingly. I had volunteers act out and/or read parts of lessons and handouts, and used visual learning games – they love to act for the most part and jump at the opportunity of some extra attention (I have a class of hams that loves charades for vocabulary). I hoped this would make it less strenuous for the more shy kids, helping them to speak in front of the group, as it was such a frequent occurrence and almost everyone participated. However, in the end I tried to give them less extroverted roles, such as collecting the reflective logs or handing out materials. I feel this may have been a disservice and I will endeavor to bring them out of their shells more next time. It is difficult not to lose the quieter ones in a room full of students demanding attention. But, I am still a bit of a wimp and do not like to make them feel uncomfortable.

I tried to keep the class engaged, but as relaxed as possible. I found that good-natured ribbing of the *clown hopefuls* worked rather well – I needed the students to know I could be both relaxed and serious, could play on their level, but would also keep the class focused and on track when required – a time and a place for everything. Some students seemed to benefit from roles with more responsibility. The kids respect a few of the more outspoken boys and girls, and one in particular has the ability to draw their attention – I made him my voice at key times. For example, I'd call him to the front during group work, I'd speak to him quietly and ask him to relay information to the class – but he had to be creative about it! This strategy kept him on task and looking out for the chance to be funny. It also drew the kids' attention, giving them an active part in their learning, some ownership over their time, and a sense of voice. A few of the kids had difficulty staying on task and were easily distracted, partly due to the seating plan. One strategy was to create a new seating arrangement as part of a lesson – a sort of pre-planned jigsaw activity that resulted in new *writing groups*. They had no idea, so it wasn't considered a punishment, but the group dynamics still changed. I walked around, especially when reading aloud, and stood near different people to hold attention. I asked questions periodically to make sure they were with me. Hopefully, the new groups balance the class. Some of the shyer students, as well as some of the more distracted, seem to be working/fitting in better.

I also decided to have a 'talk' with my group after the first few classes to let them know where I was at – I made a joke about my size and indicated that I'd pass out if I had to yell to talk over them (they know that I would if I had to, but I wouldn't ever want to). I explained that they weren't expected to be silent, but that they were also given plenty of time to work in groups – so I told them that when I needed them to listen I'd really appreciate it if they would. I related my experience at the front to their own when they worked on an oral presentation – I asked them to recall how nervous they were and how much work went into it. I couldn't believe it, but it actually worked! The more outspoken students even began shushing classmates who were getting a little too enthusiastic, if they could see I needed their attention.

Although my management situations were at times caused by my own errors, on the whole I feel I the students responded well to my strategies. I have learned a great deal from this experience. The most important lessons I learned? Get to know them, for real. Let them talk when they need to, and give them breaks. Go easy on them when you can, establish rules of conduct based on respect, and be sure to explain the reasons why you feel they're important (maybe even come up with them together), and don't be overbearing. Listening to the kids and understanding why they are behaving in a certain way is, in my opinion, the key to solving the problem and maintaining a positive classroom environment for both the students and the teacher.

***Questions*: If you deviate from your classroom management beliefs and this causes you to be very critical of yourself, is this a problem or an opportunity to learn more about yourself?**

3. Tim Rentschler – Geography

During my February/March Practicum, I was teaching two grade 9 Geography classes; one academic and one applied. The academic class contained 31 students while the applied had 18. The desks were arranged in single rows, facing the front chalkboard. The teacher's desk was at the front, left hand side of the class facing the students. There were no assigned seats in the academic class and the seating plan in the applied was a work in progress. The lessons were broken down as follows:

The lessons began with an introduction (hook) followed by some lecture (perhaps 15-25 minutes for intro and lecture depending on the subject). During the introduction/hook there would be an open exchange between the students and myself. This was followed by some lecture, and then by instruction and modelling of the activity to be completed during class that day. I would often model the activity on the overhead or chalk board with explanation and prompt students for answers. Following this, the students were given the assigned activity and I would circulate through the class to observe and assist students working. This strategy allowed me to identify specific areas where students were having difficulty and allow me to address them on the board/overhead before proceeding with the lesson. After the class had completed the activity, the questions would be taken up with the students. This also allowed me to identify and address areas that needed further explanation or clarification. Following this, students would be assigned homework unless the activity for that day was to be completed at home. This approach had a good flow to it and the students became familiar with the routine relatively fast. Establishing the routine also provided structure; thus, classroom management was relatively easy. Busy students = happy teacher.

For the most part, classroom management was not really an issue, especially in the academic class. The students were responsive to my requests for quiet and if specific students did not listen, they were moved to another desk. In the academic class, the major issue was talking. All of the students would do the work but would talk all the time. I allowed this to take place as long as it did not become disruptive and they were completing their work. If they could not do both at the same time, they could do one and that was going to be the assigned work. In the applied class, there were several identified students (6 out of 18). For the most part, if they were kept busy they were quiet and completed their work. However, there were two girls in the class that would often refuse to do their work and insisted on talking. They were spoken to individually out in the hall and instructed that their behavior was disrupting the class and that it would not be tolerated. Furthermore, if they did not complete their work during class time, they would have to do it at lunch or after school. "I'm here anyway. If you do not do it now, you will do it at lunch or after school. It's up to you." This exchange took place the second week of my practicum and resolved the problem. Both girls began to complete their work and hand it in.

Going in to this practicum, my biggest fear was classroom management. But within the first few days, I was relieved to have such *good students*. My associate told me that it was my calm and relaxed demeanor that was rubbing off on the students. I never got too excited or yelled at the students. If I had a problem with them I spoke to them and would explain my position. In the class my focus was always on the lesson content and on ensuring that every student understood the material before moving on. This approach had immediate success with the students who were a little slower at processing information or taking notes. My primary concern was the student and his/her comprehension of the material. Fortunately, I was always able to cover the lesson material using this approach. However, upon reflection I can see that I was fortunate and in the future would perhaps assign peer helpers in the class to assist the slower students. I also express a great deal of respect for the students. I feel that this is important if I want them to respect me, and it appeared to work quite well.

From a management standpoint, it is difficult for me to say what I would do differently on my next practicum. The school I was placed in was very quick to deal with unacceptable behavior and this had a positive effect on student behavior. Any swearing in the class or hallway was a two-day suspension. Any form of defiance was also a suspension. On my first day observing, a student was suspended when following her refusal to do her class work she was sent to the office. As she passed the teacher she was reminded to go straight to the office and replied "No shit." She was gone for the next three days.

Students need to know what is expected of them and the expectations must be clear. Punishment must also be swift and consistent throughout the school, a trait that was a high priority in this school. What this did was create a level of respect that was evident throughout the student body and the staff as well; everybody was on the same page.

This is not to say that the classrooms were problem-free but if you do not make a big deal out of it and address the problems quickly and consistently, your job becomes a lot less stressful. My opinion is that you must be consistent, show respect, and be aware of student needs and management issue takes care of itself.

For my April placement, I am not as fortunate. I am in a much larger high school and, from what I have been told, it is rough. There is little communication between and within the departments. Many teachers keep to themselves and as a result the students own the school outside of the classroom. I am sure I will have some questions about my management strategies after this placement. Maybe I will share them with you then.

***Questions*: When you arrive in a classroom that appears to be well managed, what can you do to improve the situation? Should you aim higher or go with the status quo?**

4. Hailey McLean – Angst

Hailey encountered feelings of uncertainty, and realized how important ownership was at the Secondary level.

I could not seem to put my finger on the exact cause of the angst that I experienced the evening before I taught my first lesson. Was it the large Thanksgiving turkey dinner that I had consumed sitting heavily upon my stomach, or was it something deeper? Was I experiencing nervousness with reference to the week ahead, jam-packed full of lesson plans, teaching, and of course managing a classroom on my own? It turned out to be the latter, but this angst quickly disappeared after being in front of the grade 12 University English Class during my first lesson.

The previous "School Days Observation" week had provided me with the opportunity to observe a number of different teachers, all of whom used a number of different management strategies within the classroom. By far, this observation session was the most beneficial experience to date that I had had in the classroom because it allowed me to sit back and see what worked well with particular grades, particular levels, and most importantly what I felt would work advantageously in my own classroom. I was able to constructively critique and analyze the manner in which management strategies worked or did not work, in turn, allowing myself to ponder and analyze a number of ideas for management techniques.

The process whereby we, as practice teachers, enter our Associate Teachers' class and are expected to teach the entire class while ensuring that the rules and guidelines set out by the AT at the beginning of the year are followed, can be somewhat challenging. Luckily, my AT employs a number of management strategies that I believe would effectively work in the classroom and therefore, maintaining their implementation was unproblematic.

I taught a grade 10 and a grade 12 English course, both at the academic level. The two different age groups provided me with the opportunity to experiment with different management techniques to better understand what works best at what grade level. There are a number of management tactics that I used during the October placement, in both or one of the classes, but the three I felt were the most beneficial were the use of non-verbal cues, the use of verbal cues for those not recognizing of adhering to the non-verbal cues, and the maintenance of a routine in the classroom.

I was quite surprised at how much I relied upon the use of non-verbal cues, especially with the grade 10 students during my October placement. I found that while I was giving a lesson I often traveled around the classroom placing myself in close proximity to those who were being disruptive, or I found myself stopping the lesson and looking at the person to catch their attention so that they would cease their disruptive behavior. It seemed to always be a repetitive pattern whereby I was always cuing the same people. This repetitive pattern became somewhat exhausting and slightly annoying as I was becoming more and more frustrated with the few students that were continuously acting in a disruptive manner.

In comparison, I did not rely as much on the use of verbal cues as I did on the non-verbal cues. When I did use verbal cues, it was usually for the purpose of asking a student to stop talking after I had used non-verbal cues on a number of different occasions, or it was to put away something that was unrelated to the lesson at hand. When I used verbal cues, I usually tried to quickly instruct the student so that I could continue the lesson with as little disruption as possible. Unfortunately, the use of verbal cues always disrupted the class. Students who were paying attention would focus their attention on the student who was being addressed and in turn, once the student had been verbally cued, I had the task of trying to get the entire class back on track.

In both the grade 10 and the grade 12 English classes, I found that the students liked to be informed ahead of time of the short- and long-term plans within the classroom. Students liked having the week outlined for them on Monday and favored a schedule for each daily class reviewed or noted on the board at the commencement of each class. This technique seemed to assist students in focusing on the task and preparing for the day. It also, in some cases, gave students something to look forward to. For example, although a student may not enjoy editing their essay, they knew by way of looking at the daily schedule that after they were done they could read their novel.

From this placement, the most valuable piece of information that I walked away with was the importance of placing ownership on the students and creating an environment where students feel safe and want to learn. Although I feel that this environment can be difficult to construct, I believe that if a teacher outlines the rules and actively allows students to participate in assisting with the construction of these rules, students will in turn be more likely to adhere to them. If students respect the school environment and, most important, their teacher, they will want to display that respect so that they in turn receive respect.

During my next placement, I plan on actively trying to create an environment whereby the students do not feel the need nor have the time to cause management problems within the class. Most important, by taking a proactive approach in creating an environment that is constantly changing so that students don't become bored, and involving students in lessons on a personal level, I believe the management within the classroom will be one in which there is little disruption and lots of learning, which is, of course, the ultimate goal.

***Questions*: Which grade do you believe is more difficult to manage and why? What did Hailey do that surprised you, or what did she not do that you might have tried?**

5. Liisa Pitre – Proxemics

Liisa remembered how she employed her knowledge of proxemics to send messages to her students.

During my October Practicum I had the opportunity to put into action several classroom management strategies. I found one strategy in particular to be especially effective and useful in various situations. The strategy is **proximity**. During my first lesson, a lecture in a grade 12 university biology class, I did not circulate throughout the room. Instead, I moved around only at the front of the class. Although the lesson passed without any major management issues, I noticed some behaviors that I decided needed to be deterred so that the next lessons would be more effective for everyone in the class. For example, a pair of girls who sit together tend to be chatty during the lecture and when given time to write notes, many students lag behind because they begin to talk too much.

During the subsequent lessons, I made sure to circulate throughout the class while lecturing and students copied notes from the board. The effect of this simple strategy was very positive. Students remained on task much more consistently throughout the period because unlike the day before, I was always close by.

Another positive effect of employing this strategy is that more students were participating and asking questions. Some students seemed to feel more comfortable asking questions when I was near them because I was more accessible and/or they did not want to be the centre of attention of the entire class when they chose to speak up. Thus, an important consequence of this strategy (circulating throughout the class), there is no focus on any one group of students (e.g., the students at the front of the class only), because as the teacher moves around the class, the students' focus moves with him/her. Therefore, ultimately, the attention is periodically on everyone in the class.

Although the proximity strategy is very effective with this senior group, some students still required management at times. When a student disrupted the class while I was speaking, one technique that I found effective was to ask the student a question, or ask whether he/she had any thoughts to share. It was a subtle technique that does not require that the flow of the lesson be disrupted. This strategy depends on knowing the student(s) name to get their attention, but it also requires that the students typically are conscientious and motivated. The rationale for this statement is that this technique is rather subtle and requires that the student recognize that his/her behavior is disrespectful for the class. A student who often disrupts the class, or who is often off-task, may not easily or quickly realize the double intention of the question. Alternatively, this type of student may not care that his/her actions are disruptive and simply choose to ignore this subtle call to come to attention.

On the other hand, when a student disrupted the class while another student was asking a question, one technique that I employed was to get the student's attention by telling him/her that a classmate is posing a question and deserves his/her respect. Admittedly, this requires that the teacher interrupt the class, which is not ideal. But, in some instances, this strategy can be effective nevertheless. A potential long-term positive effect is that the students learn to respect each other and recognize that listening to their classmates when they are addressing the class is a sign of their respect. They may also learn to recognize that when other students ask questions, they often benefit by improving their own understanding of the topic. An alternative that I may try in the future is to approach the disrupting student and get their attention using body language or eye contact. The problem with this strategy is that in the time that I have taken to do this, I have not listened/heard the other student's question and will have to have the question repeated anyway.

Another strategy that I employed was very straightforward. When trying to get the students' attention to explain an assignment or an activity, I stated what I expected of the students as well as the rationale for the expectation. This was especially important when explaining safety instructions during labs. This strategy aims to teach the students to respect the rules, but most importantly, it puts the responsibility on the students themselves to employ self-discipline. Students have accepted my expectations and now are aware of what is required to stay within the boundaries that have been explained.

I discovered that classroom management does not only occur in the moment. It requires that teachers recognize what types of teaching styles work for their students. For example, during the first lesson, I asked students to copy a rather detailed diagram into their notebooks. From my perspective, this type of task can help students visualize the process to be learned. However, the majority of the students in the class grew frustrated with the task because they found it too difficult and tedious. The consequence of their frustration was that they lost focus and interest. The next day, I chose to distribute photocopies of the diagram. Students were much more receptive to learning about the topic and remained focused throughout the lesson. Thus, I realized that as a teacher, you have to recognize what strategies work for the students, and not only what works for you.

***Questions*: The phrase, "It's not what you say but how you say it," seemed to serve Liisa well. Think of times you have been able to use this strategy, and under what circumstances has it been useful?**

6. Grade 10 English – The Reprimand

During my placement, I was able to implement a number of classroom management techniques with my grade 10 English students. On the first day of teaching, I chose not to reprimand students for minor discipline problems such as turning around and talking occasionally to someone sitting behind them or beside them. The students thought that they could get away with anything because they perceived a practice teacher as being similar to a substitute teacher; I was someone they did not know and therefore was someone they did not fully respect. I needed to show them that I deserved respect and that I did have authority in the classroom. I told them that I was the teacher in the classroom and that I would not tolerate disruptions in my classroom. This speech did not have an effect on the students because at the time of this incidence I did not have their respect. Talking to the students in this way did not affect their behavior at all.

I believe that the only way classroom management can be truly successful is if the teacher gains the respect of the students. It is when the teacher makes it clear that he or she respects and values the feelings and opinions of the students that this is achieved. In order to achieve this in my own classroom, I modelled the behavior that I expected the students to demonstrate in the classroom. For example, I listened attentively to the answers of each student. I made sure that the class was also listening attentively to each student. If a student was speaking and the rest of the class was talking I would say, “Excuse me, Joe is speaking.” The class would usually stop talking and listen to the speaker. Once this behavior was reinforced, the students seemed to realize that I cared about them and I was interested in what they had to say. It became easier to control the classroom once I had their respect. The students were more apt to listen and participate in class. I am happy that I chose to do this management technique because it became easier to implement change once I had the students’ respect. I believe it is for this reason that this was the most effective classroom management strategy I used during this placement.

As previously stated, the students usually listened to me but this is not to say that they were angels once I gained their respect. Although the class became more manageable, there were many times when I had to use different management techniques to control the classroom. One of the most effective techniques to gain the students’ attention if they were talking was to stop talking myself. I consciously chose not to yell at the students because this is a management technique that they are used to. Yelling is not the way to get their attention. When I remained completely silent, everyone stopped talking. The students disrupting the class quickly realized their mistake when other students made them aware of their disruptive behavior. They were embarrassed into realizing their mistake. I found this technique extremely effective and more preferable to yelling. Yelling at the students would not have promoted the behavior I wanted them to emulate.

After a few days, I realized that most of the behavior problems in my classroom stemmed from the fact that the students were inactive. I needed to change my teaching style in a way that would make the class more stimulating and interactive. Although my lessons at that point did keep the students somewhat active with questioning and activities, many of the students needed more activities in the classroom. I noticed in previous lessons that there were less behavior problems if I directly related the lesson to their lives. For example, when I spoke to the class about sentence fragments, I would relate it to the fact that students often use sentence fragments in their email or in MSN Messenger. I also incorporated small activities that would enable them to apply the skills I was teaching, to their lives. During one of my lessons, I taught the students how to write a news report by using a newspaper article to answer the five Ws and H. I had each student read a paragraph so that everyone would be able to participate. This gave the students an opportunity to be more active in the classroom. By asking the students more questions about themselves and relating the material to their lives and to the lesson, they were able to see the meaning and application of what I was teaching. They also became more active and interested in the material. This technique significantly decreased the discipline problems in the classroom by increasing student participation.

The next time I am in the classroom I plan to reinforce my classroom management techniques by implementing new ways of achieving these desired results. Although I noticed that there were less discipline problems when I related the lesson to the lives of the students, I did not manage to reach all the students. I particularly need to work on trying to bring the boys into the conversation. They usually stay in the background and talk. I noticed that when I walked towards them and asked them questions related to the lesson this seemed to help. I also need to find new ways of letting the students know when they are behaving badly. Achieving their respect is a step in the right direction but I also need to be able to implement other strategies besides the silence technique in order to get their attention. This worked 90 percent of the time during this placement but it may not work the next time. The most effective technique would be to change the seating of those students who are causing the disruption. I would have one person sit at a table at the back of the classroom by himself. These strategies will help me improve my classroom management skills.

***Questions*: What will you do to have students respect you? What will you avoid doing to ensure you are not disrespected?**

7. Shawn Eastwood – Resistance

Shawn taught grades 10 and 11 and uncovered some resistance.

Act

When I arrived at the Secondary School during my October Practicum I checked the placement of the desks in order to ensure students had a clear view of the front of the classroom and that there would be an unobstructed view for myself, so I could see all of my students. Students need to see me and the front chalkboard when I teach, in order to maintain their concentration. Also, if I have an unobstructed view of the students, they will not have as much opportunity to misbehave. Furthermore, I ensured accessibility to high traffic areas, such as the pencil sharpener, three-hole punch, and my desk, to keep disruptive behavior (which might result from traffic congestion) to a minimum. I also created interesting and visually effective displays in my classroom to help create a learning environment, which students would perceive as stimulating and fun. I believe it is important for students to feel that their teacher demonstrates enthusiasm for teaching, by taking the time to create a stimulating environment for them.

I researched the individual abilities and behaviors of the students by asking my Associate Teacher for advice about what I could do to prevent disruptions before they occur. My Associate Teacher identified *leaders* in the classroom who other students look up to with regards to academic ability, as well as those leaders who seem to instigate problem behavior, which others may follow. Extra attention was paid to these leaders throughout my two-week practicum to give them less of an opportunity to cause disruptions. My Associate Teacher informed me that if you "win over," or get these students on your side, other students will respect you and less disruptive behavior will occur.

I made an effort to research my students by their Individual Education Plans (IEP) and by information provided to me by my Associate Teacher. I did this so I could pay special attention to those students with learning difficulties. I feel it is important to do so in an unassuming manner, so the students do not feel uncomfortable or that they have been singled out.

Reflections

The first key element I identified, was the arrangement of the physical classroom. The arrangement of the classroom is important in order to minimize disruptive behavior. Furthermore, the classroom must be an environment which exudes warmth and facilitates learning by stimulating students' interest and creativity. In my classroom, I made sure there were no more than four students sitting at any given table. When I first arrived, there were some rows that had up to six students. I felt that the close proximity of the students to each other was causing difficulties for myself and the students due to talking and not paying attention to the lesson. After the students were separated, I noticed the amount of chatting decreased substantially. The second key element I felt was important, was researching the background of the individual students. This goes a long way towards proactively inhibiting disruptive behavior before it begins. I feel it improved my knowledge as a teacher and allowed me to prepare in advance to meet their needs. During one of my lessons, I took a moment to speak to a few students who have difficulty staying on task (identified in their IEP's [Individual Educational Plans]). They were not copying the information I provided, into their notebooks. I had to explain why it was important that they copy this information into their books. In doing so, I had responded to these students with special needs. They stopped talking and began copying the information into their notebooks.

My quality and degree of interaction with the students in my two grade 10 applied classes, in my opinion, was adequate. I made an effort to use the students' names on a regular basis during my lesson. I felt that when I called on students by their names I was maximizing the quality of the interaction between the students and myself. I believe that this makes the students feel important thus allowing them to make an attempt to answer or respond to my queries. Whenever possible, I made an attempt to involve students in the responses that other students had made. In doing so, I think the students learn to respect each other and themselves. In my grade 11 University/College Science class I have not yet learned all of the students' names. I have noticed some resistance from a few of the students in this class which may lead to more serious issues later during my practicum. I do not feel that these students respect me and I will have to work on this specifically during my next practicum.

I also noticed that many students were asking to go to the bathroom throughout the lesson. For the first week I allowed them to go one at a time. However, I noticed that they began taking advantage of the fact that I always allowed them to go to the bathroom. Not only was it disrupting my lesson and interrupting my train of thought but it was also disrupting the other students who were actually participating in the lesson. During the second week of the October placement I decreased the number of students taking washroom breaks during the class; especially those who asked to go to the bathroom immediately after the class began. I am aware this is a problem that I will have to address for my next placement. My action plan will be discussed in the next section. One student did not come back to class for 20 minutes after allowing him to take a bathroom break. When he passed by me in class, I smelt cigarette smoke on him. I confronted him by asking him why it took him so long for his break. When he did not answer I told him he had just lost his privilege to take washroom breaks. He did not respond and simply stared down at his book.

During the two-week practicum, I made an effort to establish rapport with the students. I believe it is extremely important to win over students starting on the first day, rather than try to establish a meaningful relationship later in the year, after major behavioral disruptions have occurred. I did this by inquiring about extracurricular activities and hobbies while letting them know I was also interested in many of their activities. I feel that if I take a sincere interest in getting to know the students personally from the onset, I can inhibit behavior problems before they develop.

Revise

It is my belief that one of the most important factors which can influence the learning environment, is a teacher's ability to manage the classroom. A teacher must create a positive climate in which both teaching and learning can occur in an effective manner. This climate can be compromised by the misbehavior of one or more students as the attention of both teacher and students is focused on the disruptive behavior. This disrupts the flow of the lesson, and forces the teacher and students to re-focus their attention on concepts being taught prior to the disruption. Disruptive behavior *clearly* interrupts the flow of the lesson and the learning environment.

I believe the key to effectively managing my classroom is to be *proactive* rather than *reactive* in dealing with management issues. I feel it is more efficient to take preventative measures, which would inhibit classroom management problems before they occur, rather than searching for answers regarding how to deal with issues after they happen. I have been forewarned from sources such as the university, associate, and friends and family who are teachers, about the importance of taking preventative measures to stop problems in the classroom before they arise, and of the frustration which occurs if students lose respect for you.

With respect to the issue of students taking advantage of the washroom break I will attempt to decrease the number of students going by announcing to them that there will be no bathroom breaks ten minutes into the lesson and ten minutes before the end of class. At first, I felt bad that I was not letting more than one student out at a time to go to the bathroom but now I realize that most of them are just taking advantage of the bathroom break to walk around or meet up with friends. The students have seven minutes between classes to go to the bathroom. There is no reason why they should be using my time to go to the bathroom which subsequently wastes the other student's time as well.

I intend on managing my classroom in an efficient way by forming a plan for proactive classroom management before problems arise. I believe that it is important to establish rules and routines from the first day of classes of the school year. Even more important, however, is the teacher's effectiveness in establishing a relationship of mutual respect with students. One way of accomplishing this is to use a *backbone* style of discipline, which is a combination of strict and lenient discipline styles that stresses individual self-control. The more positive the relationship a teacher has with his or her students, behavior problems become less of an issue, learning becomes more effective, and students will be given greater responsibilities as well as the opportunity for input into the decision making process. I will attempt to form a positive relationship with my students to help maintain or foster a beneficial learning environment that is both rewarding for the students and myself. Although I began to form a relationship with my students, I did not teach more than 25% of my grade 11 University/College Science class. As such, I did not interact with these students as much as I would have liked. I will have to learn all of their names as soon possible and use their names when addressing questions or responses during my future lessons. I feel that calling on students by their names builds a rapport and respect that might otherwise not be established. I will take some time before class and look over the seating plan to help with the name learning process.

With regards to special need students, I will have to refresh my knowledge of their individual learning plans as identified by the Associate Teacher and their specific IEP's. There are a few students who have IEP's, but I am unaware of their particular needs. I think this information would be invaluable in maintaining a healthy classroom environment by applying positive learning activities specifically designed for those that need them.

***Questions*: Saying 'no' to students is a big first step; Why is this sometimes quite difficult? Leaving the room is a matter of policy. How would you change classroom policy?**

8. Natalie Durant – Signals and Communication

Act

During my October practicum placement I was at Preston High School in the Waterloo Region District. I observed and occasionally taught two grade 10 academic, one grade 10 enhanced, and three grade 11 university/college classes. Since my AT had six classes, on certain days I was only responsible for two classes in a five-period day. I was never exclusively with one class but had interactions with all. The enhanced class is the only group of students who are together all year in every class; this reality exposed some interesting social dynamics both positive and negative in nature.

I gradually observed that the grade 11s responded better to discipline than the grade 10s. There were some differences in the maturity level between the grade 10s and 11s. Every class begins with ten minutes quiet reading. The grade 11s were more likely to sit down and quietly read whereas the grade 10s needed to be reminded of this routine daily. Another problem that usually occurred at the beginning of class was that students moved from their assigned seats to sit near their friends. On several occasions, students needed to be reminded that they must remain in their assigned seat. Another issue that caused problems was group work. It was very difficult to assign the students groups as they complained if not assigned to a friend's group.

When I was responsible for a class and did have to assign group work, I found it extremely difficult to command the grade 10s' full attention. I tried several different strategies to deal with off-task noise, such as turning off the lights and asking them to be quiet. However, not every class responded to the same strategy so it was sometimes confusing for me to recall on the spot which strategy to use with a particular class. I had also tried talking over the students, and during a movie, I had turned up the volume to mask the off-task noise. Neither of these strategies was a success.

Reflect

The main issue that interfered with my classroom management was off-task talking. The lights worked best to command the students' attention and address the off-task behavior but it did not work with all classes and after awhile lost its effectiveness. For example, lights out elicited silence the first few times I used the strategy but as students became accustomed to it; it did not command their attention. I spoke over students a lot as well and this was a very ineffective strategy. On the spot, however, I found myself resorting to this due to a lack of confidence in my management abilities. My AT suggested using silence but being nervous I was too impatient to properly use that strategy. I also had the opportunity to use one of my AT's techniques that was very effective. The students settled immediately when he threatened to put them in rows or to make them read all period. I have to work on my confidence before I would feel comfortable using such a strategy. Actually, I am not sure I would ever use that strategy because I am not sure I can incorporate it into my philosophy of teaching. I thought I dealt well with asking students to return to their assigned seat, though. I did not yell or centre them out but asked them politely to move back to their seats. They respected my approach and I never heard complaint as they returned to their seats.

Concerning the grade 10 enhanced class I noticed the students were very critical of one another. This is part of their dynamic and I was unsure how to deal with the unconstructive criticism. I regret not addressing it but was concerned about singling out a student. In addition, due to their academic competitiveness, it is apparently a problem in all their classes. Overall, the students I had at the high school were well-behaved and their actions were never malicious towards me. They just needed more direction from me.

Revise

There are several strategies I could employ to better my classroom management skills. I believe I need to provide students clearer instructions so they know what is expected of them. When the students were confused with my instructions, talking would erupt and it was difficult for me to deal with the talking and properly explain my expectations. I also think that I should not be afraid to circulate around the classroom while teaching and stand in closer proximity to students exhibiting off-task behavior. This may be an effective cue for them to stop that type of behavior and participate in the class. It will also help me to identify off-task behavior without interrupting the class. I also need to take more detailed notes so I can use them as a quick reference before each class to prompt my memory of which strategy to use in which class. I should not be afraid to demand that students pay attention to me. I also need to address off-task behavior more quickly as it can disrupt the class, or interfere with the learning of the student who is exhibiting the behaviors. For example, in one of my grade 11 classes, a boy near the back was doing calculations for another class therefore he could not fill out an answer sheet as he had not been paying attention. I did not realize this, however, until I collected the sheets. My AT, when he notes off-task behavior, addresses the entire class. He does not single one student out and his actions serve as a reminder of what is expected in his class. I like this approach and would like to use it myself as I do not agree with singling out one student or making an example of them. I believe I can deal with the grade 10 enhanced class in this way and simply explain to the entire class that criticizing a classmates' academic achievement is not acceptable.

I believe that my confidence as a teacher underlies my classroom management and if I can work on this and tighter planning, management will follow.

***Question*: How does confidence show itself when you manage your classroom?**

9. Christiana Johnson – Contracting

Upon reflection of my practice teaching experience during the month of October, I have realized that my classroom management skills are yet unrefined and that this is an area in which I have still much learning to achieve. I have also concluded that classroom management is an area which is also deserving of ongoing improvement and consideration for practicing and experienced teachers.

I had a number of experiences from which I learned. It is important to mention, first, that during my practice teaching, my classroom teacher and I worked primarily as a team. We discussed curriculum expectations and lesson and activity plans together, both before and after classroom practices took place. Though we operated alternately in leading and supporting roles, we also worked in a *team-teaching* style for a large portion of my stay. This is an important factor to consider while reflecting on my teaching experience, as it follows that classroom management was a shared responsibility during most of my practice teaching, and therefore my experience was different than it would have been if I had been solely responsible for the teaching.

Reflect

Daily Classroom Management Practices

I used a number of typical classroom management techniques with varying degrees of efficiency during my teaching experience. I found myself regularly roaming the room whenever I was not presenting information at the front and I even directed classroom discussion from various places in the room (the front, the back, between the aisles of desks). When my Associate Teacher was presenting material, I found myself moving towards pockets in the room in which chatter was beginning to develop. For the most part, the use of proximity had a reasonable degree of effectiveness and seemed to promote on-task behavior during group work.

When proximity was less effective and at times during which I was less free to roam, such as while illustrating material on the board, I used name-dropping, which also showed a reasonable degree of effectiveness.

At one time, while I was presenting information at the front of the class during a whole-class activity, and during which many students were becoming involved in off-topic chatter, I called their attention and requested that they demonstrate respect by actively listening to what was being said. I reminded them that respect was shown to them when they spoke or presented information in front of the class. This dialogue was effective in that it resulted in re-focusing the students' attention to the lesson. I believe the reason for the success of such a dialogue was due to the classroom teacher setting the tone for the year by identifying the principles of classroom behavior as *Responsibility* (for learning), *Respect* (for themselves, others, and the teacher), *Accountability* (for their work and their behavior), and *Pride* (in themselves, their work, and their behavior) in a contract which the students signed. Thanks to this contract, respect has been a useful keyword in achieving student co-operation in the classroom.

Classroom Routines

There were a few established routines that existed in the classroom prior to my arrival, which I carried on while teaching as a guest in my Associate Teacher's classroom. These were fairly general routines for the most part, including such things as seating oneself at the beginning of class, hand-raising during class discussion and in response to questions, and placing chairs on the desks at the end of the day. There is a school-wide late policy and late-slip procedure at my host school and the students are accustomed to this routine. They are also accustomed to the attendance-taking routine at the beginning of each class. Photocopies and handouts are distributed according to a routine in which sufficient copies are given to the first student in each row and students are expected to "Take one and pass it back."

Specific to my Associate Teacher's class is the *moniteurs et monitrices de textes* routine for text book distribution. Because text books are not assigned to each student, a class set is shared among all. On those day during which textbooks are required, the teacher calls on one student volunteer from each row to collect and distribute the textbooks to their peers in the same row. These same students are also expected to collect and return the texts at the end of the class. This routine is useful, but may run more smoothly if, at the end of the work period, the moniteurs et monitrices de textes were reminded to collect and return the textbooks from their row. I will make a point of listing these instructions in my future lesson plans as a reminder.

Classroom Transitions

There is one particular area of classroom management which I feel I could improve upon by establishing new classroom routines during my upcoming placement. I feel that transition between activities and between classes could be affected in a more productive manner, which would better promote active learning and the more efficient use of class time. In an effort to effect this change, I plan to establish a routine of bell work wherein students would have an activity in which to engage immediately upon their arrival in class. As I am teaching French language classes, these activities could be purposeful communicative tasks which have an element of play to them. Prior to returning to my host school, I hope to develop a list of such communicative tasks to which I could quickly turn while preparing my lesson plans.

A final point to which I hope to bring some change in order to encourage more positive classroom behavior is the end of period work session. Students in my host classes are in the habit of stopping to work on assignments and assigned activities anywhere between 4 and 15 minutes prior to the end of the class period. I take exception to this un-prescribed routine because this seems to lead to an unacceptable total amount of time taken from classroom learning. There tend to be application or consolidation activities taking place during the last segment of the class period, and during this time, the students are generally working independently or in small groups on the completion of some lesson-related or unit-related task. I would like to discuss this concern with my Associate Teacher and propose first, to dialogue with the students on the effect of such lost time; and second, to illustrate the amount of work that can be accomplished during those last few minutes of class by relating an experience I had with one of the students.

In this particular case, I approached a student who was not working during the allotted work period and inquired whether he might like assistance in order to complete the assigned activity. The student informed me that (he felt) there wasn't sufficient time to warrant beginning the assignment and that he would complete it at home. Skeptical of his dedication to completing work at home, I offered to assist him in working through the first few portions to ensure that he would have no trouble in finishing the remainder on his own. By the time the class period ended, the student with whom I had been working had not only clarified some grave misunderstandings on how to complete the assignment, but had in fact completed the entire assignment by the time the bell rang. These few minutes of productive activity greatly increased this student's understanding of the material and his performance on the assignment.

Revise

Overall, I feel that my classroom management skills are in the process of being developed and that my progress is developing at a natural and reasonable rate.

During my upcoming placement, I intend to make a habit of speaking directly with students during or after class when I find their behavior to be disruptive, as I previously witnessed a positive change in the behavior of those few students with whom I had spoken directly. The modification I will make is to specifically identify and follow through with students rather than only resort to this habit casually. This approach, while it may be more direct than some teachers would choose to be, is in agreement with both my developing philosophy of education and with the code of conduct established by my Associate Teacher, as it treats each student with respect, treats each student as an individual, and requires that each student take responsibility and show accountability for his or her own behavior and learning.

In order to better utilize pro-active classroom management strategies, I plan to complete a more thorough pre-assessment of learners than

I have been producing to date. With practice and with the support and guidance of my Associate Teacher, I expect to develop greater skill at planning and adjusting for anticipated behaviors.

In keeping with my humanist-progressivist orientation to classroom interactions, I expect to see an improvement in some of the classroom behavior by clearly establishing my expectations with regards to each activity before it begins. Again, this revision is generated in response to my past success when engaging students in dialogue about classroom procedures and desired behaviors.

***Questions*: Does *contracting* work, and if it does, what behavior would you consider using a contract to illicit?**

10. Lynn Manders – Awareness

The purpose of classroom management is to maintain an effective learning environment. A good classroom manager maximizes the time spent on learning and minimizes the time spent on disciplining students. Effective classroom management optimizes the learning experience for everyone in the classroom. During my October Practice Teaching Placement, I was able to reflect on my classroom management procedures.

In my grade 10 Civics classroom, the room is set up in a horseshoe fashion to facilitate group work and discussion. In the front right hand corner of the room are two students (a male and a female) who are the *talkers* of the class. These students normally talk throughout the teacher's lessons and they always finish in-class assignments as quickly as possible so that they can play cards. The teacher allows this behavior, but I find it to be a behavior management issue. The expectations for the class are that students are to be attentive when the teacher is speaking and that students must complete all in-class assignments. In an effort to mimic my Associate Teacher's style, I allowed the students' negative behaviors (as outlined) to occur, rather than properly addressing the issues, and this became my greatest classroom management mistake.

At the beginning of the lesson, I positioned myself at the front of the room to focus the students' attention on me and my lesson. I was using the blackboard and the overhead projector as my teaching resources. As the lesson turned into classroom discussion and debate, I moved about the room to try and engage all of the students into the discussion. The discussion was mostly focused on the left side of the room, as these students seemed to be participating more in the discussion. Because of the focus being on the left side of the room, I had unknowingly directed my posture towards that side, leaving a blind spot on the right side of the classroom. As I facilitated the conversation, I could hear the students whispering behind me. I quickly looked in the direction of the disruption, thinking they would notice my glance and stop talking. When the behavior continued I walked over to the students and stood directly beside them as a non-verbal cue, hoping that the talking would stop. The two students stopped talking and I stepped away from the corner of the room back to the front and centre part of the room. The students began talking again. I went back over to them and stood beside their desk. I gently knocked on the desk, as a non-verbal indication that I wanted their attention. Throughout the lesson I did not stop the lesson to tell the two students to be quiet. The third and last time that I walked over to their desks, I heard one of the students whisper to the next, "Why does she keep coming over here?"

After the lesson was completed, I assigned a task to be completed by the end of class. The same two students finished the task in approximately ten minutes and they spent the remaining time of the period playing cards. When they gave me their assignment, I remarked that they were finished rather early and I had them take back the assignment and proofread it for errors. They returned the assignment to me again within a few minutes and I took the assignment in.

Reflecting on my actions as a classroom manager, I now realize that my techniques were ineffective. Firstly, the students were being very disrespectful to me as well as their fellow students, by talking throughout the lesson. Their talking was likely a distraction to the surrounding students and it was distracting me from giving my full attention to the class discussion because I kept trying to think about strategies to stop the undesired behavior. The students disobeyed my non-verbal cues to stop the behavior and I did not want to disrupt the class to tell them to stop. I felt as though I owed my attention to the students who were actively participating in the class discussion and I knew that I would feel guilty about stopping the discussion to speak to the two misbehaving students.

After reflecting on the behavioral problems that I experienced during my placement, I have developed an action plan to revise my reaction to the undesired behavior, Firstly, I must realize that the actions of those students are affecting everyone in the class. As the teacher, the students are disrupting my ability to focus my attention on the class discussion. Other students surrounding the two disruptive students may not be able to hear what others in the class are saying and they may also be tempted to participate in the undesired behavior as a result.

Another strategy for next time can be to ask those two students a question to see if it refocuses their attention. When I heard the one student ask the other why I kept going over to them, I should have gone up to the students privately after the lesson was over and tell them my reasoning for doing so. I could have also taken a moment from the class and told them to please be quiet.

In my next placement, I will also ensure that I do not leave a blind spot while I am giving my lesson. I will stand either at the front of the room or speak from a corner of the room so that I never have my back turned to any of the students in the class. I will also tell those two students to leave the cards in their locker (or take the cards away from them), thus preventing an undesired behavior. This will remove the distraction from them and they will have to spend more time on their class-work. By telling them to leave the cards in their locker it will also show that the assignment is purposeful and that I want them to be successful on it. This will also show that I want to optimize their learning and it will put ownership on the students to make sure that they are meeting my classroom expectations. If non-verbal and verbal cues do not work in the future then I can also separate the students. Once the students are finished a task, I will suggest other activities that they may work on.

Classroom management is one of the most important aspects of teaching. I have realized the importance of preventing misbehaviors wherever possible and that they should be dealt with promptly when they do occur.

***Questions*: What can happen in classrooms that indicates you may be missing something? *Withitness* is a well-known classroom management trait – What does it mean?**

Chapter 6

Teaching and Classroom Management

Teaching Defined

You are about to become a teacher, or you may already be teaching, so it would be useful to know what teaching is. **Teaching** is, "*the use of preplanned behaviours, founded in learning principles and child development theory and directed toward both instructional delivery and classroom management, that increase the probability of affecting a positive change in student behaviour*" [emphasis added] (Levin & Nolan, 2004, p. 16). To bring this definition to life each teacher needs to be aware of the human traits expected by students, peers, and the community. Teachers need to employ a sense of humor, enthusiasm, a desire for learning, health and wellness, nonverbal qualities, and be a role model (Kirchner & Fishburne, 1998). The Ontario College of Teachers adds,

> Teachers share their *enthusiasm* for learning. They exude a passion for their subject matter that is infectious. They delight in the demands of a career that continually exposes them to new learning, new situations, new people, and new opportunities for personal and professional growth and leadership. They draw energy and satisfaction from sparking the achievement of others. Exceptional qualifications, curious by nature, dedicated to helping children grow and thrive – these are the hallmarks of good teachers. Good teachers build society one student at a time. Good teachers are organized, flexible, thoughtful, caring and nurturing. They are drawn to the profession because it's demanding, exciting, and rewarding. It attracts people who are committed to lifelong learning – for themselves and others. It inspires people to learn as they teach and teach what they love. If you're keen to learn – about students, different subjects, or even how we learn – then consider learning to teach. (Ontario College of Teachers, 2004)

As a teacher, you bring your mind, body, and spirit into your teaching. You teach *who you are* and you learn from your students just as they learn from you. You see the many faces before you with varied needs and wonder how you can teach all of these people. One means to achieve this outcome is to put in place plans, to pre-plan your day, and consider all the dimensions of the profession. We pre-plan to ensure we cover the necessary curricula, meet the needs of students, and make teaching a little more predictable, definite, and unambiguous for us. Our plans are standardized somewhat in each Faculty of Education and later in our careers we modify these to adapt to specific contexts and needs. One disquieting dimension of teaching and planning that is with us at all times is the concern for Classroom Management. In fact, "classroom management is a priority for experienced teachers, and tops their list of concerns about teaching . . . it is the centerpiece of teacher training" (Goethals, Howard & Sanders, 2004, p. 116). Viewed as a critical priority we need to have a clear understanding of what classroom management is, how we can do it, and how can we improve in this area throughout our career.

A good question for any teacher to ask is: What exactly is classroom management?

I believe classroom management involves the establishment and maintenance of a healthy learning environment. Analyze the definition and we realize that a teacher must do two things. First, *establish* a healthy learning environment; and second, *maintain* this healthy learning environment.

Establishing the Healthy Learning Environment

Before you begin to teach there is a lot of work to be done. Ask yourself, where will I be teaching (facilities, distance from home, policies, school agenda)? What grade(s) or division(s) will I be working with? Am I full-time or part-time, long-term occasional, a substitute, or a pre-service teacher? How many students will I teach each day, or each period? How diverse are the classes (special education, multicultural)? Although there are many other questions to examine, these questions are enough to propel teachers into action as they begin to pre-plan.

Planning can begin with the curricula to determine what you have to teach and to what standard. Visit Ministry of Education websites, locate your curricula, and read about expectations and about the path your teaching should follow (professionalism, accountability). Next, begin to plan a means to teach this material; an instructional strategy can be identified and numerous assessment and evaluation decisions taken. At this point, you need to ask yourself, what are my classroom management (teaching) beliefs, values, and positions? It is these beliefs that influence *what* you teach, *how* you teach it, and *when* you will teach it.

Philosophy of Classroom Management: Your Plan

When someone asks, "Why do you do it that way?" we reflect, we answer, and sometimes we connect our actions to a stance, value, and/or understanding of teaching. Each teacher carries within, beliefs about teaching, learning, students, knowledge, and ideas about what is worth knowing. These beliefs, examined or unexamined, will change throughout a teacher's career. Often, a change is brought about when the person who asks this question is the interviewer, the parent, the school administrator, a community member, or even another peer. All teachers would like to be able to connect their actions to proven theory, solid research, or a current trend just to demonstrate that we are responsible, informed, and well-prepared. However, within the hectic, fast-paced, intense world of the teacher, many of these beliefs are left unexamined.

Philosophical Underpinning

Take some time to examine John Dewey's **progressivism** where *knowledge is somewhat tentative and change is constant in life* as the whole child, who is the centre and good, picks up clues and moves forward via the ebb and flow of *active teaching* and *learning by doing* what is eclectic and democratic (learning by choice).

There are many other ***isms*** in education and over time, you will discover, or rediscover, these. You may decide you fit nicely in one area or another. If you do not fit, then develop your own philosophical orientation and your own classroom management plan (philosophy).

Reconstructionism involves students in community concerns (self and society) and global issues (war, food, and peace) as well as social involvement with crises and questioning of political standpoints. Valued in this area is examining the *now* with a view to improving and changing society via field trips, social causes, and justice from within.

Essentialism is used to produce good members of society with a focus on traditional schooling. Teachers value basic morals and values and use a traditional authoritative stance in the class. Knowledge is transmitted, the basics are emphasized, and the arts are marginalized. Students obey and demonstrate respect, work hard, and develop good character.

Behaviorism in teaching causes educators to reinforce desired behavior, structure the environment accordingly, and use rewards and consequences to alter, modify, shape, or extinguish selected unwanted behaviors.

Perennialism. This is a search for truth, independence, arts, sciences, and mind development, which is something constant (perennial) and valued. This approach is usually associated with a liberal arts education and promotes development of critical thinkers who value child-centred education and transformational teaching.

Existentialism causes students to make their own meaning and understanding of their lived experience. Students are challenged to be leaders, respect others, question, and participate in everything via individualized (choice) programs as they explore ways to construct meaning.

What do you believe is involved in classroom management? What key classroom management systems and/or strategies would you make use of in your classroom? Why do you believe classroom management should unfold in this manner in your classroom, or put another way, what is the rationale for your current classroom management approach, beliefs, stance, strategies, and systems?

Take some time now to write out your classroom management plan. There are three distinct elements to consider:

- the *first* page or section involves your **current beliefs**;
- the *second* addresses **key elements**; and
- the *third* details your **rationale** for one and two. (Why I believe this and why I chose these key elements.)

What follows is one pre-service teacher's attempt to put on paper a classroom management plan.

Exhibit A

My Personal Classroom Management Philosophy

All students in a classroom need to feel that they belong, are valued, and are contributing members of a classroom community. They need to feel they are respected and accepted irrespective of their diverse backgrounds. As such, it is important that their differences are celebrated and embraced to make them feel that they are part of the community.

One of the important things a teacher can do for her students is to provide a safe and inviting classroom and an inviting curriculum. Students are important and as a teacher I intend to provide an environment where my students will feel safe to take risks and make mistakes without fear of ridicule from me. I want my students to believe in their self- worth and their potential regardless of their background, ability level, or ethnicity. It is important to keep in mind that children learn in many different ways and so the teaching technique should be adjusted to fit the diverse group of students. It is equally important to take into consideration the different learning levels of the children in the classroom so that the teacher can teach at a level that will be challenging for all students. As such, it is my intention to use a flexible combination of teaching strategies which will include lessons that the students are interested in as well as lessons that meet curriculum expectations to keep them motivated and increase the likelihood of success.

Teaching will not only be a job for me but also a learning experience in which both the students and I can learn from each other. I believe that teachers should provide leadership within the school, community, and educational profession to improve student learning and well-being.

It is my intention to keep in close contact with parents, students, and staff. Notes will be sent home to parents to let them know the expected rules of the classroom which will be set up and agreed upon by the students. Parents will also be contacted and informed about their child's good behavior as well as challenging behavior. It is my intention to be accessible to my students at all times and I plan to establish a good working relationship with my colleagues and other staff members as well. To my students, I will show and require respect at all times. You cannot have a good learning environment without respect in the classroom. I will set my expectations high and consistently reinforce expectations for behavior and academic performance. I will have a behavior plan with classroom rules, consequences, and rewards. When it comes to behavior plans I feel that the most important thing is to be consistent. I will do what I say I am going to do all the time. It is equally important to have a good sense of humor in the classroom to help create a comfortable environment.

Classroom management is one of the most important parts of teaching. My goal is to have a fair and consistent way to establish a safe, orderly, positive classroom environment in which teaching and learning can take place. I plan to arrange my room so there will be no distractions to the students. It is important to have good strategies and skills and be prepared for anything. I will always have backup plans as well as plans for teaching students of varying abilities. I will adapt lessons to students with different abilities without the other students knowing that I did so. All these things are very important when it comes to good classroom management. However, to achieve these expectations, a well thought out proactive management plan is very necessary.

Proactive Management Plan

There are three elements to my proactive management plan: prevention, support, and correction. Of these elements, *prevention* is the most important because effective prevention of misbehavior can help reduce major problems. It is important to have some rules and guidelines established the very first day of school so all students are familiar with what the expected and acceptable behavior will be.

Guidelines for Proactive Classroom Management

1. Monitor student behavior (use an "active eye" and walk around the classroom);
2. Focus (gain the attention of the students before starting a lesson or giving announcements, and maintain a calm, quiet voice);
3. Give direct, clear instructions and provide models/examples for students;
4. Use non-verbal cues to gain attention or redirect behavior (flip light switch, musical instrument, body posture, facial expressions, pausing, eye contact);
5. Friendly environment (bring in personal items and relate personal experiences where applicable);
6. Positive discipline (state expectations/routines in a positive manner);

7. Acknowledge good behavior (verbally and non-verbally) "I like the way that H. is working quietly and following my instructions.";
8. Be consistent (strive to treat all students fairly); and
9. Manage inappropriate behavior promptly.

Guidelines for Classroom Routines

1. **Transition Time:** Clear, simple directions that decrease the possibility of management problems.
   - Be consistent.
   - Inform students ahead of time of unscheduled changes in routines.
   - Have students line up single file for rotary classes (Physical Education, Library, French, and Computers).
   - Students are expected to be prepared for class and ready to learn when they enter the classroom.
2. **Washroom/Water Fountain:** Whole class has bathroom/water fountain privileges at scheduled times throughout the day (after morning recess, after lunch recess, after last recess).
   - In case of emergency/special circumstances, student may ask for permission to use the washroom.
   - May implement system whereby student can access a pass giving them permission to go to the bathroom.
3. **Bell Work/Early Finishers:** Bell work will be assigned for 9:00 (morning bell) and 1:00 (afternoon bell).
   - The bell work will include riddles, math/language problem-solving questions, reading responses, and so on.
   - A list will be compiled by the students in September relative to what activities are available for "early finishers" (e.g., self-edit work, read a book, journal writing, ask permission to go help another teacher, help a friend, choose an educational game from the game box, brain teasers, riddle books etc.).
4. **Pencil Sharpening:** Students will be required to "trade" their broken pencils with pencils that I will have pre-sharpened on a shelf near my desk.

- They will take a sharpened pencil from my jar and replace it with their broken pencil. There will be no pencil sharpener in my room except the electric one that will be hidden in my desk.

Guidelines to Encourage Good Behavior

1. **Classroom Rules:** Work with students to come up with a list of classroom expectations and consequences (give students ownership).

When in my class, students must comply with the following policies:

   1. Common courtesy and respect for one another is expected at all times.
   2. Come to class prepared, on time and ready to learn.
   3. No hats, inappropriate attire, or inappropriate language will be tolerated.
   4. Keep hands, feet, and objects to yourself.
   5. Do not take materials out of the room without teacher's permission.
   6. Clean up after yourself.

2. **Marble Jar:** Add a marble in a jar every time the class demonstrates consistent, good behavior – once the jar is filled, the class has the opportunity to enjoy a "special" activity.
3. **Student of the Month:** The student who has demonstrated consistent model behavior and has worked diligently will be recognized with a "Student of the Month" certificate and a small token from the Treasure Box.
4. **Good Behavior Chart:** As a class, come up with a list of good, desirable behaviors and at the end of each day, review the chart and decide which behaviors were demonstrated in the class that day and give a round of applause to the student(s) involved.
5. **Special Helpers**: Roles that will be assigned from a master class list on a weekly basis – list of class duties: clean off-boards, put chairs on desks, etc.

Rewarding Good Behavior

Rewarding good behavior can also be a good thing as long as the teacher is careful not to reward behavior too much or it can actually decrease a student's intrinsic motivation. However, when appropriate, a teacher can reward behavior by recognizing good behavior at award assemblies, sending commendations home (happy grams), giving students in-class honors and awards, and posting a list of students with positive behaviors (Outstanding Students' List).

List of Reward Ideas

- Have lunch with your favorite person.
- Have lunch with the principal.
- Join another class for indoor recess.
- Have the teacher phone parents to tell them what a great kid you are.
- Draw on the chalkboard.
- Be first in line.
- Choose any class job for the week.
- Choose the music for lunch. Bring in a tape.
- Take a tape recorder home for the night.
- Use colored chalk.
- Help the teacher operate the overhead projector.
- Invite a visitor from outside the school.
- Take a class pet home overnight.
- Be a helper in the room with younger children.
- Help the custodian.
- Bring in something special for show and tell.

Guidelines for Reactive Classroom Management

Reminder: To be directed to student(s) involved before specific situation becomes a management problem (e.g., moving closer to student, calling student's name without disrupting lesson, eye contact).

1. **Verbal Warning:** Directly approach student(s) and explain what behavior is expected and ask the student to identify the "next step." Make the student responsible for making better decisions next time.
2. **Warning Cards:** Student is discretely approached and a yellow warning card is placed on his/her desk. No verbal communication is exchanged so the class is not disrupted. If student continues disrupting the class, assign a designated area for him or her to do the work.

3. **Infraction Slip:** Student's inappropriate behavior requires that a Behavior Report be completed by both the teacher and the student.
   - Student(s) is required to serve an appropriate consequence, depending on the number of previous infractions; and
   - Student is required to write down "next steps" (discussed with teacher).
4. **Sent to the Office:** Student is sent to the office with a "Time Out Slip" where the principal is now in charge of handling the situation (phone call may be required, series of detentions, etc.).

Considerations

- Steps for discipline will be clearly posted in the classroom and explained/discussed at the beginning of the school year;
- Strive to instill inner self-control in students (use responsibility training);
- Have students take responsibility for their own actions (determine the "Next Steps"); and
- Use natural and logical consequences (related to an expectation).

RID: Strategy for Reducing Anger

This strategy will be implemented in the classroom and reinforced consistently.

Recognize your anger signals;

Identify a positive way to think about a possible solution (sharing, taking turns, trading); and

Do something constructive to calm yourself down.

"Cool Downs"

- Suggest a delay.
- Agree on one point.
- Use humor.
- Apologize.
- Use a calm voice and avoid aggressive gestures.
- Ask for adult help.

Communication Strategies

Student Profile

- A student profile will be conducted at the beginning of the year so I get a sense of a student's character, strengths, areas for growth, family history, likes, dislikes, and personal/academic goals.
- These profiles will be kept in the classroom and updated when necessary.

Informal Communication Strategies

- An introduction letter will be sent home on the first day of school as a means of introducing myself to the parents/guardians (key expectations/guidelines) and as a means of initiating a line of communication between the classroom and home (parents/guardians will be encouraged to contact me at school any time for clarification, support, or "next step" planning).
- Parents will also be sent an "Entry Survey" asking them to outline what their expectations and goals are for their children during the school year. This information will be kept with the student's profile.
- Strive to respond to all communication from parents/guardians as soon as possible and in a positive manner – record all communication with parents/guardians in a Communication Log.
- A home-school folder will be given to each student that will include work they can practice regularly at home with parents.
- A weekly progress report will be sent home to parents outlining their child's behavior. If an item in this report is checked-off, parents/guardians are asked to discuss the matter with their child. Otherwise, if no items are checked off, parents are encouraged to praise their child.
- Agendas will be used on a daily basis for relaying messages between teacher and parent/guardian, and each student will be expected to have his or her agenda signed every single night.
- A monthly newsletter will be sent home to inform parents/guardians of upcoming classroom events.
- A "Homework Notification" slip will be sent home when students work is missing or incomplete. This slip requires a parent's signature before being returned.

Sample Letter to Parents

Dear Parents/Guardians,

In an effort to increase communication between home and school, I would like to encourage you to take a few minutes to consider what your personal expectations are for your child's school year. Please use the space provided below to jot down your list. This Entry Survey will be kept with your child's Student Profile, as both records will serve as a starting point of the progression of development of your child throughout the school year.

Support life-long learning,

Sincerely,

Mrs. B.

1.

2.

Home-School Folder

Dear Parents/Guardians,

This is your child's home-school folder. Inside you will find weekly dictation words, lists of high frequency words and sound/letter clusters, tips for printing/cursive writing, a monthly reading log, and practice sheets for basic math facts. Your child has been encouraged to practice these language and math skills as often as your home schedule permits. Participating in these activities with your child will enable you, as parents/guardians, to share in your child's learning through consistent monitoring and support. Any concerns or comments regarding the use of the Home-School Folder can be directed through your child's agenda.

Thank you for your support. Your effort helps to keep the lines of communication open and connects home with school.

Supporting life-long learning,

Sincerely,
Mrs. B.

Behavior Report

Name: ______________________ Date:____________

Explanation of what happened: ________________________________

____

____

____

What rules were broken: ____________________________________

____

____

____

What you think should happen (Consequences): ____________________

____

____

____

What are the Next Steps: ___________________________________

____

____

If this situation happens again, what should the consequence be:

____

____

Teacher's decision: _______________________________________

____

____

Teacher ________________________ Date: ____________

Student ________________________ Date: ____________

Parent ________________________ Date: ____________

Communication Log

Date: ______________________ Time:__________________

Name of Child: __________________________________

Name of Parent/Guardian: __________________________

Initiated by:

__ Teacher

__ Parent

__ Other

Communication by:

__ Phone

__ Letter

__ In Person

__ Other

If a formal meeting, those in attendance were: _____________________

____

____

____

Reason: ____

____

____

____

Action to be taken: _______________________________________

____

____

____

____

____

____

A second Pre-service student developed the following management plan.

Exhibit B

Classroom Management Plan

Philosophy and Rationale

The goal of classroom management is to establish and maintain a healthy learning environment. Effective classroom management maximizes the time spent on learning and minimizes the time spent on discipline. The key element in achieving an efficient classroom is proactive planning. Preventing most undesirable behavior can be achieved through well-organized and structured plans for each lesson. Planning must include activities that are engaging for students, address all developmental levels, and incorporate all styles of learning. Management issues noticeably decrease when the students are deeply involved in what is being learned.

Teacher behavior is vital for minimizing time spent on classroom management. A teacher must stay abreast of current education research and apply it to the classroom. The teacher is responsible for modelling the desired behavior for the students. Nonverbal techniques such as planned ignoring, signal interference, written notes, and proximity control are effective methods for handling much off-task behavior without disrupting the rest of the class. Other low disruption techniques include name-dropping, "I" messages, and brief reminders of established expectations.

Expectations and routines must be discussed early and posted where they are visible for all to see. Having students collaborate on developing the classroom expectations will give them a sense of accountability. A list of the established expectations and routines are sent home to parents for review and signing. The students themselves must also sign the list of expectations indicating they are aware of and understand them. Teacher and students must jointly understand each expectation and why it is in place.

The **Collaborative Management Theory** is employed to encourage both teacher and student input into classroom management. The teacher and students work together towards a harmonious classroom environment. Rapport building and the development of mutual respect ensures that each student feels valued within the classroom and is therefore less likely to have undesirable behavior. Extra-curricular involvement with students promotes a positive relationship between students and teacher. In addition, awareness of and sensitivity to a student's home life and other issues can enhance the teacher's ability to effectively handle management issues. Students are provided with choice and options, both in learning and for discipline issues. Discipline measures must be linked to the behavior itself and classroom or individual meetings are used to resolve problems. Effective classroom management promotes students' self-esteem and sense of self-worth, while maximizing learning.

Key Elements

Classroom Arrangement

- The student desks will be arranged to promote collaboration and group work.
- The seating arrangement will change periodically throughout the year to encourage students to work with new groups of people or in response to classroom management issues that arise.
- The teacher's desk will have a clear line of sight to all students and areas of the room.
- Supplies and resources will be set up in well-labelled centres throughout the room for easy accessibility.

Classroom Routines

- Each lesson will begin with Bell Work that will be posted prior to the beginning of class. Students are expected to begin work immediately.
- Students will be assigned a variety of ongoing projects and activities that they may work on once they have completed the day's work.
- Transitions between periods will be run consistently and each student will be expected to be prepared for class by the beginning of the period.
- Students are expected to be prepared for class each day, with homework completed and all supplies available, ready to begin.
- Bathroom breaks and pencil sharpening will be done independently, without disruption to the class.

Classroom Expectations

- At the beginning of the year, the students and teacher will collaborate on creating a list of acceptable expectations.
- The expectations will include respect for self, respect for each other, respect for property, and respect for the teacher.
- The list will be discussed with the students and signed by each member of the class, including the teacher.
- Each parent will receive a copy of the classroom expectations and return a signed form stating that they have read and understood each expectation.

Behavior Plan

- First, students will receive a non-verbal cue (e.g., written note, proximity).
- Second, students will receive a verbal cue (e.g., name-dropping, reminder of expectations).
- Third, student will attend a student/teacher conference to discuss the issue.
- Fourth, student will receive a written note sent home to parents to be signed and returned.
- Finally, the teacher will arrange a parent/student/teacher conference to develop solutions to resolve the issue.

Communication Plan

- Parents will be contacted on a regular basis and updated about the progress of their child.
- Communication will take the form of: notes, phone calls, e-mails, or parent/teacher conferences.
- Parents will be provided with several methods to contact the teacher, should they have any concerns: available meeting times, call the teacher at school, send a note, or send an e-mail.
- The teacher will strive to respond to every communication ASAP, preferably same day.
- Regular class newsletters will be sent home to all parents, updating them on current and upcoming classroom events.

A third Pre-service Teacher constructed this next plan.

Exhibit C

Proactive Classroom Management Plan

Philosophy

My classroom will be a safe and pleasant environment where student participation will be encouraged. I will build a rapport with students and create a trusting relationship, where students know I care about them and that I am consistent. Classroom management is critical to the development of such an environment and a relationship. I will need to be prepared to address long-term and daily management issues. I believe one of the most important aspects of management is teacher preparation and reflection. I will be aware of my students' needs and interests and reflect continually on their achievements and contentment. I will need to be adaptable and change what isn't working. My responsibility is not only to understand my learners and to prepare effective academic long-range plans, but to prepare for successful daily instruction. Students must be engaged and prepared to participate; most important, they must understand what is expected of them. Teachers need to not only be enthusiastic and engaging, they need to have a clear picture of the concepts they are directing students towards, and effective strategies for them to arrive at those concepts. My classroom will be fun and students will enjoy many privileges once their work is completed.

Students in my classroom will understand their decisions affect their lives and the lives of those around them. Students need to learn to be responsible citizens and to make good decisions. Development of classroom rules and logical consequences will be student-centred at the beginning of the year. These rules will be focused around concepts of self-respect, respect of others, positive attitude, and class participation. I will strive to understand the forces influencing student behavior and address student needs with programs to develop personal skills. I will help students develop important life skills including problem-solving, conflict resolution, teamwork, goal-setting, and self-control.

The physical aspects of my classroom will be ever changing as the year progresses. Students will be curious to explore the different displays related to all subject areas and will be motivated by positive reinforcement and displays of their own work on the walls. I will utilize a variety of seating plans and arrangements to address the needs of the students and the requirements of the tasks we are completing.

Implementation

In order to create a safe environment in my classroom I will work towards creating a sense of community and a trusting relationship between students and myself. This will be achieved using cooperative learning strategies, self-esteem and positive reinforcement exercises, group discussions, team competitions, and by providing class incentives using positive interdependence (i.e., popcorn Fridays, pizza parties, etc., where everyone or no one is rewarded with the same reward). This will further be developed through student input into classroom rules and daily activities. As the classroom teacher, I will demonstrate self-control and I will follow an intervention hierarchy for dealing with daily discipline issues; beginning initially with non-verbal cues and working towards verbal cues and logical consequences if difficulties increase. I will understand my students to the best of my ability by initially reviewing OSRs, talking to other educators, and by having students complete interest surveys. I will maintain awareness of their needs and interests through communication with parents and by having students periodically complete course evaluations. I will reflect daily on student contentment and achievement and the success of the classroom environment.

I will be prepared to engage my students everyday through thorough preparation of the material, effective team teaching, and by using a diversity of teaching/learning strategies (i.e., cooperative, indirect, etc.). I will practice authentic assessment so that learners of all intelligences feel they are demonstrating their abilities to their fullest potential. My expectations of the students, both academically and in terms of their participation and behavior, will be clear and will be stated in a positive manner. I will post a daily outline of activities and will keep them informed a month in advance of where the class is heading, so they can be prepared. Students will have the opportunity to participate in directing their learning. They will be expected to use an agenda system, which parents must sign daily; this will help students to remain organized and will help parents to remain informed. As previously mentioned, my classroom will be equipped with an incentive system, whereby students earn rewards for appropriate behavior, completing tasks, and maximum participation. Incentives will be directed towards both individuals and the class as a whole. Students will enjoy their time in my classroom through use of this system in addition to a variety of thematic days, field trips, games, kinetic activities, and with a diversity of resources.

Students will come to understand how their decisions affect themselves and others through numerous opportunities to make decisions in class (assessment, projects, units, etc.). I will also utilize a *self-check* system, whereby students are given a warning for behaviors the class predetermines as unacceptable. The student will have to mark the warning off a list posted in the classroom (using student code names to maintain confidentiality). After a number of warnings, a logical consequence will be assigned (i.e., small essay, classroom chores, detention, etc.). Having the students mark off the warning themselves offers them an opportunity to self-correct their behavior and refocus on the task. In a similar manner, I will use *antiseptic bouncing* (offending student sent out of the room) to offer aggressive students the opportunity to briefly withdraw from the classroom to self-correct their behavior.

My students will participate in a variety of programs to meet their needs and to help them develop excellent personal skills. These programs will include role playing, goal-setting exercises, problem solving and conflict resolution seminars and games, group work and group evaluation (sharing circles), group discussions, and frequent self-assessment of these skills. In addition to offering these programs, I will model many of these skills to the best of my abilities on a daily basis.

My students will be greeted every day with a smile and friendly words. My classroom will feature a student "Wall of Fame" where students can feature their most recent accomplishments. Students will be encouraged to contribute material to decorate the classroom walls including posters, uplifting quotations, and thoughts, et cetera. Music will frequently be played during student work periods and student contributions will be accepted for this as well. I will pre-determine the seating arrangement in the classroom and I will frequently change its shape and orientation based on student needs and task requirements.

Support

The fundamental notions of this plan are based on several concepts. Developing a community of learners and a safe learning environment is presented as a primary emphasis of all effective educators (Levin and Nolan p114). They stress the importance of peers to individual student development. Other important characteristics of an effective educator as presented by Levin and Nolan that are utilized in this plan include: the importance of effective lesson design, the importance of communicating positive expectations, the importance of student interests, needs and success, as well as addressing multiple intelligences with a diversity of teaching/learning strategies (based on Howard Gardner's theories). These concepts are also supported by the work of Bandura who believed that "When feelings of self efficacy are high, individuals are much more likely to exert effort toward task completion" (Levin & Nolan, p. 118). All of these characteristics are thus essential to securing student motivation, classroom management, and, therefore, teacher success.

In observing a diversity of classrooms, I have reviewed and attempted to analyze the four main teacher power bases (Levin & Nolan, p. 75). In implementing this plan I hope to rely primarily on referent and on reward/coercive power-bases. I hope to establish a referent power-base by being actively involved in students' lives inside and outside of the classroom. I will try to communicate my concern for their well-being and practice positive reinforcement. It is, however, impossible to predict if this power base will, or can, be developed in a particular classroom. I will also therefore, heavily rely on a reward/coercive power base, as I have described. I have observed many such systems in a majority of the classrooms I have been in and found them to be quite effective. In managing misbehavior outside of the reward /coercive system, I will rely on the intervention hierarchy as provided (Levin and Nolan p170). This hierarchy suggests approaching students using non-verbal techniques initially, then gradually moving to verbal cues, and finally to logical consequences if the misbehavior continues. It considers effective use of classroom time, reducing power struggles, and maintaining student attention and respect while achieving the desired intervention.

Finally, with respect to the various theories of classroom management, this plan draws heavily on a collaborative management approach (Levin & Nolan, 2000, p. 88). This approach is reliant on the belief that both the teacher and the student are responsible for controlling student behavior. This connection is evident in my plan, through my initiation of student skill development programs and my student self-check system (Levin & Nolan, 2000).

Each of these classroom management plans would be good to have in hand – and in mind – before you begin to teach. Each plan communicates a philosophy (beliefs, values, moral stance, informed decisions, and awareness). Each plan illuminates key elements such as behavioral techniques, community building ideas, communication policy, and organization devices. Each plan details a rationale for many of the points detailed. Once you have your plan, it will need to change as you do and in response to the positions you assume and the needs of each class.

Each teacher's position is complex and at times overwhelming; however, there are several traits that can ease the pressure to be perfect! Each day, simply try to exercise discipline, be positive, consistent, and communicate effectively. Sounds easy as you read this, but add to this, any pressure from your personal life, political pressure, professional duty, and we begin to compress. Understanding the terms may help. For instance, **discipline** is "*a form of control imposed internally by an individual or externally by another person in control of the learning environment*" [emphasis added] (Kirchner & Fishburne, 1998, p. 702). Teachers are required to exercise self-control to extremes, as they are models of self-management. The behavior of a teacher should be supportive, encouraging, and refined. The problem is that as pressure builds, some of the less appealing human traits can surface to the point where a teacher's behavior becomes the problem. So, look at yourself and when you sense you are about to show behavior that is not what you would like to see exposed, just back-up, withdraw (time-out), get a breath of fresh air, take a sick-day, or do something that will help you cope with the pressure of the day, moment, or week.

Chapter 7

Nonverbal Communication

Communication: The Teacher's Craft

An article in the Canadian Teachers' Federation (CTF), Fall *HORIZONS* (2003) publication, included a survey that asked, "What determines a child's success in school?" The data suggest that almost nine in ten Canadians surveyed (87 %) said the quality of the teachers has *a lot* of influence on whether children fail or succeed in school and this aspect ranked the highest among six factors surveyed. With this belief firmly entrenched in Canadian society, it is important from many perspectives to ensure that Canadian teachers strive to be their best and standards are in place to remind educators what is required.

Various provinces have certification bodies that regulate teachers and teaching in an effort to ensure teaching excellence. For instance, Ontario's College of Teachers is a body that produces a publication called *Standards of Practice for the Teaching Profession*. Key elements within this document include ongoing professional learning, professional knowledge, teaching practice, leadership, community, and commitment to students and student learning. Each teacher today requires many skills and abilities to demonstrate excellence in these key areas. One inherent trait that pervades each of the main elements, and possibly the most important skill that can be viewed in the classroom, the school, and the community, is an ability to *communicate effectively* with students, parents, and peers since teachers must often show-and-tell to teach effectively. Among the many requirements to teach, we can highlight a few critical ones. For example, teachers *model* appropriate behavior, offer instructive guidance, illuminate content via discussion, and "foster a convivial atmosphere in their classrooms" (Ryan & Cooper, 2004, p. 168). They do this by using cognitive, psychomotor, and affective knowledge and skills. Teachers are required to be sensitive and sense emotional tones within the class in order maintain a healthy learning environment. As well, "activities connected with rules and procedures require the teacher's most salient verbal and nonverbal communication skills" (Goethals, Howard & Sanders, 2004, p. 117), as it is these rules and procedures that can be utilized to establish and maintain a functional classroom. Communication requires teachers to make informed decisions because what you choose to say as a teacher, and how it is said can be the difference between effective and ineffective teaching, community relations, and classroom management. In addition,

> Successful classrooms are not a direct result of the implementation of abstracted principles of teaching, learning, development or management. Rather, the successful implementation of any educational, psychological or administrative theories relevant to the creation of effective classroom environments ultimately depends on the quality of the moment by moment interactions that occur between teachers and their students. Effective communication is the "bedrock" on which productive teaching and learning are built. (Martin, Sugarman & McNamara, 2000, p. 22)

However, some teachers lack insight, knowledge, and skills in the area of communications. It is to these ends that we embark to examine both verbal and nonverbal elements of communication. "Human communication is the process of one person stimulating meaning in the mind of another person (or persons) by means of verbal or nonverbal messages" (Richmond & McCroskey, 1995, p. 1). Communication happens when we speak, write, listen, see, and sometimes by sensing something. These messages and our sensing of them result in human stimulation. This stimulation affects your classroom each moment of each day. Therefore, we need to prepare to communicate, rehearse our communications, and check for effect and understanding. If we can do this, we can manage our class in a manner that we intended. As we teach, we must remind ourselves that "effective communication is one of the most important skills a teacher must understand and use" (Kirchner & Fishburne, 1998, p. 77). Once we achieve effective communication means, we have to maintain our efforts because "effective classroom management requires the building of communities, and to do so, teachers must evaluate the manner in which they communicate with students, find alternatives to traditional punishments, and eliminate the focus on rewards and praise" (Hardin, 2004, p. 125). We need to first take a deeper and wider look at the nonverbal variable.

> Nonverbal behavior is any of a wide variety of behaviors in which humans engage that also have the potential for forming communicative messages. Such nonverbal behavior becomes nonverbal communication if another person interprets the

> behavior as a message and attributes meaning to it. (Richmond & McCroskey, 1995, p. 6)

Nonverbal behavior is in our appearance, our way of dressing, our mannerisms, our energy, and our dedication which people can sense and attach meaning to. So when someone asks, why are you wearing a tie or a dress today, the answer is not a simple one: it is within our philosophy of communication and within our attitude towards our profession. *Appearing* to be a good teacher and *being* one may not be too far apart. We are told by the Ontario College of Teachers (2004) that "good teachers build society one student at a time. Good teachers are organized, flexible, thoughtful, caring, and nurturing. . . . Today's teachers wear many hats and perform different roles. They are communicators, counselors, classroom managers, and role models" (p. 3). How we speak to students, parents, colleagues, and school community members sends messages.

If you were lucky enough to be a Wolf Cub and studied the text of Baden Powell, the founder of the organization, his motto was "Be Prepared." Carry this message into teaching and we find that all aspects of our job as educators can benefit from being prepared. A readiness to communicate at all times with all stakeholders, and being aware of failed communication, are important teacher skills.

Dress

Ask yourself, am I wearing something that communicates respect for the profession, my school community, my school colleagues, and students? Do I feel professional yet comfortable and at ease with what I am wearing? Being real, teaching who you are, and accomplishing professional goals is often a complex task. Self-understanding can be communicated via dress and "interactions between teachers and students evoke many emotions from both parties" (Hennigar, 2004, p. 68). Show you care enough to send the message that elicits the kind of stimulation you are looking for in the school community. Dress the part by asking: Am I a coach, an artist, or a manager? How could each belief of self, change the way a teacher dresses for his or her role? If you are a bit of all three then you may need to explain why you are dressed that way. Often I would get into character if we were studying some period or celebrating an occasion (Christmas, Halloween, or Easter) and the message sent was that I was an actor who had spirit and a sense of humor.

Are we guilty of judging a book by its cover? Think about your feelings if you visited a hospital and were confronted by a person wearing jeans, sandals, tie-dyed shirt, and had shoulder-length hair who then introduced himself or herself as a doctor. Would you question their credentials and ask to see identification? If a police force had no dress code, would they be able to serve and protect as well? What if they drove old, rusty pick-up trucks and wore old, casual clothes? Would this affect your feeling of security or respect? Most large stores have uniforms and standards of behavior. The dress code serves many purposes and makes your shopping experience better.

Students are often proud of their teacher and their school. Meeting students out of class, I sense their pride as they introduce me to their family or friends, and I am glad I look respectable and professional most of the time. Clothing can communicate how you feel, what you're doing, what your job is in society, and it can be either a negative or a positive element that creates your image. This image is one that may last for a lifetime. You only have one chance to make a first impression so you decide what message you would like to have cast in the minds of others.

Gestures and Posture

As you teach *who you are*, your students will make observations and report these to you. They might say: "Why did you wave me over in the hall? Why were you standing like that?" It could be that the messages sent were not read accurately. Students are now finding out from you, what, if any, messages you were sending. Personal characteristics cannot be overestimated in effective teaching. "These characteristics [including gesture and posture] in conjunction with other key behaviors interact to produce the child's learning environment" (Kirchner & Fishburne, 1998, p. 79). A teacher can quiet a class by raising a finger to their lips and a gym class can be herded into a corner of the gym by a wave of a hand. Stopping someone from entering a door or passing you in the hall requires a firm forward arm movement with the palm up to signal stop. It is these common gestures that are quite powerful yet we may not appreciate just how effective a communicator we can be just by gesturing. Think of the sports referee with their gestures and cards, whistles, flags, and bells that instantly send messages to players.

For instance, to stand straight with your hands on your hips sends a firm, "I mean business" message to your students. Can you think of some other gestures and/or postures that send messages that are appropriate in your classroom? Practice these in front of a mirror and with peers. Have your peers guess what your message is. Send a "be quiet" message nonverbally. I recall being pulled over on the highway by a police officer who was standing at the side of the road. All he did was point at me and then point to the side of the road. All I saw was this recognizable uniform and I knew immediately what was happening. The nonverbal message caused me to decelerate from 80 kmh and quickly pull over. You can guess how I might have felt if this has happened to you.

Your Face and Your Eyes – Show Me That Teacher 'Eye'

We do not have to look far to read about teachers and how they are "proficient in curbing disruptive behavior . . . [and] are experts in the use of a variety of proactive interventions skills" (Levin & Nolan, 2004, p.171). We remember as students looking up only to be confronted with the teacher's stare or perhaps just an eye movement that said, "get serious and stop that." "Teachers' facial expressions can affect how students feel about the classroom environment" (Richmond & McCroskey, 1995, p. 267). A teacher's smile along with head-nodding *yes*, signals that we have the teacher's approval. Conversely, a stern look of disapproval and the head-shaking *no*, sends a negative message perhaps to stop and reflect on your behavior. Teachers communicate emotion with their face and eyes. Surprise is that wide-eyed look, while disgust requires some twisting and squeezing of the face. As students become accustomed to your body and facial expressions and the many messages they contain, they will not need any words to read you and your messages. Take a moment and practice these emotional message transmissions either on your own in front of a mirror, or with another person.

1. Show us your look of *fear* – You have just seen a ghost.
2. Show us your *happiness* – You have just won $500 000.
3. Show us your *sadness* – Your pet has just died.
4. Does surprise look a little like happiness?
5. Does your angry look have some fear in it?
6. Does your sadness contain disapproval?

Every teacher brings to his/her class unique means to communicate and various strengths, weaknesses, and attitudes that can enhance or reduce communicative effectiveness. A student might say, "I do not understand that teacher, they are hard to read." It could be that at the moment you are attempting to convey the message of anger you were actually thinking about something that was quite funny in your personal life hence the message to the student may have been unclear or muted. A teacher needs to smile even when it's raining, he or she forgot to bring a lunch, and got a speeding ticket on the way to work. I have worked in many schools where the staff room is full of things to cheer us up. It could be the coffee, a box of treats, a funny joke on a bulletin board, a happy colleague, or that big comfortable chair that just relaxes us and helps us to smile. "Smiling has long been associated with liking, affiliation, and immediacy. The teacher who smiles and has positive facial affect is perceived as more immediate and likable than one who does not" (Richmond & McCroskey, 1995, p. 267) So if you are reminded to smile or someone asks what is wrong with you, just grin and bear it.

Voice in the Classroom

Suppose you are from South Africa and you are teaching a class in southern Ontario; what would the students notice about your voice? Some students may notice the accent and ask where you were from while others may just say that you speak funny. I have heard such a comment from students who had an exchange teacher from Ireland. *Accents*, *inflections*, *tone*, and *mood* all impact the message you send beyond the words you speak. The point then, is that your voice does influence how your students receive your messages. Your *vocal behavior* can put people to sleep, or cause them to laugh. Richmond and McCroskey (1995) surveyed students and found that "the monotone voice was the most objectionable behaviour of a teacher . . . the monotone voice projected the image of boredom, noncaring, and nonimmediacy . . . they learned less" (p.269). Therefore, we can suggest that teachers need to avoid the monotone voice and inject some *pitch*, *energy*, and *intensity*. Reflect on the adjustments you make to your stereo to get the right tone (treble, bass) and volume that you require. Ask students if your voice is too soft or too loud and ask: "Can you hear me?" Students will give you feedback just as passengers in your car give you feedback about your car audio, whether you want to hear about it or not.

Listen to students speak and you will hear in their voice, certain disfluencies (non-linguistic verbalizations: um, er, uh) that send you messages. This *paralanguage* tells you about the person: they may be tired, angry, or highly motivated and excited. We need to listen to this paralanguage to pick out meaning. Think of a student saying, "Great sweater, nice color." Was the comment sincere or sarcastic? It may be the paralanguage that tells us.

Proxemics

You are driving your car and you notice a police car coming up behind you. How close does the police car get before you get nervous, check your speedometer, or reflect upon the rules that you may not be following? Do you have your seatbelt on? It is a relief when the police car passes you. Maybe you have a bad memory of getting a speeding ticket that causes this reaction. Actually, what is at work here is something called **proxemics** which is "*the study of the communicative aspects of space and territoriality*" [emphasis added] (Richmond & McCroskey, 1995, p. 14). Sometimes all you have to do, to stop a student's maladaptive behavior, is to appear on the scene. I have stepped out of my class, reappeared suddenly at the door, and have often been confronted with several students running back to their seats or freezing in place just because of the proxemic impact of my movements.

As you walk around your class people respond to the closeness in discrete ways. Teacher proximity can promote desired behaviors. All you need to do is to stand near students, relocate a student's desk near yours, briefly interact (praise, reprimand, or consequence) with students while moving around the room, and constantly monitor student movement. Doing this requires teachers to both cue and prompt antecedents for suitable classroom behavior. Nonverbal cards can be used as they are in soccer and volleyball games to indicate classroom noise levels, or appraise group or individual behaviors without using words.

Some students will smile at you, some look down and fidget, some feel obligated to ask a question or verbalize. You want to use proxemics and not abuse it or use it in a negative way. Deliberately invading their space or being too close just to send your message is too aggressive and may lead to other problems.

> Personal space is an invisible bubble that surrounds us that expands or contracts depending on personalities, situations and types of relationships . . . the intimate zone . . . ranges from touching to a distance of 18 inches. This zone usually is reserved for the very few special people in our lives. . . . The casual-personal zone . . . ranges from 18 inches to about four feet . . . [and] is used during conversations with close friends and interactions with relatives. (Richmond & McCroskey, 1995, p. 123)

Teachers may find themselves coaching in huddles, or shoulder-to-shoulder solving problems in class, and need to remind themselves that the closeness of the two people is a sign of mutual respect and trust, and nothing else. Be aware of the distance between you, the professional educator and your students. Personal space is to be respected and ever-present in the minds of educators.

Listening

A social skill that is often taught at the elementary level, and one many teachers need to practice, is careful listening all day, each and every day. Two actions produce effective listeners. First, we look at the person speaking, and second, we do not speak when listening. In addition, "forensic listening is listening with the senses and with the heart. It is much like emphatic listening in that one listens to be understood without being judged" Cantrell & Cantrell, 2004, p. 79). So, you not only look at the person; you attempt to read their expressions which illuminate emotions such as boiling mad, scared white, shaky, trembling, shocked quiet, and the like. Try listening to someone while you look away; or calculate the interest on your loan while someone is giving you directions. Can you do these listening tasks? Probably not, because listening involves focus, attention, and energy. If you are lacking any of these then your listening may be impaired, blocked, and/or diminished. This is why teachers wait until a classroom is quiet before they speak and stop when others speak as teachers know students can not listen while there is noise, distractions, or competing messages.

Touch

When I began teaching I recall my union sending a memo to me and all other teachers informing us of contact (touch) that is inappropriate within certain contexts. I appreciated the information and reflected on the usefulness of such a memo. I also read about teachers who were in serious trouble for touching that was inappropriate (See: Ontario College of Teachers periodical entitled *Professionally Speaking* – Blue Pages – Disciplinary section.). The topic is something I had not given much thought to until I began teaching. I asked myself what I would do if an allegation was launched against me. It scared me so I recall keeping my hands off and even in my pockets to avoid such an allegation. As I gained experience, I relaxed my attitude and even got to the point where touching was not a big issue anymore for me as an educator. I found that many elementary students would hug or climb on you, and the older elementary would high five, pat you on the back, and touch you in a playful manner (flip your hat off or step on your toes in jest). Touch at the elementary level is an important part of building a healthy relationship with students. In fact most education acts use the phrase '*In Loco Parentis*' which means in place of the parent, meaning you are the surrogate parent for each of your students when they are at school. This affects relationships, discipline (suspension, expulsion), and can be an area of confusion as we are now looking at each persons' definition of *parent* within the role of the *teacher*. A staff discussion of these roles would hopefully clear up much of the misunderstanding.

At the Secondary level touch was quite frequent when I coached sports and less so when I was in the class. My approach to touch was not to initiate it unless it was appropriate. For example, as a volleyball player scored an ace and came to the sideline, I would often pat him or her on the back or shake hands. Obviously, when we consider classroom management, touch should be a last resort in a conflict and only used to stop a student from hurting themselves, others, or you. Most education acts outline the duty of teachers to maintain good order yet this is usually via the creation of healthy learning environments, healthy relationships, and effective communications.

Touching is a science and some argue it is an art that has healing properties yet this is an area for another book. The communicative "aspects of touch are known as *haptics*. Touch has been called the most potent message in human communication" (Richmond & McCroskey, 1995, p. 13). In education, teachers see touch as both a good thing and an area of concern when the touch becomes harassment, abuse, or physical discipline. Teachers protect students in all situations by being friendly, professional, firm, consistent, aware, and informed. A teacher today must be informed of abuse (verbal or nonverbal) and harassment (sexual or other) since "teachers can be held liable for physical abuse . . . 75% of teacher abuse cases involve corporal punishment. Students who are hit, spanked, or restrained excessively by teachers can file charges against teachers for causing bodily harm or emotional abuse" (Feilstein & Phelps, 2001, p. 362). Your best approach is to avoid situations where you may be subject to allegations, so do not work in any room with only one student. Always detain two students so that you have a witness and keep the standards of practice in mind at all times.

Chapter 8

Verbal Communication

Learning the Language

To develop a positive classroom atmosphere each teacher uniquely models expected behaviors. Teachers communicate these classroom and school standards using their nonverbal channel first, as we have just learned in Chapter 7. In this chapter, we address a teacher's second means to communicate via the verbal channel and verbalization.

Each day, a teacher sends thousands of messages, both intended and unintended, to students, peers, and the school community. Effective teacher communication requires each teacher to monitor the communication process to ensure we are getting the responses we hope for when we speak or gesture. However, we can *demand*, *request*, *repeat* ourselves, and *make appeals* to students so frequently that it causes us to look for more efficient alternative means of communication and this is why professional development is so important throughout a teacher's career as new research and theory can be used to make improvements in all areas of education.

Teachers today verbalize to provide *feedback*, *motivate*, *question*, *instruct*, *manage,* and *encourage* communication with students, peers, and the school community. Communication is a craft that requires all of the nine multiple intelligences – musical, bodily-kinesthetic, logical-mathematical, verbal-linguistic, visual-spatial, interpersonal, intrapersonal, naturalistic, and spiritual. However, it is the *verbal-linguistic intelligence* that is fundamental to a teacher's success. Teachers are required to use words, actions and language in spoken and written tasks as they interact with students, staff, and the school community each day.

> An interactive communication process invites dialogue and clarification and helps ensure the message sent is the message received. You understand the importance of two-way communication when you see quizzical looks, dejected faces, blank stares, and other signs of distress on your students' faces! Taking time to read and respond to these visible signs of

> miscommunication lessens discouragement and confusion for the students and the teacher. (Goethals, Howard, Sanders, 2004, p. 78)

To be a good communicator requires speaking skills; some of our best public speakers are recognized in competition due to their clarity, enunciation, and smoothness of expression while sending quality messages. The top speakers produce emotional responses within listeners and they get attention. A teacher needs to be a good speaker who can establish a connection with people (rapport) because, "underlying all effective relationships is rapport – a feeling of harmony and connection that leads to positive outcomes. Rapport is established by mutual respect, trust, and open communication. Underlying all relationships characterized by rapport is the notion of respect" (Feilstein & Phelps, 2001, p. 67). Respect can be shown by listening with both our eyes and our ears (attending behavior), by thinking about the words you hear, and the nonverbal behavior you see. These two channels provide clues to the emotional tone of the message so attending requires you to listen with your heart (emotional message). For instance, if someone swears, you can decode the message by listening for pitch, intensity, and tone. Think of your own expletive when you are frustrated and how you might say it. Do tone, pitch, and intensity change when you are tired, angry, frightened, sad, or overwhelmed? Listeners learn a lot from your nonverbal behavior as it *supports* the verbal message.

Language

Language is symbolic, governed by rules (semantics, syntax), and instills meaning and images within the minds of listeners. The images you create in the minds of students can be enhanced or diminished depending upon your verbal and nonverbal communicative impact. Miscommunication happens as one word may mean many different things to many people due to their backgrounds. So, a teacher who says simply, "complete a *short* journal entry," will get multiple products from a class. Show what you mean and give detailed information to create the image you are looking for (exemplar). Teachers use emotive language that denotes (objectively describes) and connotes (emotive description). For instance, describing the act of smoking objectively appears to be a scientific stance yet using emotive language can communicate your personal attitude towards smoking and this may enhance or diminish your message. Martin, Sugarman, & McNamara, (2000) explain: "The two most important ingredients of effective communication in the classroom are a teacher's own self-discipline, and a teacher's communication style. The former emphasizes the personal and interpersonal maturity of the teacher, while the latter emphasizes the interpersonal manner of the teacher" (p.23).

You teach who you are and the perceptive students will react accordingly. As well, language in the classroom needs to be *nonsexist*, often objective, and not too abstract. For instance, I recall talking to my grade 10 class about the office of the Prime Minister and how important this was. However, it was not until I mentioned the person's name that they were fully aware of my topic, as most of my class did not identify with my message. I was speaking too abstractly and from an adult perspective that was informed via years of experience and travel.

Questioning

Questions play a central role in teaching. Asking the wrong question may cause students to be defensive. Coming upon students who are off-task, you could ask, "What are you doing?" However, this question may just lead to student defensiveness and resentment. A better question would be, "What should you be doing?" This recognizes the student is off-task and needs to be prompted to get back on task. I have realized over the years that this alternative question gets results. Questions can be a means of intervention, a means to manage a student, students, or an entire assembly. I can ask, "Why do we *walk* down the hall?" I know the answer yet I want to raise the awareness within the student so I ask this question. Asking a question can be a means of redirection and it involves the teacher's message, verbal and nonverbal, which can interrupt inappropriate behavior and prompt students to engage in appropriate behavior. Think of a question you could ask for each of the following situations:

1. Student is talking when you are explaining something to the class.
2. Student is making tapping noises during a video.
3. Student is about to throw a snowball.
4. Student asks you a personal question.
5. Student makes a homophobic remark to another student.

Your questioning is a controlling tool, a lever to be used as necessary to raise awareness within the person who is being questioned. If you can send a clear and easily understood question to a student, this will increase the likelihood of success for that student. For every successful interaction you have with a student, the more social reinforcement (positive rapport) is realized and the interaction can extinguish inappropriate behavior. **Extinction** is a strategy in which *the positive reinforcers maintaining a behavior are withheld, terminated, or diminished, resulting in a reduction of the behavior to pre-reinforcement levels.* You need to be aware of behavior frequency and duration before your intervention and track the behavior while offering necessary reinforcement (negative/positive). Much of the extinction process can be facilitated via questioning and statements such as, "What should you be doing? Now lets get back to work!" If this is not for you, consider the following common elements.

Effective questioning in a classroom involves ten key elements.

1. Consider the **clarity** and conciseness of the question;
2. Higher Order Question (evaluative, synthesis, analysis);
3. Question is **connected** to lesson;
4. Question **stimulates** thought (provocative);
5. Social **reinforcement** follows (positive teacher response);
6. Question **encourages** and **motivates** students to respond;
7. Teacher provides enough **wait time** (thinking time: 5+ seconds);
8. **Alternative** (secondary questions) probes are supplied to broaden, deepen, prompt and **cue responses**;
9. Questions are **open** to all students; and
10. Students know how to **respond** (hand up, quiet, eye contact, clear voice).

If you are able to complete these actions in your class, you still may find that you do not understand the answer given. Naturally, you ask a supplementary question to try to understand or place the first response. A student, upon answering the second question, may reveal that they really do not understand, in which case you need to be supportive and not critical or sarcastic (negative reinforcement) as this will only create uncomfortable stress for the student. In the past, during wait time, I have suggested to the student that I will come back to hear from that student. I am attempting to shield the student from discomfort yet by coming back later, there is still a chance for positive reinforcement (Skinner's behaviorism). In summary, teachers' questions need to encourage students to respond and supplemental questions are there to uncover additional information. A teachers who carefully listens to the answers is then in a position to respond and draw out further information by asking tertiary questions that cause students to respond further. A final point in the interaction between student and teacher would be the alternative level in which we want students to look for alternative answers, possibilities, and remedies to the question posed.

Humor

Language is a perfect tool for intervention as the right word or phrase can deflate a negative situation immediately. Think of your favorite comedian and how he/she uses words, accent, nonverbal expressions, and sounds to create laughter. Consider your favorite comedic movie and how the language can change the way you feel. It is a powerful and useful tool to build rapport. Most of us would like to be with people who make us laugh, so if you can humor your class, you may create many fans and that may work for you. Be tactful and cautious so you do not make a joke at someone's expense.

Peer Reinforcement

This technique uses peer pressure and social reinforcement to stir a positive ripple effect in the classroom. I like to address the situation first and not make it a personal attack when I see someone not doing as they should. I will draw attention to the good things other students are doing in both nonverbal and verbal ways. Praise a fellow peer for being quiet, on-task, or ready to work ("Good Job," "Perfect," "Best one yet."). Add the student's name ("Excellent work, Pat.") so the target of the praise is clear to the peer you are trying to cue. A pat on the back of a fellow peer, high five, or thumbs-up might be called for in some contexts. It causes the other students to look and see who is getting the social reinforcement. Lastly, it is important to be consistent when giving positive reinforcement. Your actions demonstrate equity, predictable behavior (trust is built upon this trait), responsibility, and may even teach positive behaviors.

Feedback

Teachers are required to respond and the feedback is an opportunity to reinforce behavior.

> [Feedback is there to] give students specific information about their performance at scheduled times and within reasonable

> timeframes. There are several ways and means to encourage positive classroom behaviour, for instance, creating positive rules with the class, using positive reinforcement regularly, and adding novelty such as a classroom lottery, game or contest. Teachers can also, select reinforcers following a survey of reinforcement (what students perceive as positive). Teachers can use reinforcement contracts and encourage self-management by coaching the student and setting up unique communicative signals such as a teacher wink, nod or gesture. Teacher feedback should be frequent and as close to the task as possible. (Feilstein & Phelps, 2001, p. 219).

Feedback can be positive and it can be negative. Take, for example, these guidelines when you verbally reprimand a student:

- Do not verbally reprimand in front of peers (loss of dignity);
- Respond immediately to the behavior (quick connect);
- Keep it short and to the point (no philosophy);
- Solicit information from student (what); and
- Conclude with discussion (teacher listens).

You cannot use sarcasm and must try not to judge while objectively describing your perception of the observation. Address only one student behavior item at a time, even though you are aware of the many that need attention, and always end with a positive note, something to build on.

Feedback that is in the form of praise builds positive rapport and as Stipek (1998) points out, there are 12 guidelines for offering effective praise.

> Effective Praise
>
> 1. Is delivered contingently.
> 2. Specifies the particulars of the accomplishment.
> 3. Shows spontaneity, variety, and other signs of credibility; suggests clear attention to the student's accomplishment.
> 4. Rewards attainment of specified performance criteria (which can include effort criteria).
> 5. Provides information to students about competence or the value of their accomplishments.
> 6. Orients students toward better appreciation of their own task-related behaviour and thinking about problem solving.

7. Uses students' own prior accomplishments as the context for describing present accomplishments.
8. Is given recognition of noteworthy effort or success at difficult (for this student) tasks.
9. Attributes success to effort and ability, implying that similar successes can be expected in the future.
10. Fosters endogenous attributions (students believe that they expend effort on the task because they enjoy the task and/or want to develop task-relevant skills).
11. Focuses students' attention on their own task-relevant skills).
12. Fosters appreciation of and desirable attributions about task-relevant behaviour after the process is completed.

(Stipek, 1998, p.36)

Conversely, the absence of any of these actions may render praise ineffective. Your feedback is offered after you analyze the student response and your feedback is both a personal comment and a professional response to a student. Teachers can use these discussions to build their assessment (gather data). These discussions lead to report card comments or could be offered as evidence during future conversations with administration and parents. It is up to you to document on a regular basis in order to construct an accurate (valid) record.

Instruction

Discipline/*disciplino*; the latin root actually means to instruct. This is the time you need to be "on," prepared, organized, calm, inspiring, energetic, and sharp because there is no second chance to make a good first impression. Each day, period, unit, or subject is a new beginning. As you interact, you put into practice what you have planned. It is as if you are marketing something: you sell your audience on the idea, topic, or task in order to motivate action. A trial and error process never catches everyone so you end up selecting strategies that work with most students. Teachers must engage all learners regardless of culture, economics, or learning styles. You need to have a menu of instructional modes in order to discipline and instruct your class. Still, the best plans can fail to meet your expectations and this is when your need to reflect upon the Antecedent-Behavior-Consequences sequence that is present within everything we do. For instance, it is commonplace for teachers to observe a student and list the events that happen before and after a particular behavior. This contextual information is vital to understand and further examine the connections. To review, the **Antecedents** are the elements that precede the behavior, **Behavior** is the trait we are interested in (i.e., speaking out) and **Consequences** refer to what happens following the behavior (i.e., class laughs). Being aware of this a teacher can then examine the **ABC**s to develop and identify strategies for either decreasing or increasing the student's behavior.

Direct Instruction

You can choose to address the class as a whole group (whole-group instruction/direct teaching); however, a teacher needs to be aware of the *duration* of the address and the *timing* of the same as this can mean success or failure if the teacher misreads the audience. First, you need to command attention via the signal: hand-up, lights on/off, count down from five, shout for quiet, or clap your hands. You decide what is good for you. You want to train the students to respond the same way players respond to a whistle in a sports match. They stop, look, and listen. You may need to verbally prompt one or two students who want to go on doing their own thing. I would say, "Devon, I need you to stop what you are doing and listen." Be positive and if the student ignores you, move onto your lesson and come back to that student in a few minutes when all are working for a one-on-one discrete conference. The student may be off in another world and unaware of the magnitude of what just occurred.

Direct teaching/instruction requires you to explain, show, present, distribute work, and manage as you are the centre of attention. Using this teacher-centred approach, you follow your own highly detailed plan (script). This is not a new approach or strategy, nor is it the only choice of instructional mode. It is, however, a mode of instruction that is quite entrenched. The Association for Direct Instruction (http://www.adihome.org/phpshop/members.php). defines it as a system based on Zig Engelmann's theory that children can learn at an accelerated rate if educators can deliver instructions that are clear, are able to predict likely misinterpretations, and thereby reduce confusion, and assist in forming generalizations. In addition, it is pointed out that G.P. O'Neill, in the *Canadian Journal of Education* (1988, Vol. 8), reviewed 150 past studies and concluded that **Direct Instruction** is correlated with improved learning among primary children from working and middle class backgrounds – a conclusion supported by almost every relevant study on the topic. Likewise, a 1987 U.S. Department of Education booklet, *What Works: Research about Teaching and Learning*, concludes that direct instruction enables students to learn more, especially in conjunction with well-designed homework assignments. (Lindsay, 2004)

All teachers use direct instruction at some point and it is something that does get results; however, if your teacher-centred approach is not yielding the results you want there are alternatives such student-centred teaching (Piaget) and indirect instruction (nondirective teaching, Vygotsky).

Indirect Instruction

The nondirective (student-centred) approach grew out of the work of Carl Rogers who was a counsellor using nondirective counselling; that is, he wanted to ignite curiosity and let students use their *own* motivation to explore and discover their world. In education, nondirective (student-centred) teachers are in the class early in order to talk with students and they leave late so that they can be accessible. Not only are these teachers available before class they are available after class to facilitate communication, problem solve, and build rapport. Your nonverbal *receptive* attitude (demeanor) is important as students need to perceive this as positive. As a student-centred teacher, you go looking for feedback from students by asking for their opinion, suggestions, and evaluations (survey, Q/A). Student-teacher relationships require effective communication, so any technique that encourages students to communicate will help build rapport.

It is important that students feel valued (social reinforcement) if they are asked for their comments. Most students need slight encouragement; however, vigorous requests of student input will advance associations with the less at ease (shy) student. Teachers can encourage student communication by requesting it in writing (journal, comment cards), visual (video), audio (tape recording), or spoken word (1:1 meetings). It is possible to be a demanding teacher and still have positive rapport with students. The key is not to be too aggressive or autocratic. As John Dewey wrote (1933), we need democratic schooling that is progressive and thought-provoking. As an indirect instructive teacher, you plan to use words cautiously; you suggest, imply, and provoke responses rather than ordering or directing students. You understand that human communication includes many subtleties within, and outside of, the language that can influence the relationships within the classroom. We want to build a team and not promote sabotage or mutiny in any small or large way.

Constructivist

The approach has roots that stretch back to Piaget, Vygotsky, and Bruner who realized, through cognitive research, a schematic-construct related means to instruct. This mode can be realized through a **constructivist approach** one that "*encourages learners to make sense of their world through taking an active role in acquiring, building, and understanding meaning and knowledge in social contexts*" [emphasis added] (Naested, Potvin, & Waldron, 2004, p. 329). We do this because constructivists believe that transmission of knowledge from the mind of one person (teacher) to the other mind (student) is not an accurate depiction of what is really going on. In fact, constructivists believe that new knowledge must be deconstructed and then rebuilt so that it fits in with existing knowledge of the learner. So, a lecture on the danger of fire may not be the learning tool required; however, building a campfire on the weekend may teach the student far more. This new knowledge is then organized into a mind-map called a schema (schemata). Knowing this may help the teacher teach, cause communication to change, or it may change the plans of teacher.

Cooperative Instruction

Naested, Potvin, & Waldron (2004) suggest "cooperative instruction is a learner-focused instructional process in which small, selected groups of three to five individuals work together on a well defined learning task for the purpose of increasing mastery and/or understanding of course content"(p. 329). I have used this mode in many classes at all levels and have enjoyed the results.

Jigsaw

Once you have groups of students orchestrated (for example six per group) – and I do mean *carefully* prepared groupings given the personalities of each group member – you can proceed to hand out the task to each group. Each member is then assigned a number from one to six. One member from each group teaches/leads the others (train the trainers) and when each group member has learned the task they can leave their group to reform another group: put all ones together, all twos together, and so on until all are reassigned in new groups. The new group has only one member from each of the previous groups. The new group is then taught what each member has to offer (skill, process, and product).

You can add order by assigning time limits and overseeing group dynamics and behavior.

Squads

Groups complete learning, take tests, and scores go towards squad (group) points – borrowed from the Physical Education curriculum.

Learning Circuit

Sometimes called *Centres*, as found in most kindergartens, these workstations provide different tools and tasks for student learning.

Pair work

Partners can lead, give peer evaluation, and motivate others (peer-helper). Having a policy explained and noted on the walls of a classroom can save many teachers from repeating themselves. One I have used relates well to the idea of pair work. My sign reads, “When you are finished your work you become a peer-helper.” The first student to finish comes to me and I mark the work. After that point, the person who has their work corrected becomes a peer-marker. The helping multiplies until all have completed the task and all assignments are marked. Some problems will arise but it is a policy that has largely worked over the years.

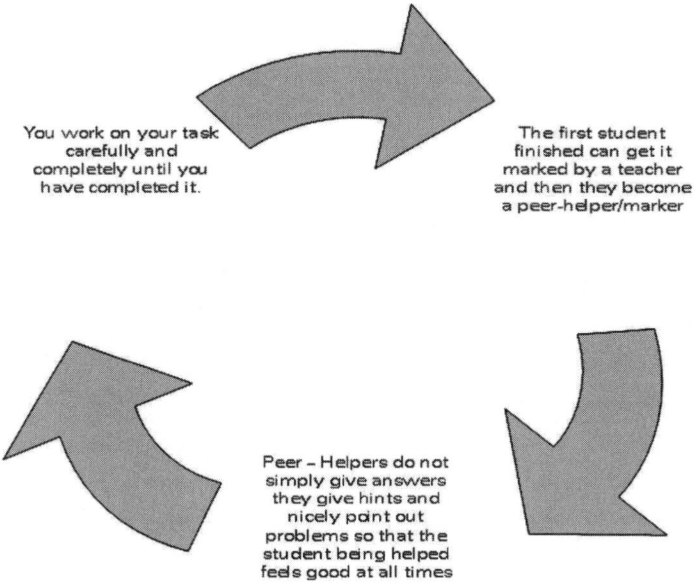

Figure 4. The peer support system continues until all students have completed the assignment.

Chapter 9

365 Days of Teaching

The Numbers

A school year traditionally lasts from September until June which is ten months. That's two months shy of a full year and if you eliminate holidays and weekends, we end up with about 190 teaching days, give or take a few days. Within these 190 days of school, we must squeeze in a tremendous amount of curricula, teaching, coaching, and community activities, not to mention the other 476 items that need to be attended to during the year. As you gain experience in education, you learn to prioritize and invest your time efficiently. From this 190 days of teaching, eliminate five to ten special event days, a few winter weather days, and you will probably miss a few days due to illness, professional development, coaching, or special education duties depending on your level (secondary or elementary). You will be left with 175 days to cover all of the expectations. Do not dwell on this fact – just push it to the back of your subconscious in order to cope.

Unfortunately, Professional Development has steadily diminished over the years and class-size has increased. Yet, to a new teacher, your first year will be the *norm* so that much of what I have just stated may seem somewhat uninteresting or not applicable to your situation. However, with very little professional development (seminars, conference time, on-the-job-training) this can be a problem or it can be just another challenge – it depends on how you frame it. I view it as a challenge; one that can be met and overcome each year. I have found that I need at least ten classroom management modes (I will explain later) to keep the students focused, motivated, and self-managed. As well, there are some actions that I take each year that seem to meet my expectations and hopefully these same steps will serve you well.

I started teaching in 1985 after completing my B.Ed. that year, and I honestly was not ready to teach. I wondered, "What is teaching?" Levin & Nolan (2004) define teaching as "the use of preplanned behaviors, founded in learning principles and child development theory and directed toward both instructional delivery and classroom management, that increase the probability of affecting a positive change in student behavior" (p. 4). For a new teacher, a definition of this complexity is not comforting; it merely serves up more angst. I believe that feeling anxious about teaching is a good thing since this state can energize you to become more aware, prepared, and sincere. I recall thinking to myself in 1985 that I was able, skilled, and qualified; however, I felt I needed more lessons. I *did* get these lessons – though they came on the job and not in the safety of a university classroom.

I recall being offered a job following an interview and signing my contract at the Board office. I was officially on probation. This is just what the new teacher needs – the stress of being on *probation*. I thought you had to be found guilty in the courts to be on probation. In addition to probation, most of us had large student loans, new teaching responsibilities, and now we needed to move and find new residences with little money. It didn't seem fair since we had proved ourselves repeatedly; we had to prove ourselves again for at least ten months. We need not have worried as much as we did since most of us were hired following the probationary period, and we signed permanent teachers' contracts. This time of probation can deflate even the most energetic, prepared, and likable teachers. Even the Ontario College of Teachers (2004) found that according to their survey of first and second year teachers:

- More than half of new teachers are hired after school starts in September;
- One in five are asked to teach subjects they haven't been trained to teach; and
- Almost one in five is at risk of leaving teaching altogether early in their career.

If we lived in an ideal world, you would finish your B.Ed. and find the job you want, in the location you want, have no debt, and have lots of time to prepare. It probably will not happen that way for you and if it does not, be positive and smile (enduring teacher trait). Each one of these elements (stressors) can affect your classroom management and probably will.

The Informed New Teacher

Most provisions in Education can be traced back to The Canadian Charter of Rights and Freedoms, and the various provincial Human Rights Codes. To manage your class make sure you are aware of provincial policy (curricular), documents, and laws (Education Act, regulations and memos) that guide teachers and others in education. Your union websites will provide you with the newest guidelines, information, and hot topics. Visit your Ministry of Education websites to locate the code of conduct which details the roles of all stakeholders including you. For example, in Ontario there is an Ontario Code of Conduct which states,

> **Teachers and School staff**, under the leadership of their principals, maintain order in the school and are expected to hold everyone to the highest standard of respectful and responsible behaviour. As role models, staff uphold these high standards when they:
>
> - help students work to their full potential and develop their self-worth;
> - communicate regularly and meaningfully with parents;
> - maintain consistent standards of behaviour for all students;
> - demonstrate respect for all students, staff and parents;
> - prepare students for the full responsibilities of citizenship.
>
> (Ontario Ministry of Education, 2004)

Within this document, we read about standards and what is not up to standard; however, it becomes your call as soon as you are hired and this is why you need to discuss standards of behavior at your second meeting with school administration. Why not suggest the whole first staff meeting be about the code and its inherent standards? Your first staff meeting should consider the following *Standards of Behavior:*

> **All school members in Ontario must:**
>
> 1. **respect** and **comply** with all applicable federal, provincial, and municipal laws;
> 2. demonstrate **honesty** and **integrity**;
> 3. **respect** differences in people, their ideas, and opinions; (tolerance)
> 4. treat one another with **dignity** and respect at all times, and especially when there is disagreement;

5. respect and treat others **fairly**, regardless of their race, ancestry, place of origin, colour, ethnic origin, citizenship, religion, gender, sexual orientation, age or disability;
6. respect the **rights** of others;
7. show proper **care** and **regard** for school property and the property of others;
8. take appropriate measures to **help** those in need;
9. respect persons who are in a position of **authority**;
10. respect the need of others to work in an environment of learning and teaching.

(Ontario Ministry of Education, 2004)

We expect students to be respectful, honest, fair, caring, helpful people who embrace differences and respect authority, and we teach this by example. This ideal person is in each one of us yet with the pressures from political, personal, and professional elements, even a teacher can find it difficult to achieve this ideal every day. If a person is not all of these things, we need a system that is realistic, forgiving, and meditative.

Another area of concern for all stakeholders is safe schools. The province of Ontario has put forward an act (*Safe Schools Act*) to deal with this.

The Board, Your School, and the Community

When you secure your teaching position, you need to know where everything is and what may be expected of you, so take some time to visit the Board's web page, prior to your physical arrival at the school. Following this cyber visitation, head down the road to your school and get accustomed to your class, or the classroom in which you will teach.

Community contacts are important and will help you to build an identity for yourself with key members/leaders in the local community. To be involved is to be informed and it keeps you aware of current issues and political activity in your area. An additional step is to be involved with a school council as a staff representative. However, it may be best to wait until your fourth or fifth year to get in this deep. The school council can be very taxing and time consuming depending upon the issues.

School

Once inside you need to proceed to the office and begin to form a good relationship with the lead/head secretary as they essentially run the school and have the most information. Of course, if the head secretary is also new, talk to the person with the most seniority who will explain the school's history and evolution to this point. Find the *School Parents Manual* and calendar and read these carefully (they can often be found online as well). The parents' handbook illuminates the information the parents are getting. You need to be aware of this because they may call you or want to speak in person to discuss some aspect of the handbook with you. Also, locate the Board policy manual and study it. It may be online by now but in any case, if you do encounter head lice or pinkeye there are policies on them you will need to learn.

Locate the student records at your school and ask the head secretary about the protocol for access as some schools have unique policy. Take some time to read about each one of your students. Make notes and find your Ministry of Education website at http://www.edu.gov.on.ca. It would be ideal to do this before you begin your school year to uncover which students are identified exceptional, who has medical conditions (alerts), or who has custody orders or access papers on file. The student record reveals valuable information. Some educators may say this is not necessary; however, only you know what will put your mind at ease when it comes to being prepared to teach.

The Custodian

The Custodial staff at your school is vital in the scheme of things. They can inform you of policy concerning fire regulations and other safety issues which affect your room arrangement. For instance, the use of extension cords is detailed in government policy and the custodian usually can tell you what can be on the walls and what should not. They can tell you where or how you can get School Board furniture and/or where to put furniture. They can clean anything for you and will clean your room at some point. They often make repairs (even pencil sharpeners) and you can arrange to have them place on your desk certain items they sweep up during the evenings so you can recycle (pencils, pens, erasers). When it comes to room arrangement, which is very important in classroom management, you may need to eliminate current, or get hold of alternative, types of furniture. The custodian may be helpful.

Furniture, Decor, Tone, and Classroom Management

This is really an element of nonverbal communications and I have ten desk arrangements (seating plans) that have attached rationales. This would be a good action research project. Ask yourself, can classroom management be improved via arrangement of the furniture?

September

Rows. No two desks touch each other until you understand the tensions between certain students in the classroom community. I recommend this arrangement as individual behavior is easy to see and the organization of the desks sends a message. This is a high-energy month when people realize their own identity in this new context.

October

Pairs. Partners, critical friends, and peer-helpers can be arranged using this orchestration. Give some thought to who can help whom and who needs to be separated from whom and parental requests. It may be that a student will change once they are paired and we hope it is for the better but only time will tell. The last day of the month turns into 'Hell Week' but if you meet that energy with your own (dress up for Halloween), you tend not to notice it. *Booo!*

November

Triads can be useful to employ certain instructional strategies such as role plays and problem solving tasks as long as you are clear, define student roles, provide adequate time, and are available to mediate when interpersonal turbulence is encountered. Remembrance day sets the tone for this month as energy levels are leveling out and generally are calm.

December

Varied. This is a challenging month with the anticipation of holidays. I generally reduce the amount of content expectations and make my tasks eclectic by having them work *individually*, in *pairs,* or in *groups of three*. Once they have mastered this working arrangement, and many have by this point, we can move on to *quads*.

January

Quads. A return from a break and holidays means a reintroduction of the rules, guidelines, and protocols. The energy is quite good in January and I find working in quads works well. "Build a snowman" competition is a fitting festive event at any level with any class as it is interdisciplinary.

February + March

Farch – my term for the feelings I have during this time of the year and the emotional tone in my classes. Farch requires unique classroom furniture arrangements such as the *circle*, the *horseshoe,* or the *T*. With Valentines day, some silliness before and after the 14th can be problematic if you are not prepared for it. Take the pulse of your class daily and try to complement it. Discuss the history of valentines, reflect on you experiences, speak in emotional terms, and address it as it can be fun.

April

Groups. April is generally all wet and yet the energy levels are high again as some eager souls wear sandals and shorts. I counter with small group tasks and limit the size of the groups to no more than six. Performance assessments work well as groups make presentations and your marking is less frequent as you assign peer and self-evaluation tasks.

May + June

Two things generally happen as the students know what is expected of them, when, where, and to what extent. I ask them to arrange the class as they would like and abandon the seating plan for May. June is really the opposite so I often go back to rows to keep a lid on things. June is high energy and silly things do happen as the students who have been together for nine months have changed so much together that new tensions appear so watch for this.

If you would like to have plants in your room ask each student to bring in their own plant and label it. It can be a project. This worked well in a Secondary homeroom I had and also within the elementary level.

As a rotary secondary teacher you travel so your rooms are less appealing and some items you put up go missing. There will be vandalism when no one is supposed to be in the room but a few students who shouldn't be there, are.

At the elementary level, you may be able to claim a room and be in that room all day (hopefully not all night too). I have placed a couch and a big old chair in the corner to make the area more comfortable. I have brought in rugs, tossed others, and hung just about anything – found, purchased, or thrown out – on my walls to decorate, provoke thought, and stimulate students. I have had nature rooms, animal rooms, science rooms, artsy rooms, drama rooms, and theme rooms of any description. I have been known to let the students decorate so I begin in September with a barren room and they do it for us.

Duty Schedule – Your Supervision

Try to get your duty (supervision schedule) before Day One and try to meet all staff before students arrive in September, as this is a more relaxed portion of the year. You may want to talk about the school, students, or professional issues. Meet the Administration as they are generally the first to arrive each year and each day, as well as the last to leave. Ask about the duty schedule and how they would like you to be on duty (supervision). Are there areas of concern on the grounds and issues of which you need to be aware? This will ease your angst somewhat and give you an understanding of what is expected. "Be seen and be heard" is the motto. Be firm, fair, and calm on duty and know when to urge people to move along in halls, areas of concern, and washrooms. What is *in-bounds* and what is *out-of-bounds* during certain times of the day? Check online for schools with posted supervision schedules for an example of what you can expect.

Day One – Entry Plan

You only have one chance to make a good first impression as do your students. Ask yourself, do I understand this school and the community? Do I understand the needs of each student in this new class? Having a group activity ready allows you to meet with your students individually. For example, a game of baseball, a checkers tournament, a tic-tac-toe tournament, or board games can be run by students while you chat with each student. You need to assert yourself but do not be too aggressive. Think rapport, rapport, rapport. Build bridges, allies, and look for supports. What would make you comfortable? Each day spend some time working on rapport as communication reduces fear and angst, and promotes understanding.

Most teachers plan chronologically, and gradually end up planning like most other teachers in a particular school due to timetable realities, sports, bussing, and peer pressure. Having a means to diffuse tension leads many teachers to opt for games, competitions, and academic challenges. The internet is constantly enlarging and the number of good web sites dealing with a day one entry plan has as well. A search online for "day one," "first day," or "teaching tips" may generate some useful sites containing ideas you'd like to try.

Rules

There are regulations at every level of society and we need to develop classroom rules (values to laws) that complement not only the Board policy, school culture, and the community, but also have rules that empower. Day One, I have students make up the rules (submissions) and later I bring back a synthesis. Often I hear the question, "Why is it important for students to be involved in creating the rules for the classroom?" We need to do this for several reasons; the process leads to and demonstrates the following:

- Student empowerment (we made these);
- Shows respect for students (we observe and follow);
- Encourages professionalism (reminds and becomes habitual);
- Order, details consequences (structural classroom community);
- Builds leadership (leaders assume roles and followers observe);
- Encourages responsibility (self and shared);
- Promotes and facilitates logical thinking and problem solving; and
- Supports and fosters classroom equity (democracy).

The process usually leads to five simple rules: (1) we keep our *hands to ourselves*, (2) we are *honest*, (3) we are *nice to each other*, (4) we are *not silly*, and (5) we use our *manners*. I frame each future situation using these underlined words and I usually communicate effectively since the words are well known and understood once I explain them on Day Two. Always address the context and if necessary suggest that the observed behavior was silly and not the person. I try to help the person (teachable moments) and not make them feel bad when a problem arises and they appreciate this approach.

Activity

Build your reputation, you need to ask all stakeholders many questions, as the status quo does not look for new teachers usually. Get involved wherever you can.

Clubs

Join the associations that interest you and if nothing existing does, then start a club for students who share your passion – how about a *philatelist* club? I have started clubs solely to improve the rapport with just one student, even though in one particular case, I had no personal interest in snowmobiling!

Classroom Management

What is classroom management and do the people who supervise you (pre-service or in-service) have a definition? If they do, you need to know what it is because two competing definitions may lead to confusion in your workplace if a school leader sees it one way and you see it another. Let's look at a few definitions.

Classroom management involves, "the techniques a teacher uses to create a positive learning environment, which includes classroom control, discipline, and governance" (Naested, Potvin & Waldron, 2004, p. 328). Feilstein and Phelps (2001) suggest classroom management involves "teacher decisions and actions intended to create an environment conducive to learning" (p. 458). Classroom management is a system, a discipline, and a means to instruct. It is a system because it requires a number of micro-systems to build community via planned instruction and management. Classroom management is discipline because it requires the establishment and maintenance of control, and consequences await those who are undisciplined (self-control, personal management). It then follows that classroom management is instruction since both a system and the required discipline need to be taught through on-going instruction.

Also, we need to keep in mind that students are responsible for their behavior at all times and the *Education Act* actually details the students' responsibilities. The students must cooperate and work within our system. However, there are a number of self-management points that need to be raised before we look at classroom models. Students can self-manage. You may need to supply a few self-management interventions such as,

1. Self-recording'(Every time you talk put a check on this sheet of paper this period.);
2. Self-reinforcement (Each question you complete, give yourself a checkmark on this recording sheet.);
3. Self-managed Free-token Response-cost (Give yourself a sticker for each thank you and take away a sticker for each time you yell out an answer.);
4. Self-evaluation (Any task can use a self-evaluation grade.); and
5. Self-instruction (Self-talk through problems.).

Most students like the independence that comes with these **self-management interventions** and need only timely support to enable them to achieve success. As a teacher, you are a privileged observer who can study student behavior within a setting to realize what triggers (Antecedent) offending behavior. Teachers can then record the triggers and work to shape behavior – perhaps by asking for the desired behavior which can be modelled by peers. Your task is to maintain consequences for offending behavior just as we see in our society. Perhaps a chart, such as the one shown in the sample below, would help you sort the issues.

Most students when interviewed and coached, can be taught social skills to deal with triggers and the behavior is extinguished as students are empowered.

Setting	Antecedent (trigger)	Problem Behavior	Desired Behavior	Consequences
Gym	Name-calling	Hitting	Walk Away	Time Out

Figure 5. Sample of a Self-Management Intervention Chart, which can be used by teachers and students for effective behavior management.

Group Interventions

Group – Token (Economy) Response-Cost Scheme

Like our driving points system, each of us have so many points and if we break the rules of the road by speeding, failing to stop at a stop sign, or whatever, we usually lose some of our dollars and are issued demerit points. Keep up the bad behavior and you may find yourself walking. Similarly, your class can be given a fixed number of tokens. A token is removed each time a student member breaks a rule. If tokens remain at the end of the day (or period), a reward is given to the whole group (pizza party, free-time, computer time, or leave early).

Good Behavior Contest

Students are divided into groups (tribes, teams) and a scoreboard is made and posted. Inappropriate behavior by a team member is recorded or *scored.* League tables can be developed and maintained throughout the day, week, month, or year just as they do in the NHL. Standings could be sent home and posted and a trophy constructed for award. For a change, why not catch them being positive and reward, observe, and record only good behavior points?

Group Assessment/Evaluation

Forms are developed and given to each student in the group/class. Students rate their own, their peers', or other groups' behaviors. Establish a group rating system and compare ratings with yours. Points are earned and exchanged for reinforcers such as prizes – old toys students bring in, ones you buy at garage sales, or purchase at dollar stores.

Group Timeout (Prop)

A prop such as a can, flag, sign, or Teddy-bear Mascot, is positioned where all students can see it. The prop remains in place if students behave appropriately and the class earns tokens that can be exchanged for prizes or other rewards. If unsuitable behavior surfaces the prop is removed for a few minutes, during which the group loses the opportunity to earn tokens. As the class becomes familiar with the system, student leaders (captains) can assume responsibility for removing the prop and dispensing tokens – hopefully!

As a society, the token economy is used daily by big business as we carry cards and gather points for air miles, free stuff, and credit. This system can lead to brand or store loyalty; however, it also has a place in education as it prepares students for citizenship. If you do not follow rules, you are put in detention and not allowed to earn money and your freedom is severely reduced. Most young offender units use these powerful systems with a great deal of success and mostly everyone would like to get something for spending a dollar on a product or within a store.

Models, Strategies, Principles, and Theorists

We need to consider what other theorists, researchers, teachers, educators, and stakeholders have to say about classroom management. First, I believe classroom management is systematic (akin to action research). It is strategic (another action research element) in that a strategy is applied and all classroom management requires modelling. Traditionally, classroom management is embedded in rules, consequences, reinforcement, and community values, however, how these elements unfold is very much up to the adult in the classroom and the students within the system.

Model 1 – Assertive Discipline

Assertive discipline is a system (program) developed by Lee and Marlene Canter in the 1970s who told us that we (teachers) have professional rights (Ontario College of Teachers, Education Act) in our schools and all educators should expect appropriate student behavior. Students have the right to choose how to behave and educators need to set limits (rules) for inappropriate behavior. They explained that teachers need to assert themselves in classrooms by stating their expectations in a firm, clear voice and explain the limits (thresholds). Generally, this is where I tell students I will intervene if they are about to hurt themselves, other peers, or people in authority. Next, the Canters wanted educators to explain what the school and classroom consequences are (code of conduct: swear at teacher = suspension) and note how they will try to be consistent in applying the rules and consequences.

Model 2 – Democratic

Rudolf Dreikurs, a student of Alfred Adler (who was the founder of *individual psychology*), put forward several **effective teacher principles**. Dreikurs encouraged teachers to be democratic (Dewey), fair, firm, and friendly in the school. One of the goals is to empower students by having them develop and implement class rules thereby ensuring that all students are informed and aware of limits. Post rules and consequences and encourage peer pressure to follow the rules. Promote the family sense of belonging and encourage goal setting in order to develop feelings of fellowship, status, and recognition while ignoring some unwanted behaviors such as attention-getting, power-seeking, revenge, and social isolation.

Model 3 – Behaviorism

Even though B.F. Skinner never proposed a model of school or classroom discipline, he has had a tremendous impact on all school systems, teachers, and students due to his work with animals, behavior, and reinforcement. Others such as Dreikurs, William Glasser, and Haim Ginott have used Skinner's theory and developed **Behavior Modification** (B.Mod.) which teachers can use in all classrooms. To use B.Mod., identify the problem behavior to be modified and then make frequency and duration observations (baseline data) of the behavior, noting the context in which it occurs. Plan to positively reinforce, through positive consequences, the behavior you want to occur and when the behavior has reached the target level, gradually diminish the reinforcement randomly. The process has been called *shaping* and strengthens the desired behaviors. You can also negatively reinforce an undesirable behavior in order to reduce and extinguish it.

Model 4 – Choice Theory

William Glasser, throughout his career, has suggested that student failure and the school context was the root of problematic student behavior, and that students need to make better choices (*Choice Theory*). For instance, I can choose to skip my exam and fail the course, or I can choose to study. Glasser has further noted that students need to have fun, a sense of belonging, have freedom, and be empowered in order to be successful. An informed, democratic, and sensitive teacher can support and guide students to do the right things and Glasser also supports the family approach with class meetings and one-to-one discussion.

Model 5 – Withitness

Jacob S. Kounin concluded that the way in which a teacher reacts or handles maladaptive/misbehavior once it occurs is not critical; however, the key to successful classroom management is what teachers do to prevent management problems from occurring (precorrection/proactive). He came up with the term **ripple effect** (*behavioral dominoes*) and **withitness** (*awareness*) and teachers need to be aware of these factors at all times. Once you begin teaching, your challenge is to keep the teaching momentum going to avoid down time, pit stops, awkward transitions, and the like. Make sure each student is responsible and accountable for his or her actions.

Model 6 – Self-Discipline

From the 1990s, there emerged Alfie Kohn, who believes in no stickers, rewards, bribes, or grades. Instead, students need to be taught how to be responsible and respectful (social skills) as this meets their emotional needs. Kohn believes the goal of education is to help students realize that they can think, learn, act, and change things (confidence). Kohn explains that it is also human nature when children act aggressively, selfishly, or demonstrate empathy and generosity. Kohn adds,

> We are more caring than we give ourselves credit for, and . . . our generosity cannot be reduced to mere self-interest. Students are not receptacles to be filled with knowledge, or clay to be molded. They, like all of us, are active meaning-makers. So, we need rethink the use of lectures, worksheets, textbooks, and, for that matter, our preconceptions about what makes a good teacher. (www.alfiekohn.org/teaching/topics.htm)

Teachers need to develop curriculum with the students in mind, and not traditional educational norms. Also, students who were not graded at all did just as well on the proficiency exam as those who were. "Students interests may therefore help shape the curriculum and a growing facility with words and numbers derives from the process of finding answers to their own questions"

This model will be difficult to use for most teachers as many of the responsibilities which Kohn condemns are actions teachers *must* take as required by law (education act). The curricula is mandated and provided by the Ministry of education and the Board ensures via its administration that these documents are followed.

Model 7 – Child-Centred

Haim G. Ginott promoted a communications model and wrote best-seller books in the 1960s mostly for parents; however, teachers could adopt the elements. Teachers tried to send clear messages about the situation (context) and not the character of the student. Teachers would model expectations, teach students how to communicate feelings, how to empathize, and how to cooperate in the classroom and school community. Today we might describe Ginott's model as an emotional intelligence mode that would complement the multiple intelligence curricula. Ginott suggested that teacher-child communication should not blame, shame, accuse, ridicule, threaten, bribe, label, punish, preach, or moralize. Instead, teachers, parents, and other adults should express their angry feelings when a child does something wrong but without attacking the child's character. They should also acknowledge the child's feelings (emotional first aid). This model is quite similar to Alfie Kohn's model/approach.

These seven models, only superficially dealt with here, cover much of what is being done in schools today. We need only to observe ourselves in our classroom or school and label our action to discover what model we are using. I have found that I use bits and pieces of each model and all of these support learning efforts of both students and teachers. Your philosophy may tie into a little of each one and I believe no one model is better than another as they all have strengths. Create your own model and build from it.

Chapter 10

Effective Strategies

We learn by doing yet there is a need to study – away from the action – the theory behind the action. This *theoretical knowledge* helps us to interpret new situations and can guide us as we solve problems or dilemmas. Alternatively, *personal practical knowledge* is most useful when we are confronted with a problem that is familiar; for instance, the teacher in the classroom always seems to have a student who is out of line, rule breaking, or just off-task. A teacher can use personal practical knowledge in this familiar problematic situation. Conversely, a once-in-a-career crisis in the classroom demands that theoretical knowledge be called upon. For example, the student with a weapon threatening to hurt someone requires teacher action that may have been learned in theory (theoretical knowledge) but has yet to be used in practice.

A less traumatic experience that requires both theoretical knowledge and physical skill is a driving test which involves a practical component and a written exam. One is a performance assessment and the other a traditional written test. One supports the other and supplies the examiner with evidence to make a decision. Actually, there are three sources of data here if we include the examiner's opinion and evaluative position.

Scenarios

A few years ago, a game was released called "Scruples." In the game, points are scored based on how well players assess one another's responses to scenarios that question personal morals and societal mores. I used some of the scenarios from the game in the classroom to promote critical thinking about personal values, ethics, and morals. The discussions caused students to think about the **natural and logical consequences**. Students reflected upon societal issues and what was *right*, *good*, and *proper* ethical conduct. For example, a child leaves the house without a coat on and is cold. A natural consequence, "denoting the natural results of ill-advised acts" (Dreikurs, 1968, p. 63), is the physical discomfort of being cold. The logical consequences "are consequences that are arranged by teachers or other adults" (*Ibid.* p. 65).

Sometimes it is useful to draw the problem (*sociogram*) on paper to help you and others see how the issues and people relate within the studied context. This process works well with visual learners who have trouble sorting and visualizing words and related issues.

Student-Focused Scenarios

See code of conduct for province, Board, school, and consider your own classroom rules when reacting.

- A student swears at you;
- A student gives you the middle finger;
- A student refuses to work;
- A student pushes another student to the floor in your class;
- Two students continue to talk while you are talking to the class;
- A student repeatedly sharpens a pencil;
- A student calls out answers and does not raise his or her hand;
- A student makes a homophobic remark that is heard throughout the class; or
- A student is crying.

Teacher-Focused Scenarios

Next, consider the teacher behaviors – is there a problem?

- A teacher repeatedly yells at a student to sit down;
- A teacher refers to a student as a monkey;
- A teacher sends a student to the office for talking;
- A teacher interrupts a student who is answering;
- A teacher pushes a student down into their seat;
- A teacher asks a student where they live; or
- You see a male coach tap the buttocks of a female player in the hallway. What could happen next and if *you* did the above what could you or would you do next?

Common Scenarios

What do you do?

- You notice a student taking food (cafeteria, school store) without paying;
- You see a student taking a book out of the library without signing it out;
- You see students hugging and kissing at the back of the school;
- A student comes to class with no materials and smells like alcohol;
- A fellow teacher comes to school and smells like alcohol; or
- You see a student put a hunting knife in their locker.

Role Plays

- Two female students are making rude comments (name-calling) about another female student as she passes them in the hall. You hear this from your desk in your class. The next sound you hear is that of bodies falling to the ground and swearing. You hear other voices encouraging what you believe is a fight. What is your next move?
- You are supervising an exam (test, quiz) and you notice a student repeatedly looking at their wrist. So, you . . . ?
- You are in the office speaking to the Principal when another teacher rushes in with a student who has just struck another student repeatedly. The Principal begins to belittle the student in front of you and the other teacher to the point where the student begins to cry. What is your next move?
- You arrive back in your class from lunch supervision and notice your desk drawers are open and your trip money is missing. It is 1 p.m. and students are coming in. What are your next steps?
- Compose your own role-play with your group. Write out each person's role on paper and then rehearse. After several minutes of rehearsal, the roles can be acted out. Ask your audience for solutions, next steps, and paths to take.

Interventions, Problem Solving, and Mediation

Interventions are *strategies employed to redirect student behavior.* In earlier chapters, we learned about *nonverbal* and *verbal interventions* and in this chapter, we look at intervention via **problem solving** and **mediation**. Conflict resolution is the goal in our problem solving efforts and in combination with mediation can lead to enhanced classroom dynamics.

Problem Solving

Teaching and learning problem-solving strategies creates vital and creative thinking skills that address both the product (outcomes) and the processes in the classroom. Certain instructional strategies lend themselves to problem-solving lessons. For instance, debates increase intensity in a controlled arena of discussion. Interviews, research, role-play, simulations, questioning, moral dilemmas, and rehearsals expose students to each person's perceptions and perspectives. We know that when children work together and listen to the opinions of their peers, they become aware of individual differences. Being able to *listen* to others is a social skill that may need to be taught. Jean Piaget found that opportunities for becoming less egocentric are more common when children discuss things with each other because then they face the reality that not everyone has the same perspective on a situation. Psychologists have based most of their research in this area on Piaget's theory, and have examined children's performance on conservation tasks, working in pairs and individually. Several researchers have found that a child who is paired with a more advanced child were later able to solve conservation tasks at a higher level, while children who worked individually did not improve (Tudge & Caruso, 1989).

Within the classroom community, it is necessary to possess problem-solving skills that do not break classroom rules. If there is a dispute, the students need to know how to resolve the problem via acceptable means. In simple terms, teachers need to communicate three key elements,

1. Problem identification and clarification (fact finding, or "What just happened?");
2. Analysis of the information or data (multiple perspectives, or "How do you see it?"); and
3. Clear communication of the results (decisions understood: logical/natural consequences follow).

Mediation

Teacher and Peer

Mediation is *the process of a third party meeting with people who are in conflict and listening to each person's perspective in order to realize middle ground and remedies that are acceptable to both parties.* For instance, a dispute between students over a pencil can be dealt with when a third person (peer or teacher) sits down and listens to both positions. Each party is asked to propose a resolution and if the mediator negotiates a settlement that both accept, the students have been successful. Sometimes the mediator can impose a settlement in order to move the process forward, however, this can only be achieved when both disputants agree to this step.

Checklist for Mediation

Trained mediators follow a simple procedure, such as the model outlined below:

Part I. Introduction

1. Have participants introduce themselves.
2. Explain the mediator's role.
3. Explain the ground rules. An example of a good ground rule is: Respect each other.
4. Explain steps of mediation.
5. Ask for any questions before you begin.

Part II. Telling the Story

1. Both parties tell their side of the story to the mediator.
2. Summarize both parties' side of the story.
3. Make sure you understand the conflict.
4. Make sure the parties understand the conflict.

Part III. Identifying Facts and Feelings

1. Parties tell their side of the story to each other.
2. Bring out facts and feelings of what the parties say.
3. Have parties change roles.
4. Summarize the facts and feelings of both sides.

Part IV. Generating Options

1. Ask both parties how they can solve the problem.
2. Write down all solutions.
3. Check off only the solution(s) both parties can agree to.

Part V. Agreement

1. Use only the solutions that both parties agree to.
2. Write the contract up in parties' own words.
3. Everybody signs it.
4. Remember to thank the people for being there. (Trevaskis, 1994)

Lastly, a must-have resource for teachers who must deal with behavior in schools, buses, and on playgrounds is the 'PRIM' or *Pre-Referral Intervention Manual,* which can be located online using a standard search-engine.

Teacher Tactics

A list of Teacher Tactics to use when surface behaviors arise in your classroom – Plan, plot and proceed with caution.

Antiseptic bouncing

Offending student sent out of room

Authoritative Verbot

"NO!"

Chaining

Link desired behaviors

Conflict Outcomes/Approach

(Win:win),(Win:lose), (Lose:lose), (Lose:win)

Contracting

Sign to the terms laid out

Daily Report Card

See the positives every day

Direct appeal

Emotive language and use emotions

Dual Perceptions

Voice your perception and then ask for theirs

Humor to ease tension

Adopt a red clown nose in the heat of the moment

Hurdle Help

Get to the student before frustration sets in

Hypodermic Affection

Sudden positive attention

Interviews

Student/teacher or student/teacher/parent or teacher/parent

Limits

Tools, toys, boundaries, space

Modelling

Student observes you and follows

Peer Culture-Pressure

Counselling or pressure by peer-helper

Permission

It's OK to be angry or ?

Physical Restraint

Only when someone is bound to get hurt physically

Planned Ignoring

I didn't see that!

Premack Principle/Grandmother's Rule

Eat your veggies(-) and get dessert (+)

Proactive Interference

Distract student before behavior surfaces

Promise – Reward

Promise to give something in return for behavior

Proximity

Be at arms length

Punish/Threat

You will have to go to the back of the line if you continue

Relocate

Change seat of offender

Restructure

Go to back-up plan if mood of class sours

Shaping

Reinforce desired behavior

Sudden Interest

Ask student about themselves/activity completed

Target behaviors

Plan to get behavior to surface

Token Economy

Points for positive behaviors

Bibliography

Action Research International Journal (1997). Action research defined. "Action Research International Journal," 5 (2), p 32-34. Retrieved 24 November 2003 from [http://www.triangle.co.uk/ear/].

Adelman, C. & Carr, W. (1988). "Whatever happened to action research?" British Educational Research Association Annual Conference, University of East Anglia.

Adler, M. J. & Van Doran, C. (1972). *How to read a book.* Toronto, ON: Simon & Shuster.

Albert, L. (1989). *A teacher's guide to cooperative discipline: How to manage your classroom and promote self-esteem.* Circle Pines, MN: American Guidance Service.

Alberto, P. A., & Troutman, A. C. (1995). *Applied behavior analysis for teachers.* (4th ed.). New York: Merrill-Macmillan.

Altrichter, H., Posch, P. & Somekh, B. (1993). *Teachers investigate their work: An introduction to the methods of action research.* New York: Routledge.

American Psychological Association. (2002). Ethical principals of psychologists and code of conduct. *American Psychologist*, 57, 1060-1073.

Association for Direct Instruction (12 April 2004). Teachers' perceptions of direct instruction teaching. "Direct Instruction News." Retrieved 10 April 2004, from [http://www.adihome.org/phpshop/members.php].

Bailey, B. (1997). *There's gotta be a better way: Discipline that works!* Oviedo, FL: Loving Guidance, Inc.

Barnsley, J., & Ellis, D. (1987). *Action research for women's groups.* Vancouver, BC: Press Gang Printers.

Canadian Teachers' Federation (Fall, 2003). *HORIZONS*, 11. Canadian Teachers' Federation, Ottawa, ON.

Canter, L. (1990). *Back to school with Assertive Discipline: Grades 1-6.* Santa Monica, CA: Lee Canter & Associates.

Canter, L., & Canter, M. (1976). *Assertive Discipline: A take-charge approach for today's educator.* Los Angeles, CA: Canter & Associates.

Canter, L., & Canter, M. (1992). *Assertive Discipline: Positive behavior management for today's classroom.* Santa Monica, CA: Lee Canter.

Canter, L. & Canter, M. (1993). *Succeeding with difficult students: New strategies for reaching your most challenging students.* Santa Monica, CA: Lee Canter.

Cantrell, G. G., & Cantrell, G. L. (2003). *Teachers teaching teachers: Wit, wisdom & whimsey for troubled times.* New York, NY: Peter Lang Publishers.

Carr, W. & Kemmis, S. (1986). *Becoming critical: Education, knowledge and action research.* London, Falmer Press.

Connelly, F. M. & Clandinin, D. J. (1988). *Teachers as curriculum planners: Narratives of experience.* Toronto, ON: OISE Press.

Corey, S.M. (1949). *Action research, fundamental research and educational practices.* Teachers College Record, 50, 509-514.

Deshler, D. & Ewert, M. (1995, May 25). "Participatory action research: Traditions and major assumptions." (PARnet On-line, p. 1-6) Retrieved from [http://www.parnet.org/tools/tools].

Dewey, J. (1933). *How we think: A restatement of the relation of reflective thinking to the educative process.* Boston: D. C. Health.

Dinkmeyer, D., & Dreikurs, R. (1963). E*ncouraging children to learn: The encouragement process.* Englewood Cliffs, NJ: Prentice Hall.

Dreikurs, R. (1964). *Children: The challenge.* New York: E. P. Dutton.

———. (1968). *Psychology in the classroom: A manual for teachers.* (2nd. ed.). New York: Harper & Row.

———. (1972). *Discipline without tears: What to do with children who misbehave.* New York: Hawthorn Books.

Dreikurs, R., & Loren, G. (1968). *Logical consequences.* New York: Meredith Press.

Earl, L., & Cousins, B. J. (1995). *Classroom assessment: Changing the face; facing the change.* Mississauga, ON: Ontario Public School Teachers Federation.

Edwards, C. H. (2000). *Classroom discipline and management.* (3rd ed.). New York: John Wiley & Sons Inc.

Elliott, J. (1987). What is action-research in schools? *Journal of Curriculum Studies*, 10 (4), 355-57.

———. (1991). *Action research for educational change.* Milton Keynes: Open University Press.

———. (1994). Research on teachers' knowledge and action research, *Educational Action Research*, 2 (1), 133 - 137.

Englemann, S., & Carnine, D. (1982). *Theory of instruction:Principles and application*. New York: Irvington.

Epanchin, B. C., Townsend, B., & Stoddard, K. (1994). *Constructive classroom management: Strategies for creating positive learning environments*. Pacific Grove, CA: Brooks/Cole Publishing.

Feilstein, L. & Phelps, P. (2001). *Introduction to teaching: Rewards and realities*. Belmont, CA. Wadsworth/Thomson.

Feldman, A. & Atkin, M. (1999). Embedding action research in professional practice In Noffke, S. E. & Stevenson, R. B. (Eds.), *Educational Action Research: Becoming Practically Critical*. New York, NY: Teachers College Press.

Flores, E. & Granger, S. (1996). The role of the collaborator in action research. In Noffke, S. E. & Stevenson, R. B. (Eds.), *Educational Action Research: Becoming Practically Critical*. New York, NY: Teachers College Press.

Freud, A. (1968). *Normality and pathology in childhood: Assessments of development*. New York: International University Press.

Fullan, M. & Hargreaves, A. (1991). *What's worth fighting for: Working together for your school*. Toronto, ON: Ontario Public School Teachers Federation.

Galloway, C. (1976). *Silent language of the classroom*. (Report no. 130 337). East Lansing, MI: National Centre for Research on Teacher Learning. ERIC Document Reproduction Service.

Glasser, W. (1968). *Control theory in the classroom*. New York: Harper & Row.

———. (1969). *Schools without failure*. New York: Harper & Row.

———. (1975). *Reality therapy: A new approach to psychiatry*. New York: Harper & Row.

———. (1992). *The quality school: Managing students without coercion*, (2nd ed.). New York: Harper-Collins.

Glasser, W. G. (1990). *The quality school*. New York, NY: Harper and Row.

Goethals, S. M., Howard, R.A. & Sanders, M. M. (2004). *Student teaching: A process approach to reflective practice*. (2nd Ed.). Upper Saddle River, NJ: Pearson, Merill Prentice Hall.

Griffin, P. (1998). Outcomes and profiles: changes in teachers' assessment practices. *Journal of the Australian Curriculum Association*, 18(1), 9-19.

Grundy, S. (1996). Towards empowering leadership: The importance of imaging. In Ortrun Zuber-Skerritt (Ed.) *Action Research for Change and Development*, Aldershot: Gower-Avebury.

Grundy, S. & Kemmis, S. (1982). Educational action research in Australia: the state of the art (an overview). In S. Kemmis & R. McTaggart (eds) *The Action Research Reader*. Deakin University Press, Victoria.

Hannay, L. M. (1998a). *Action research: Facilitating teachers' professional learning*. Kitchener, ON: OISE/UT Midwestern Centre.

Hardin, C. J. (2004). *Effective classroom Management: Models and strategies for today's classrooms*. Pearson, Merill Prentice Hall: Upper Saddle River, NJ

Hargreaves, A. & Fullan, M. (1998). *What's worth fighting for out there?* Toronto, ON: Ontario Public School Teachers' Federation

Henniger, M.L. (2004). *The teaching experience: An introduction to reflective practice*. Upper Saddle River, NJ: Pearson, Merill Prentice Hall.

Hodson, D. (1993). Against skills-based testing in science. *Curriculum Studies*. 1(1), 127-148.

———. (1994). Seeking directions for change: the personalization and politisation of science education. *Curriculum Studies,* 2(1), 71-98.

Hopkins, D. (1993). *A teacher's guide to classroom research* (2nd ed.). Philadelphia: Open University Press.

Jones, F. (1987). *Positive classroom instruction*. New York: McGraw-Hill.

Jones, V. F., & Jones, L. S. (1998). *Comprehensive classroom management: Creating communities of support and solving problems*. (5th ed.). Boston: Allyn and Bacon.

Joong, P. & Ryan, T. G. (2004). *Teachers' and students' perceptions of the nature and impact of large-scale reforms in ontario secondary schools.* Presentation – American Educational Research Association Annual Meeting – (17 April 2004):San Diego, California, U.S.A.

Kemmis, S. & McTaggart, R. (Eds.). (1988a). *The action research planner*. Deakin University Press, Victoria, Geelong.

———. (1988b). *The action research reader*. Deakin University Press, Victoria, Geelong.

Kircher, G. & Fishburne, G. J. (1998). *Physical education for elementary school children*. (10th Ed.). New York: McGraw-Hill.

Kohn, A. (1996). *Beyond discipline*. Alexandria, VA: ASCD.

Lebacqz, K. (1985). *Professional ethics: Power and paradox*. Nashville, TN: Abingdon Press.

Lemlech, J. K. (1999). *Classroom management: Methods and techniques for elementary and secondary teachers*. Prospect Heights, IL: Waveland Press.

Levin, J. & Nolan, J. F. (2000). *Principles of classroom management.* (3rd Ed.). New York: Allyn & Bacon.

———. (2004). *Principles of classroom management: A professional decision-making model.* (4th Ed.). New York: Allyn & Bacon.

Lewin, K. (1946). Action research and minority problems. *Journal of Social Issues*,2, (4), 34-46.

Lindsay, J. (2004, April 12). "What the data really show." Retrieved from [http://www.jefflindsay.com/EducData.shtml].

Martin, J., Sugarman, J., & McNamara, J. (2000). *Models of classroom management.* (3rd Ed.). Calgary, AB: Detselig Enterprises.

McCroskey, J. (1992). *An introduction to communication in the classroom.* Edina, MN: Burgess International Group.

McLean, J. L. (1995). *Improving education through action research: A guide for administrators and teachers*. Thousand Oaks, CA: Corwin Press, Inc.

McNiff, J., Lomax, P. & Whitehead, J. (1996). *You and your action research project*. New York, NY: Routledge.

McTaggart, R. (1991). *Action research: A short modern history*. Deakin University Press, Victoria: Geelong.

———. (1996). Issues for participatory action researchers. In Ortrun Zuber-Skerritt (Ed.) *New Directions in Action Research.* Washington, D.C.: Falmer Press.

———. (1997). *Participatory action research: International contexts and consequences*. Albany, NY: State University of New York.

Melrose, M. J. (1996). Got a philosophical match? Does it matter? In Ortrun Zuber-Skerritt (Ed.) *Action Research for Change and Development*, Aldershot: Gower-Avebury.

Mertens, D.M. (1998). *Research methods in education and psychology.* Thousand Oaks, CA: Sage.

Naested, I., Potvin, B., & Waldron. (2004). *Understanding the landscape of teaching*. Toronto, ON: Pearson-Prentice Hall.

Noffke, S. E. (1995). Action research and democratic schooling problematics and potentials. In Noffke, S. E. & Stevenson, R. B. (Eds.), *Educational Action Research: Becoming Practically Critical*. New York, NY: Teachers College Press.

Noffke, S. E. (1997). Professional, personal, and political dimensions of action research. In Apple, M. (Ed.). *Review of Research in Education*, 22, (p. 305-343). Washington, D.C.: American Educational Research Association.

O'Neill, G. P. (1988). *Canadian Journal of Education*, Vol. 8: 162-185.

Ontario College of Teachers (2004). "How to become a teacher." Retrieved 23 March 2004, from [http://www.oct.ca/en/CollegePublications /PDF/becoming.pdf].

Ontario College of Teachers (2004). "Transition to teaching: New teachers of 2001 and 2002 report on their first two years of teaching in Ontario." (News Archive). Retrieved 23 March 2004, from [http://www.oct.ca/en/ CollegePublications/news-archive/20031210_e.asp].

Ontario Ministry of Education and Training (1997c). *Key directions in secondary curriculum development: A synthesis of the recommendations of 24 expert panels*. Toronto, ON: Queen's Printer.

Ontario Ministry of Education (2004). "Ontario schools: Ontario code of conduct." Retrieved 22 April 2004, from [http://www.edu.gov.on.ca/ eng/document/brochure/conduct/conduct.html].

Pedretti, E. G. (1994a). "Action research in science-technology-society education: The road less travelled." Unpublished doctoral dissertation, The Ontario Institute for Studies in Education, University of Toronto, Toronto, ON.

———. (1994b). Facilitating action research in science, technology and society (STS) Education: An experience in reflective practice. *Educational Action Research*, 4(3), 307- 327.

Piaget, J. (1965). *Moral judgment of the child* . New York: Free Press.

Richmond, J.C. & McCroskey, J.C. (1995). *Nonverbal behaviour in interpersonal relations*. (3rd Ed.). Allyn & Bacon, New York: NY.

Rosaen, C. & Schram, P. (1997). Professional development for beginning teachers through practical inquiry. *Educational Action Researcher*. 5(2), United Kingdom: Cambridge University Press.

Royal Commission on Learning. (1994). *For the love of learning*. Toronto, ON: Queen's Printer for Ontario.

Rudduck, J. (1991). *Innovation and change*. Toronto, ON: OISE Press.

Russell, T. & Mcpherson, S. (2001). "Indicators of success in teacher education: A review and analysis of recent research." Paper presented at the Pan-Canadian Education Research Agenda Symposium Teacher Education /Educator Training: Current Trends and Future Directions (22-23 May 2001) Laval University, Quebec City

Ryan, K. & Cooper, J.M. (2004). *Those who can, teach.* (10th Ed.). Houghton Mifflin, Boston: MA.

Ryan, T. G. (2000). "An action research study of science assessment praxes." Unpublished doctoral dissertation, Ontario Institute for Studies in Education, University of Toronto, Toronto, Ontario.

———. (2001, May, 26). The role of leadership within an action research study of science assessment praxes. *International Electronic Journal for Leadership in Learning*, (5) 3 [http://www.ucalgary.ca/~iejll].

Sagor, R. (1992). *How to conduct collaborative action research.* Alexandria, VA: Association for Supervision and Curriculum Development.

Saskatchewan Teachers' Federation. (1992). *Building for success.* Saskatoon, SK: Saskatchewan Teachers' Federation.

Schon, D. (1983). *The reflective practitioner.* London: Maurice Temple.

Schoonmaker, F. (1998). Promise and possibility: Learning to teach. *Teachers College Record*, 99, 559-591.

Smith, F. (1988). *Insult to intelligence: The bureaucratic invasion of our classrooms.* Portsmouth, NH: Heinemann.

Smith, M. K. (2001). "'Kurt Lewin, groups, experiential learning and action research', the encyclopedia of informal education," Retrieved 15 March 2004, from [http://www.infed.org/thinkers/et-lewin.htm].

Stevenson, R. B., Noffke, S. E., Flores, E., & Granger, S. (1995). Teaching action research: A case study. In Noffke, S. E. & Stevenson, R. B. (Eds.), *Educational Action Research: Becoming Practically Critical.* New York, NY: Teachers College Press.

Stiggins, R. J. (1994). *Student centered classroom assessment.* Toronto, ON: Maxwell Macmillan.

Stipek, D. (1998). *Motivation to learn: From theory to practice.* (3rd ed.). Toronto, ON: Allyn & Bacon.

Stringer, E. T. (1996). *Action research: A handbook for practitioners.* Thousand Oaks, CA: Sage Publications, Inc.

Trevaskis, D. K. (1994). *Mediation in the Schools.* (ERIC Digests: ED 378108) Bloomington IN: ERIC Clearinghouse for Social Studies/Social Science Education.

Tudge, J., & Caruso, D. (1989). *Cooperative problem-solving in the classroom.* (ERIC Digests: ED310881) Urbana IL: ERIC Clearinghouse on Elementary and Early Childhood Education.

Webb, G. (1996). Becoming critical of action research for development. In Zuber-Skerritt, O. (Ed.) *New Directions in Action Research.* London, UK: Falmer Press.

Wideen, M., Mayer-Smith, J., & Moon, B. (1998). A critical analysis of the research on learning to teach: Making the case for an ecological perspective on inquiry. *Review of Educational Research*, 68(2), 130-178.

Winter, R. (1996). Some principles and procedures for the conduct of action research. In Ortrun Zuber-Skerritt (Ed.) *Action Research for Change and Development*, Aldershot: Gower-Avebury.

Wolfgang, C. H. (1995). *Solving discipline problems: Methods and models for today's teachers*. (3rd ed.). Boston: Allyn and Bacon.

———. (1996). *The three faces of discipline for the elementary school teacher*. Boston: Allyn and Bacon.

Wolfgang, C. H., & Glickman, C. D. (1980). *Solving discipline problems: Strategies for classroom teachers*. Boston: Allyn and Bacon.

Yonemura, M. (1982). Teacher conversations: A potential source of their own professional growth. *Curriculum Inquiry*, 12,(3), 234-256.

Zuber-Skerritt, O. (1992). *Professional development in higher education: A theoretical framework for action research*. London: Kogan Page.

Additional Resources

1. Please visit this action research web site at [http://www.nipissingu.ca/oar/]. The following description was taken from this site and explains,

    The Ontario Action Researcher is a refereed electronic journal intended for elementary, secondary, and university teachers. It is made possible through a partnership of the Grand Erie District School Board, the Elementary Teachers' Federation of Ontario, and Nipissing University. While our primary aim is to serve the needs of teachers in Ontario, we welcome readership and writing from elsewhere in Canada and the world. The Ontario Action Researcher promotes the development of educational knowledge through action research by elementary, secondary, and university teachers. Within this context, the journal strives to support personal and professional growth by:

    Providing models of effective action research

    Enabling teachers to share their action research.

    Supporting teachers who are beginning action research

    Demonstrating classroom connections between practice and theory

   Informing educational practices in elementary and secondary schools and in universities

2. The following site at Queen's University also supports and encourages action researchers to move forward: [http://educ.queensu.ca/~ar/].
3. The University of Alberta supports Reflection as a means to increase knowledge at [http://www.phenomenologyonline.com/max/epistpractice.htm].
4. A journal of Reflective practice is located at [http://www.tandf.co.uk/journals/titles/14623943.asp].
5. A pre-service students struggle with classroom management is located at [http://educ.queensu.ca/~ar/].
6. Action Research at the Grand Erie Board of Education in Southern Ontario is located at [http://www.actionresearch.ca/].
7. OISE/UT site for Teacher Research supports Action Research at [http://education.ucsc.edu/faculty/gwells/networks/].

8. British Columbia Teachers Federation supports Teacher Research at [http://www.bctf.bc.ca/inquirer/].
9. Action Research is in the Hastings & Prince Edward County Board and one study can be located at [http://educ.queensu.ca/~ar/reports/MP 2002.htm].
10. The Upper Canada Board has Action Researchers at [http://educ.queen su.ca/~ar/reports/JWebster.pdf].
11. Be sure to read the Naked Truth of Action Research at [http://educ.queensu.ca/~ar/oerc97/].
12. A Master's Thesis making use of Action Research can be found at [http://educ.queensu.ca/~ar/801a/suzinmcp.htm].
13. A UK guide to Action Research at [http://celt.ust.hk/ideas|/ar/start up.htm].
14. Dr. Ryan's contribution to Action Research at [http://www. nipissingu.ca/oar/oarCurrIssue/v614new.htm].
15. Dr. Ryan's Action Research effort in the International Journal for Leadership and Learning at [http://www.acs.ucalgary.ca/~iejll/].
16. The Association of Chief Psychologists with Ontario School Board [http://www.acposb.on.ca/pub.html.].
17. Tips and hints on creating questionnaires: [http://edresearch.org/pare /getvn.asp?v=5&n=3].
18. Software for organizing data can be found at [http://www.qsrinternational.com/index.htm].
19. For help with surveys, try [http://www.oct.ca/en/default_e.asp].
20. Quantitative research help.

    [http://www.wadsworth.com/psychology_d/special_features/ext/workshops/workshops.html].

    [http://www.mste.uiuc.edu/hill/dstat/dstat.html].

    [http://trochim.human.cornell.edu/kb/statinf.htm].

    [http://www.psychstat.smsu.edu/multibook/mlt00.htm].

    [http://www.apa.org/journals/amp/amp548594.htm].
21. Coding software:

    [http://www.code-a-text.co.uk/].

    [http://www.researchware.com].
22. Safe Schools Act: [http://www.ontla.on.ca/documents].